The Story BEHIND THE NICKNAME

The Origins of 100 Classic, Contemporary, and Wacky Minor League Baseball Team Names

On the Cover: Front: Lawrence–Dumont Stadium in Wichita, Kansas, home of the Wichita Wingnuts of the independent American Association. Back: FirstEnergy Park in Lakewood, New Jersey, home of the Single-A Lakewood BlueClaws.

ISBN: 978–1718879751

SportsLogos.Net is a website providing a history of sports logos and uniform graphics for most sports, leagues, and teams from around the world. The site is used often as a resource for current and historical sports logos by major media organizations and the general public. It is also a source of news regarding changes to team logos and uniforms and home to a community forum allowing users to discuss the subject.

Contents

TO RAMSEY

For the fire and the light

Foreword

BY CHRIS CREAMER

There's something special about Minor League Baseball. Representing communities all across the United States of America, towns small and cities large, you always know there's a pro ball park somewhere nearby thanks to Minor League Baseball. Easily accessible, affordable, a night out with the family, and by far the best way to introduce your kids to the world's greatest game.

Part of what makes the Minor League games so magical are the identities these clubs roll with. You'll never see a Major League team call itself the RubberDucks or the Jumbo Shrimp or the Baby Cakes—but my kids will excitedly throw on an El Paso Chihuahuas T-shirt or slap a Richmond Flying Squirrels cap on their head even though they may not even really be into baseball yet. It's fun, it's carefree, and that's what baseball's supposed to be about.

These names, logos, and uniforms give a small town, almost otherwise unknown to the majority of the United States, a chance to tell its history and to share what makes their town special. I can't imagine I'd have ever known that Binghamton, New York, was the "carousel capital of the world" without seeing the logo for their Rumble Ponies or that a "yard goat" was an old train car on the New York, New Haven, and Hartford Railroad without the Eastern League's Hartford Yard Goats. There are stories like this all across Minor League Baseball's landscape, and Paul is just the guy to share these stories with you.

My first encounter with Mr. Caputo's passion involving this subject was about five years ago, a Tweet about a story Paul had written regarding the origin of a Minor League team name came across my feed, and being someone who enjoys such stories, I clicked and was quickly impressed by what I read. Paul was clearly someone who shared my fascination with the topic. I checked out Paul's site and found it was chock full of stories just like this one; I decided right then and there that I had to have Paul write for my site, SportsLogos.Net, and share similar stories with our readers. To my delight he loved the idea and since then he has been writing and we've been publishing the stories you'll find here in this book.

Unsatisfied with simply passing on rumours and folklore, Paul went and spoke directly with those who made the decisions to pick the names they picked: team owners, front office staff, and the designers who created the logos and uniforms; to find out exactly why they chose their names, why they picked their colours, and why their logos and uniforms look the way they do.

This is by far the most definitive collection of origin stories behind Minor League Baseball's best and most interesting team names. I'm certain you will enjoy it as much as I have.

Chris Creamer
SportsLogos.Net
May 2018

Introduction

I was startled in 2008 when I learned that my favorite Major League Baseball club's Triple-A farm team would be called the Lehigh Valley IronPigs. Growing up in the Philadelphia suburbs, I was accustomed to stability in the Philadelphia Phillies' farm system. For most of my formative years, the Triple-A team had been the Scranton-Wilkes Barre Red Barons, the Double-A team had been the Reading Phillies, and the high-A team had been the Clearwater Phillies. Then all of the sudden, the team in Clearwater was called the Threshers; the team in Scranton-Wilkes Barre changed parent clubs to the Yankees and the Phillies signed on with the Ottawa Lynx, who would become the IronPigs a year later; and the steadfast Reading Phillies would rebrand as the Fightin Phils and feature an ostrich in their logo.

I was smitten. Where did these wackadoodle team names and logos come from, and what did they mean? Would this wave of wackiness peter out, or would it continue to crescendo? As a person whose professional and educational background is in graphic design, I was charmed by minor league baseball logos new and old alike. Before I started writing this series, my interest in the subject manifested itself in an extensive collection of helmet sundaes (many of which are pictured throughout this book), simply because I enjoyed the logos (and, if I'm being honest, the ice cream).

Intrigued, I set out to learn as much as I could about the increasingly crazy nicknames and logos I was seeing in the ever-shifting landscape of minor league baseball. Along the way, I learned more about small-town America than I ever thought I could. I can tell you where "Star Spangled Banner" author Francis Scott Key is buried because of the Frederick Keys. Because of the Stockton Ports, I know that Stockton, California, claims to be the asparagus capital of the world—and it's one of four towns in the USA alone to make that claim. I know that the tightest hairpin train track turn in the USA is located in Pennsylvania's Allegheny Mountains because of the Altoona Curve.

I have not included every affiliated Minor League Baseball (capitalized) club in this book. There are 160 of those, but some are named for their parent clubs, and that's boring, and some I just could not get a hold of. Some of the teams included in this book are not affiliated with Major League clubs. There are great stories to tell about the teams who play in independent and collegiate summer leagues, part of the larger landscape of minor league baseball (lower case).

I started writing these articles in 2014, at first, and briefly, for a (now-defunct) blog that I had started as an outlet for my enthusiasm for minor league baseball logos, and then for SportsLogos.net, a website I had followed and enjoyed for many years. Once a week, I called teams and spoke with whoever knew how their respective team's name came about. I also talked with logo designers, either in house or with outside firms, who very frequently were involved in the name selection process. And there have been a few thrills along the way. I spoke with actor Jamie Farr about the Toledo Mud Hens gear he wore on the TV show MASH; noted "Nancy and Sluggo" cartoonist Guy Gilchrist, who created logos for the Portland Sea Dogs and New Britain Rock Cats; and former Major Leaguer Pete Incaviglia, who played on that infamous 1993 NL Champ Philadelphia Phillies team from my youth, and later went on to manage the now-defunct Laredo Lemurs. Over the years, I found that minor league baseball is populated by people who are generous with their time and enthusiastic about their industry.

Researching these teams and telling their stories has been a labor of love. Collecting as many of them as I have been able here in this book has been of a dream come true.

The Classics

STEPHEN BOBB / STEPHENBOBB.COM

DAWN OF THE MINORS

The term *classic* is relative in minor league baseball. The industry has been around for years, with many teams dating back to the late 1800s. But the sport has surged in popularity in the last couple decades, and its branding has seen seismic shifts in that time. So it's easy to call teams that have been around since most of us were born—the Durham Bulls, Buffalo Bisons, and Toledo Mud Hens—classic. But there are other, more recent teams that have had a significant influence on the current era in branding minor league baseball. This chapter includes those teams that set the stage for where we are today, whether they've been around for more than a century or a few decades.

Durham Bulls Athletic Park in Durham, North Carolina, home of the Triple-A Durham Bulls

Arkansas Travelers

Arkansas Travelers
1963–present

Current Team Data

Parent
Seattle Mariners

Class
Double-A

League
Texas

There are two versions of a mid-1800s legend of a minstrel who gets lost in rural Arkansas and stumbles across a squatter playing a never-ending tune on a fiddle. The first is told by Arkansans themselves, and has its roots in a tale told by Colonel Sanford Faulkner, an important figure in the state's early history. Faulkner sang the story of losing his way and asking directions at a log home. In exchange for showing the fiddler how to finish his interminable tune, Faulkner was offered hospitality and the only dry spot under the cabin's leaky roof. It's a story that's meant to celebrate Arkansas's diversity and the warmth of its people.

A second version of the story was performed around the same time by Mose Case of Buffalo, New York. While the basic story remains the same, Case's version paints an unflattering picture of the local population and ends by saying that the traveler "has never had the courage to visit Arkansas since."

In spite of a widely circulated version of the story that basically portrays them as hillbillies, the people of Arkansas reclaimed the legend and embraced the traveler as a symbol of their state. "The Arkansas Traveler became a catch-all phrase for almost anything or anyone from Arkansas," according to an article on the *Encyclopedia of Arkansas*. "The term found itself as simply a name on riverboat, racehorse, newspaper, and newspaper column, as well as a nickname for any number of people from Arkansas."

One of Arkansas's many cultural institutions named for the traveler dates back more than a century—minor league baseball's Arkansas Travelers. Born in 1901 as the Little Rock Travelers, the team is the poster child for longevity.

"It's pretty cool that the Travs have never taken a different nickname dating back to 1901," said the team's Director of Broadcasting & Media Relations Robbie Aaron. "There have only been seven seasons since 1901 when there's not been a team, obviously because of the war. Every other season there's been either the Arkansas Travelers or the Little Rock Travelers baseball."

Not only that, but the team has played in only three stadiums in their entire history. They celebrated a decade in their current home, Dickey Stephens Park, in 2016, but 10 years is kind of a drop in the bucket of the team's history. "If you think about it, 10 years in this ballpark seems so significant, but there's over 100 years of Travelers baseball before that," Aaron said. "You're talking about over 100, almost 115 years now of Travelers baseball playing in only three fields. That's amazing."

The Travelers have a unique claim to fame in their name. When they switched from the Little Rock Travelers to the Arkansas Travelers in 1963, they became the first professional sports team named for a state instead of a city.

The team's current logo, created by Brandiose in 2014, focuses more on the traveler's ride than the traveler himself. "When they said 'Travelers,' they said, 'What can we associate with Travelers?'" Aaron said. "Well, he's on a horse, it's perfect."

The 2014 update to the Travelers' logo was a welcome relief, as it replaced one of minor league baseball's blandest and most reviled. The team's previous primary logo, which was designed by an intern at the Little Rock Department of Motor Vehicles (probably), was once voted one of baseball's 50 worst.

Another of the team's previous logos plays on a different definition of Traveler—the name of Robert E. Lee's horse. With the Arkansas state flag replete with Confederate symbolism and a tie to a Confederate general in the Travelers' past, the 2014 brand update endeavored to link several meanings of the term traveler.

The old Travs' logos, retired in 2013

"There's a visual language that's very Confederate, and so you have a horse, you have this flag," Klein said. "There was a question of how do we reimagine this idea and celebrate everything?"

The new identity took the various meanings behind the term *traveler* and wrapped them up in a look that reflects the architecture in Little Rock. "It's the capital and everything is chiseled out of this rock," Klein said. "We had this idea of, we like the horse—there weren't a whole lot of horse mascots in minor league baseball that were dominant—the Robert E. Lee thing's probably not a great thing to hang our hat on, but maybe we can take this horse concept and evolve it. What if the horse is chiseled out of limestone?"

The foundation in stone is a theme that carries throughout the new identity. "We realized this idea of the capital, and might, and chiseling the horse," Klein said. "[Brandiose partner] Casey [White] was really up for doing something that was not typical Brandiose that you come to expect from us."

What baseball fans *have* come to expect from Brandiose is character-based logos, and when it came to the Travelers, Jason and Casey couldn't resist themselves.

As Robbie Aaron puts it, "The biggest crowd reaction has come from the secondary mascot, which has nothing to do with the Arkansas Travelers, but more of the area. It's a swamp possum named Otey."

Just as the legend of the traveler can be seen two ways, Otey plays off the image outsiders might have of Arkansas. "Here's this swamp possum, it was a little tongue in cheek—stereotyped, but in a fun kind of way," Klein said.

As with all things related to minor league baseball logos, the reaction from locals was hesitant at first. "That first time they unveiled Otey," Aaron said, "there was this big uproar and outcry in the community of what the heck is a swamp possum? Now everyone loves it. It's turned into this great, lovable, ugly mascot to the point where we're doing a bobblehead night this year and people are begging to know what date this bobblehead is going to be."

From the mid-1800s legend of a lost minstrel to a Confederate general's horse to a hillbilly possum, the identity of Little Rock's baseball team has embraced local lore. Over more than a century of baseball, the Travelers' identity has collected layers of meaning like sediment settling on the bottom of a swamp.

Asheville Tourists

Asheville Tourists
1976–present
1915–1971

Current Team Data

Parent
Colorado Rockies

Class
Single-A

League
South Atlantic

For nearly 100 years, the minor league baseball team in Asheville, North Carolina, has gone by the name Tourists. If you're familiar with the area, you know that tourism is a major industry in Asheville—with visitors coming for attractions like the Blue Ridge Parkway, the Biltmore Estate, all sorts of outdoorsy adventures, breweries, and, of course, the world-famous pinball museum. So it makes sense that the baseball team is called the Tourists, right?

"We're a very tourist-driven town," said the team's president, Brian DeWine, "so everyone just assumes that is why we are the Asheville Tourists." However, Asheville's status as a tourist destination has nothing to do with the name of the local team. Rather, it was local writers who coined the name a century ago. "None of the players were from Asheville," DeWine said, "so the local sportswriters and fans kind of said, 'It's just a bunch of tourists.'"

When the team undertook a major rebranding effort after the 2010 season, it was with a responsibility to respect a team name that dated back to 1915. Even though the origins of the team name are not necessarily common knowledge ("The casual fan may not know the history," DeWine said), there's still a strong attachment to the name in the community.

So with respect to the history of the name in Asheville, the team changed the logo but left the name as it was.

The decision to change the logo in 2010 was driven in large part by the fact that the logo at the time looked like it was designed by Bob "Happy Little Trees" Ross on a Mac Classic. "It was just an A with some mountains and trees going through it," DeWine said. "It looked kind of like a cross between the Atlanta Braves logo and the Oakland A's logo. It was just not very distinctive."

The Tourists, a Rockies affiliate, based their new look on nighttime colors and a character called Mr. Moon. The colors all have a specific meaning to the local community, according to Mr. DeWine: "We nicknamed the colors midnight navy, Blue Ridge blue, for the mountains behind us, and Biltmore jade, for the Biltmore House, which actually has jade on top of it." Also, something some fans are surprised to learn after they purchase souvenir caps and get them home, everything that is white on the logo glows in the dark.

According to DeWine, some fans had a specific complaint about the new colors: "I got emails within the first week or two saying, 'You took the red out of our logo and that was un-American. All baseball teams should be red, white, and blue.'" So the colors are relevant to Asheville, but what does the moon have to do with Asheville or tourists?

"We joke, what is the ultimate tourist destination?" DeWine said. "Well, it's the moon."

But if you go way back in the team's history, there's a much more fun reason for the team's connection to the moon. "In the late 1800s we were the Moonshiners," DeWine said. "That's where we got the moon from, to pay homage to that first team."

Wherever the term came from, this particular moon wears sunglasses that reflect a baseball field and carries a hobo-style baseball bat, presumably with all of his worldly possessions contained in a bandanna pouch tied to the end.

COURTESY BRANDIOSE

Early sketches from the designers at Brandiose show different renditions of Mr. Moon. They also show a grimacing bear, a throwback to the team's logo from 1980 to 2004, who still appears as a mascot at the ballpark and on the occasional item at the souvenir stand.

The bear, named Teddy, continues to be a fan favorite. Even though Teddy had not officially been a part of the team's logo for more than five years when the team rebranded, there was some trepidation about the fan reaction to the new look.

"There was definitely the sentiment, you killed Teddy," DeWine said. However, "Teddy's still a character at the ballpark. He's at every game. He still does stuff in our community."

Another idea that appears in early sketches from Brandiose appears an anthropomorphized rack of ribs. "There's a lot of good rib restaurants in Asheville," DeWine said. "That was just one of their ideas."

One of the distinctive features of the Tourists' identity is a unique letter A—certainly not one that will be confused with the Braves or A's anymore. Brandiose tinkered with a number of designs, but the one they settled on has its roots in the region.

"Historically in Asheville, there are a lot of craftsman-style houses, and the thought was that kind of Crafstman-style look," DeWine said. "Part of that was we really wanted our own A. We wanted our A to stand out, to be the Asheville Tourists' A."

The Tourists' wordmark can be traced back through the team's history. According to DeWine, "You see that script Tourists, the Tourists written in cursive, if you look back in the history of Asheville, I would say over 100-year period, maybe 70 or 80 of the years, they've had that form of Tourists somewhere."

The Tourists have one of the more obscure nicknames in minor league baseball, to the point where even many local fans don't know its origins (or worse, they think they do but are wrong). The team had an opportunity to dump their city's longstanding team name in favor of some newfangled name that might have sold more merchandise, and it's to their credit that they resisted. It's a much more interesting story this way, and any mascot whose origins are rooted in a team called the Moonshiners has to be a good thing.

Birmingham Barons

Birmingham Barons
1979–present
1964–1965
1901–1961

Current Team Data

Parent
Chicago White Sox

Class
Double-A

League
Southern

Beneath the surface of the tidy identity of one of minor league baseball's most storied teams lies a decidedly untidy, twisting, turning history—or rather two separate histories that converged under the banner of today's Birmingham Barons, Double-A affiliate of the Chicago White Sox.

To start with, the team's identity is untidy just because of the sheer length of its history. Since 1885, the Barons have collected leagues and affiliations like an old house collects clutter. They've played in the Southern Association, the Dixie Association, and several iterations of the Southern League, and they've been affiliated with the Cubs, Reds, Pirates, Athletics (of the Philadelphia, Kansas City, and Oakland varieties), Red Sox, Yankees, Tigers, and White Sox.

For a team with that much change in its past, the Barons have stayed remarkably consistent in one aspect: their identity. Since 1901, Birmingham's team has gone by the name Barons every year they've played (there were some years without a team) except for a period in the late 1960s and early 1970s when they went by their parent club's name, the A's. Prior to 1901, it was something of a grab bag of team names, including the Ironmakers, Maroons, Grays, Blues, Bluebirds, and Reds.

In the early days of the Barons, the team was called the Birmingham Coal Barons, a direct reference to the area's biggest industry. "Back in the late 1800s, teams were representative of companies," said Michael Guzman, the team's media relations manager. "In Birmingham, a big part of the industry back then was coal."

According to the *Encyclopedia of Alabama,* coal mining in the region dates back as far back as 1815, with booms and busts over the decades until the industry's decline in the area in the 1950s.

That said, the origin of the team name is not exactly common knowledge, even among locals.

"Barons has been the name of the team for so long, I don't think that people connect the dots," said Barons general manager Jonathan Nelson. "Last night I spoke at an event…that was the first question that was asked, what's the genesis of the Barons name?"

While the coal industry was the inspiration for the Barons' name, it's not the only factor that shaped the visual identity of the team that takes the field today.

From 1920 until 1960, the Birmingham Black Barons played in the Negro Leagues, hosting the likes of Willie Mays and Satchel Paige along the way.

The Birmingham Black Barons and Birmingham Barons shared the city's Rickwood Field, alternating home series over the course of the season. The Black Barons won three titles in the 1940s with a roster that featured numerous players who would go on to play Major League Baseball after Jackie Robinson broke the color barrier in 1947.

The current Birmingham Barons' history is so closely tied to the Black Barons that the Negro Southern League Museum, which opened in 2015, is located adjacent to the team's home at Regions Field. Not only that, but the team's uniform set includes a look that is familiar to students of baseball history in the area.

"When we redesigned our uniforms back in 2008, we wanted to connect with that Birmingham Black Barons past," Nelson said. "If you look at our road uniform, it is incredibly similar to the Birmingham Black Barons uniform, whether it's the piping on the jersey or the piping on the pants, or just the type of font that says Birmingham. I know that that is an important part of our history, especially here in Birmingham."

The current iteration of the team dates back to 1981, when the Barons resurfaced after a five-year baseball hiatus in Birmingham. The Birmingham A's had folded in 1975 because of poor attendance, in spite of a roster that included the likes of Reggie Jackson and Rollie Fingers. While new stadiums and the continued presence of high-quality players like Frank Thomas, Robin Ventura, and Ray Durham helped this current version of the Barons, the thing that really put the team on the map was a certain #45, who played one season in 1994.

"The Barons have such a rich history of great teams and great players," Nelson said. "Michael Jordan, when I speak to civic clubs, continues to be the most commonly asked question."

The Jordan-era identity, which was used from 1993 through 2007, evokes the Chicago White Sox, the team's parent club since 1986. That said, the Old English B on the cap, while consistent with the White Sox brand, actually pre-dates the affiliation with Chicago. According to Nelson, the Old English B goes back to the days even before the Birmingham A's, when the Barons were in the first of their two stints as a Tigers affiliate (1957–61, then again 1981–85).

The updated logo introduced after the 2007 season, designed by Hartwell Studio Works in Atlanta, reintroduced red as an important part of the team's identity.

"We decided to dive in, really update and modernize our brand," Nelson said.

That's said, it's still a conservative look in a minor league baseball landscape that features sea horses and turtles and tiny dogs, but that's an appropriate choice for a town defined by a baseball heritage that runs deep. The name and the logo call back to aspects of Birmingham's past—it's a tidy, solid identity for a team that plays in a city where many teams in many leagues have been built, torn down, and built again over and over.

Buffalo Bisons

Buffalo Bisons
1979–present
1877–1970

Current Team Data

Parent
Toronto Blue Jays

Class
Triple-A

League
International

1985

I thought this one was going to be easy. The Buffalo Bisons are the Triple-A affiliate of the Toronto Blue Jays. They play in a town called Buffalo, which is the common name of the animal technically called a bison. Case closed. My shortest Story Behind the Nickname ever, right?

But if the team is called Bisons because they play in Buffalo, where did Buffalo get its name? In this instance, the only fact that historians seem to agree on is that the town of Buffalo was named for Buffalo Creek. The name of Buffalo Creek might have come from the big ol' bovid itself, whose original range included western New York before overhunting and introduced disease reduced its populations and range to tiny specks of the North American West.

But historians are not convinced that it's that simple. Rather than just being named for the animal, the creek's name could have come from a Native American person named Buffalo, a mispronounced Native American word (though no one is sure which one), or mumbling French traders, who might have been calling the place *beau fleuve* (pretty river) or *boeuf a l'eau* (beef of the water). So if the team is named for the city, it's possible they should have featured a Native American, a river, or a French dictionary in their logo.

To get to the bottom of where the baseball team's name came from, I called to talk straight with the source.

"I'll tell you this," said Brad Bisbing, the team's director of public relations. "You're not going to be able to find anybody to comment about why we are called the Bisons because, unfortunately, they're all passed on."

While this might be startling at first, the reason why anyone involved with naming the first iteration of the Buffalo Bisons is dead is that it happened almost 140 years ago.

"We have been the Bisons since 1877," Bisbing said. "Every year of our professional baseball existence has been as the Buffalo Bisons."

Having a brand that's been established for 14 decades can help a team build some impressive numbers. "We were established almost a hundred years before the Buffalo Sabres first took the ice," Bisbing said. "We have 20 players who wore a Bisons uniform that are in Cooperstown. Stuff like that is really cool."

While the team's longevity has made it one of the most solidly established brands in the minors, the name itself seems to make people want to correct each other—for lots of reasons.

First up is the pronunciation. Whereas most people pronounce the word *bison* with a

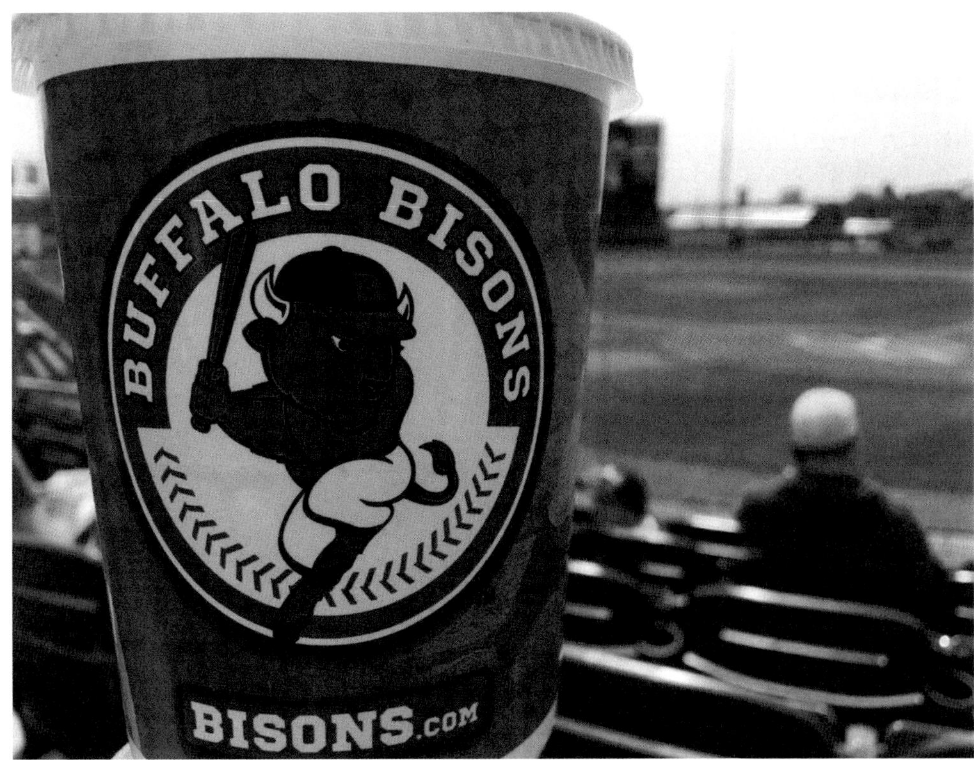

hard S, as demonstrated by the online *Merriam-Webster Dictionary*, the Buffalo Bisons use a soft S. "It's almost like there's a Z in there. Maybe that'll help," Bisbing said. "When we have voiceovers and commercials and PA announcers and local sports media, we use that as a teaching tool, because it is the Bizzzons. That's the correct way to pronounce it."

Next up is an issue of grammar and usage. "The question that I deal with multiple times every season is, 'You know, that's not the right way to pluralize bison,'" Bisbing said. "And the correct answer is yes, we know that's the not the correct spelling. The plural of bison is, of course, bison. We know that it's not bisons. What we tell them is that we've been the Bisons every year since 1877 so that's what we're going to be."

Finally, there's the question of just what this animal is called. The American bison is commonly referred to as a buffalo, but this derives from the fact that early settlers thought the animal looked like African and Asian buffalo, which are, scientifically speaking, completely different animals. So people who like to be pedantic about this sort of thing will tell you that bison and buffalo should not be used interchangeably.

I asked Brad Bisbing about this, because he must deal with it all the time. I mean, if the team is named for a city that is named for a creek that's (maybe) named for an animal, you'd at least want it to be the right animal, right?

"I'll be honest," Bisbing said. "This is my 12th season as director of public relations for the Bisons and no one has ever brought that question up." (People tell me this a lot.)

Lots of teams called the Bisons have played in Buffalo since 1877, but the current Triple-A iteration of the Bisons debuted in 1985, when their logo featured a red, white, and blue drawing of Buster, the team's mascot. They played two seasons as a White Sox affiliate (1985–86), then one season with the Indians (1987) before taking up with the Pirates from 1988 to 1994, then switching back to the Indians in 1995.

In 1998, the team changed colors and went with a logo that features Hunter Pence with horns sliding into home plate. (Okay, not really, but it looks like Hunter Pence, doesn't it?)

That look lasted until 2009, when the team switched its parent club once more. "When we aligned with the New York Mets, we wanted to celebrate the changing of a new affiliation with a new logo and a new brand, so that logo obviously mirrors a lot of what the New York Mets logo was," Bisbing said. "During the four years that we were affiliated with the Mets, it was a more realistic-looking animal."

1998

2009

That realistic buffalo (er, bison) was a departure from the classic swinging Buster logos, and fans reacted enthusiastically whenever the team busted out its retro gear. So when the Bisons switched to their current parent club before the 2013 season, they went back to their roots with a logo designed by a local firm called ADPRO Sports (the one on my soda cup in the photo that accompanies this article).

"We wanted to obviously celebrate a great partnership that we have with the Toronto Blue Jays, but we also wanted to reestablish an independent Bisons brand with the logo," Bisbing said.

But it's more than just an independent brand—it's a look that conjures nostalgia and captures the hearts of longtime fans.

"One of the main things that we wanted to do was celebrate a logo from the past, from when we first opened up Pilot Field, now Coca Cola Field, in 1988. We wore red, white, and blue colors and we had a Buster swinging the bat," Bisbing said. "That's why we went back to that with this recent logo, because we wanted to get back to what fans remember the Bisons looking like and the colors Bisons fans are used to."

Given the history of the team, it's appropriate that their current look reflects the past (though it's certainly a more recent past in the context of the history of baseball in Buffalo). Wherever the name of their city came from and whatever the animal is called and however it's supposed to be pluralized or even pronounced, the Bisons are right up there with the Toledo Mud Hens and Durham Bulls as icons of minor league baseball.

Durham Bulls

Durham Bulls
1980–present
1913–1967

Current Team Data

Parent
Tampa Bay Rays

Class
Triple-A

League
International

The Durham Bulls recognize that having Kevin Costner and Tim Robbins as the de facto (and pro bono) spokespeople for their brand for the last 25 years has been a blessing, but there's one specific challenge that the movie *Bull Durham* poses to the team. To be sure, when the movie came out in 1988, it brought international recognition to a team that was already popular and well established in its own community. And it's a classic film—argued by some, including yours truly, to be the best baseball movie there is. But in the family-friendly world of minor league baseball, the Bulls have had to tread lightly around one issue.

"The fact that it's an R-rated movie, it's kind of a double-edged sword," said Bulls Director of Marketing Scott Carter. "We're not going to be playing clips throughout the game. It's not like we can say, 'Hey, guess what, Saturday night we're playing *Bull Durham* after the game on the video board.' Because it's an R-rated movie, you have to be really careful about how you incorporate it into the game experience."

So while there's no bizarre love triangle subtext when the team's racing characters, Nuke, Annie, and Crash, take the field, there are winks and nods to the movie all around the stadium. Crash Davis's uniform number 8 is retired, along with Joe Morgan's, Chipper Jones', and Hall of Fame manager Bill Evers'. There's still a bull mascot, Woolly Bull, though he is not the same one Crash Davis has Nuke Laloosh purposefully bean in the head in the movie. But more than anything else, Carter said, "you walk around this ballpark and hear people shouting out *Bull Durham* quotes at you ad nauseum."

The most obvious nod to the movie at a real-life Bulls game is the "Hit Bull Win Steak" sign over the outfield wall. "The snorting bull sign, as we call it, that was something that didn't exist until the movie came out," Carter said. "That was a prop that the movie producers actually put into the old ballpark as part of the movie, and then left it up after the movie was done shooting."

In fact, the sign—now in it's third iteration after the original "basically disintegrated," according to Carter, and the second was damaged in a hurricane—was one of the few items that made the move with the team when the Bulls moved from their old stadium, Durham Athletic Park, to their new stadium, Durham Bulls Athletic Park, in 1995.

The Bulls franchise, currently the Triple-A affiliate of the Tampa Bay Rays (and the only Triple-A affiliate the Rays have ever had), has been around since 1902, when they were called the Tobacconists, an obvious nod to the local agricultural industry. They became the Bulls in 1913, and have existed as such on and off ever since. There have been occasional

deviations, like a brief period in the 1960s when they were call the Raleigh-Durham Triangles after the area's famous Research Triangle, but those have been the exception rather than the norm. The baseball team's nickname is tied to the city's nickname, the Bull City, which is tied to a popular brand from the early 1900s, Bull Durham Smoking Tobacco.

The team's logo, the iconic snorting bull through a big, slab-serif D, has been the same since 1980, when the then Single-A Bulls of the Carolina League were reinstated after a nine-year absence. "There was some upheaval in the league," Carter said, "and there was about a decade when the Bulls didn't play baseball. Back in 1980, they were reinstated as the Bulls and had the logo we have today."

Before that, according to Carter, there wasn't a logo, per se. "There was a script B on the hat and it just said 'Bulls' across the chest." Personally, I'm disappointed by this, because I would love to see what a logo for those 1902 Durham Tobacconists would have looked like.

In a minor league baseball landscape littered with a steady stream of new logos and team names every year, the Bulls have been a cornerstone. They are a fixture on the list that Minor League Baseball puts out every year of the top 25 teams in terms of merchandise sales.

"You look at that list, and it changes from year to year based off of who the new logos are and who the hot teams are," Carter said.

But while the Bulls have to compete with increasingly wacky and distinct logos, those other teams have their own challenges to overcome. "It's awesome right now," Carter said. "Is it going to be awesome in five years? Is it going to be awesome in ten years? Some of them are built to last and some of them may not be, and that's for the fans to decide. That's a problem that we, luckily, are never going to have to deal with."

Some of those new, wacky teams may have the Bulls and Kevin Costner to thank for their own popularity. According to Carter, "What the movie did—and it wasn't just for the Bulls, it was really minor league baseball—it really kind of kickstarted the renaissance of minor league baseball nationally, to bring people's attention back to, 'Hey, there's another brand of baseball being played.'"

It's true that the Bulls themselves will never have to go through a major rebranding effort because an enduring Hollywood motion picture does much of their marketing for them. But locally, the team has always been popular. "The Bulls were always drawing well," Carter said, "and at the time the movie was made, led the Carolina League in attendance, and were playing in front of packed houses at the old ballpark where the movie was shot."

More than anything else, the movie expanded the team's merchandise sales outside the local fan base. After the movie came out, in the days before online team stores, the Bulls were selling merchandise through text-only print ads in baseball publications. "They just couldn't keep merchandise in stock because everyone wanted the hat that they were wearing in the movie," Carter said. The team store continues to thrive thanks to the movie, and I am absolutely going to have to buy a Bulls Lollygaggers T-shirt now that I've found it.

The Bulls logo is to Minor League Baseball what the Yankees, Red Sox, or Dodgers are to Major League Baseball. It's a classic, unquestioned in popularity because of consistency, recognizability, and one very good movie. They're a standard-bearer, and they're going to be around for a long time.

Nashville Sounds

Nashville Sounds
1978–present

Current Team Data

Parent
Oakland A's

Class
Triple-A

League
Pacific Coast

Original Sounds logo

Slugger circa 1998

Nashville, Tennessee, had been home to a rich music scene since the late 1800s, but it was the debut of two clear-channel radio stations in the 1920s that cemented the city's reputation as Music City, USA. WSM and WLAC launched in 1925 and 1926 respectively, drawing performers who hoped to find their own stylings carried on the near-nationwide radio waves emanating from Nashville. Though the city's music scene was diverse, it became known specifically for producing country and western talent, so much so that the genre earned the nickname "that Nashville Sound," a phrase first seen in press in 1958.

"It might be somebody in Texas or somebody in California talking about music," said Brandon Yerger, vice president of fan experience for the Triple-A Nashville Sounds. "They're saying it has 'that Nashville sound.' Back then, it was that country-western music that was coming out of Nashville."

Twenty years after the phrase "that Nashville sound" first found its way to the printed page, the city's minor league baseball team, then a Double-A affiliate of the Cincinnati Reds, debuted. When your city is home to the Country Music Hall of Fame & Museum, the Grand Ole Opry, the Johnny Cash Museum, the Musicians Hall of Fame and Museum, and the "Mother Church of Country Music," The Historic Ryman Auditorium, you don't have to look far for inspiration for a team name.

"Now Nashville is known for so many different sounds," Yerger said. "We have bands from Kings of Leon coming out of here all the way to the Oak Ridge Boys, a wide range of different sounds that Nashville is known for. We thought it was appropriate even though the meaning has changed a little bit with the different audience."

The team's original logo featured type that reflected musical notes and treble clefs and a guitar-swinging baseball character named Slugger. Slugger was updated in 1998 to be a muscle-bound power hitter (before steroid testing for logo characters was implemented) as part of a major rebrand.

That rebrand featured a primary logo with a silhouetted baseball player hitting a ball toward the Nashville skyline, including the city's distinctive "Batman building," as well as musical note cap logos.

In October of 2014, the Sounds updated their look again, introducing a new super-orange identity produced by Brandiose. As is often the case with new minor league logos, this one received some pushback, but instead of fans eventually coming to embrace it, the chorus of negativity grew louder and the team took the unusual step of doing an about-face.

"It was just the overwhelming amount of people saying, 'You know I don't want to wear orange,'" Yerger said. "So we heard it, and the fans are who we need to make happy. We need them coming out and enjoying ballgames, we want them to want to wear this jersey and show it off proudly around town. So if they're telling us that orange isn't something that they want to wear while they're supporting their team, we knew we needed to find a combination that they liked."

1998 primary logo

That combination was red and black. When the team reintroduced its new look in a more palatable palette, fans embraced it, and the Sounds embarked on their new era with a new look in a new ballpark with a new Major League parent club (switching from the Brewers to the A's during the offseason) on a positive note (as it were).

With fans approving of the new color, they have been able to focus on some of the nuances of the identity. For one, while the typeface is obviously meant to evoke the stylings of country and western music, there's another inspiration for it. The dimensionality of the look comes from a part of Nashville that locals are well familiar with.

"When you're walking on Broadway, you have all these neon signs," Yerger said. "[The new look] references the neon sign look. It raises a little bit from the left to the right on the Sounds script, and the border of it is supposed to give off that neon look. It's supposed to be a thick, bold lettering style that you'd be familiar with if you were walking down Broadway if you were looking for a bar to go into."

The ill-fated orange update

Not only is the primary cap logo set against a guitar pick the way many logos are set against baseball diamonds, but the diagonal stroke emulates a guitar's F hole (a term I was not familiar with—and one that I had to ask Yerger to repeat several times to make sure I didn't make a horrible, horrible mistake in this article).

On Fridays, the Sounds wear black MC caps and jerseys with "Music City" emblazoned on the front. It's an homage to the city's nickname, attributed to 1950s WSM radio announcer David Cobb.

The 2014 update was much better received in red

On its own, the meaning of the MC logo is not always completely evident. "It is something that we have to explain. We match it with the Music City jerseys on Fridays so that people will get it," Yerger said. "It probably would click for most people in Nashville.... Nationally, it probably needs a little bit more of an explanation."

And while many teams host Throwback Thursdays, the Sounds throw *way* back for every Thursday home game. Their new stadium, First Tennessee Park, is built on the site of Sulphur Dell, an early-1900s stadium that played host to the Nashville Vols of the Southern Association.

"Everybody came through it. Babe Ruth, Jackie Robinson played here," Yerger said. "We use it as a way to honor the past, and also, on the site where we're playing, to teach the fans about the history of baseball in Nashville."

The Sounds have had a handful of MLB parent clubs and have even switched classifications from Double-A to Triple-A in their history, but the one constant since 1978 has been their name. While their logo has evolved over the years (for the better, in my opinion), the team name, which is about as appropriate to the local community as it could be, is entrenched, and as a result is one of the most recognizable in the minors.

Rochester Red Wings

Rochester Red Wings
1928–present

Current Team Data

Parent
Minnesota Twins

Class
Triple-A

League
International

Red Wings 1928 logo

The Triple-A baseball club in Rochester, New York, has a remarkable history. Founded in 1899, it lays claim to being North America's longest continuously operating non-Major League franchise. It also lays claim to being part of the longest baseball game in professional history—a 33-inning affair against the Pawtucket Red Sox over 8 hours and 25 minutes in April 1981.

The team has been called the Red Wings since 1928, when a certain hockey team in Detroit was going by the name Cougars. (It would be another three years before the world was introduced to the Detroit Red Wings.)

When it debuted, the Rochester Red Wings nickname was a wink and a nod to the team's new parent club, as well as an aspect of western New York's heritage: "The team came to be called the Red Wings in 1928, when their affiliation with the St. Louis Cardinals began," says an article on the Red Wings' website. "The name was intended to reference not only a link to their parent club, but also the region's rich Native American history."

That affiliation with the Cardinals would last more than three decades until 1960. And while the Red Wings' nickname was inspired by the team's association with St. Louis, Rochester maintained it well after that affiliation ended, through more than 40 years as an Orioles affiliate and another 15 in their current tenure as a Twins farm club.

Prior to adopting the Red Wings name, Rochester's club went by the names Tribe (1922–1927), Colts (1921), Hustlers (1908–1920), and Bronchos (1899–1907). Red Wings is not the oldest team name in the minors, but it may be the name with the longest uninterrupted use. Teams like the Buffalo Bisons, Birmingham Barons, and Durham Bulls, among others, date back to the late 1800s and early 1900s, but their franchises have had gaps and changes along the way. Rochester, on the other hand, has played every season since 1928 as the Red Wings.

When the team rebranded before the 2014 season, there was a responsibility to pay homage to the club's considerable history. There would be no wacky new nickname or outrageous cartoon for a logo. The team turned to Dan Simon of Studio Simon to refresh a look that was starting to show its age.

Simon spoke with Red Wings team president Naomi Silver at the 2012 winter meetings in Nashville about the team's then-current logo.

"I said, it's been around for a while," Simon recalled. "It's getting a little long in the tooth."

Naomi Silver, it's worth noting, is the daughter of Morrie Silver, who in the 1950s coordinated the stock drive to raise funds to purchase the team from the St. Louis Cardinals, who were making noises about moving the franchise. The purchase kept the Red Wings in town, and to this day the team (which can be found at One Morrie Silver Way on the map) is owned by community stockholders.

In discussing the redesign, Naomi Silver wanted to maintain the visual approach the team had used in its recent history.

"Their mascot is very popular in the community there," Simon said. "She wanted to make sure that the updated identity reflected that mascot."

So, like the logo from 1997, Spikes the bird is front and center. While the 1997 version looks like it may have been dipping into the HGH and andro, Simon's current version appears to have adjusted to baseball's ban on performance-enhancing substances.

"That was an intentional change," Simon said. "They don't need to be looking like they're on steroids to be tough. It could still be tough. It could still be a big, strong, baseball-playing bird without Charles Atlas- or Arnold Schwarzenegger-defined muscles. That was something we wanted to do on our end, was not make this so overboard with regards to that."

In developing the new look, Simon recognized that minor league baseball is about family entertainment and should be fun, but at the Triple-A level, these professional players are just a breath away from the Majors, so there's a reason to be serious as well.

"What we try to develop are characters that are approachable to a certain degree," Simon said, "but are also rendered in a bolder, more graphic logo fashion, as opposed to a Disney or Warner Brothers cartoon character fashion."

In a baseball market with a storied history, the Red Wings' identity strikes the balance between fun and serious effectively. Owned by stockholders in the community and older than the vast majority of its residents, Rochester's Red Wings are as much a part of their hometown as any club in sports.

1997–2013

St. Paul Saints

St. Paul Saints
1993–present
1901–1960
1894–1899

Current Team Data

Class
Independent

League
American Association

If you look at a list of sports teams that play in the city of St. Paul, Minnesota, they seem to have one thing in common: Hockey's Minnesota Wild, lacrosse's Minnesota Swarm, and roller derby's Minnesota RollerGirls all seem a little sheepish about broadcasting exactly where they play. Only the St. Paul Saints of baseball's independent American Association truly embrace their hometown.

"Everybody else in town is the Minnesota Somethings," said Tom Whaley, the team's executive vice president. "It was important to us to be named the St. Paul Saints because that's the town where we play."

Of the two Twin Cities, outsiders sometimes overlook St. Paul in favor of Minneapolis. "Say you're from out of town and you come here, you don't say, 'I'm flying to the Twin Cities' or 'I'm flying to St. Paul.' You say, 'I'm flying to Minneapolis,'" Whaley said. "St. Paul sometimes gets a little short shrift in that regard."

But when it comes to baseball, there's no reason for St. Paul to be sheepish. "St. Paul is the baseball town—the baseball twin in the town," Whaley said. "You've got Joe Mauer, Dave Winfield, Jack Morris, Paul Molitor, they're all St. Paul kids, who grew up on the playgrounds of St. Paul."

The current iteration of the St. Paul Saints was founded in 1993, but the name's religious origins go back to 1884, when the St. Paul Apostles played in the city. The first team to go by the name Saints was owned by Charles Comiskey and played in the Western League from 1894 to 1899. That team would move to Chicago's south side in 1900 and become the American League's White Sox. Another St. Paul Saints team would play from 1901 to 1960 as a White Sox and Dodgers affiliate in the Triple-A American Association.

"In the case of our team, it was just kind of a no-brainer to pick that up again," Whaley said. "We were interested in providing the team with the identity of St. Paul." (While the Saints' name doesn't have much to do with religion, they did once do a St. Paul bobblehead promotion.)

As for the team's visual identity, "We're pretty much meat and potatoes," Whaley said. "We've had two main logos on our shirts in the 22 years, and that won't change."

The first of those logos carries on the timeless tradition of interlocking letter logos in baseball, echoing such classics as the New York Yankees, St. Louis Cardinals, and Los Angeles Dodgers, to name a few.

"We'll always wear that STP that we wear on the hats. It's a classic," Whaley said. "When we talk about branding and marketing and whatever, that's kind of the one universal, that everyone is like, yeah that ain't going anywhere."

The second logo is a traditional script that's appeared on the team's jerseys for the duration of the team's existence.

While the Saints' visual identity is conservative, they make up for it in other aspects of their operation, beginning with the team's noteworthy co-owner, Bill Murray. "He's a fan and has a genuine interest in the business," Whaley said. "I would say as owners go, he's real involved. He's got a real job, but when it comes to baseball, he's real active and involved."

And while Murray doesn't spend a ton of time in the Saints' offices, he's not just involved with the Saints on a lark. "It has to do more with our general approach, our outlook on life and baseball and baseball fans," Whaley said. "That's where I think he's a tone setter."

That tone has come in to play in the form of some of the team's promotional events, including the now-infamous Night of Unbelievable Fun—dubbed Atheist Night by the media. On August 10, 2012, the Saints removed the S from their name and became the Mr. Paul Aints, wearing custom jerseys and covering the S in Saints all around their stadium.

106 GROUP

Saints fan Chris Evans enjoys a helmet sundae, St. Paul-style

The event was sponsored by the Minnesota Atheists, who were holding a conference in town. "The idea for making us the Aints came from the Atheists," Whaley said. "They thought it would be kind of a fun play on words and we agreed."

A Night of Unbelievable fun has become an annual tradition in St. Paul, despite a fair amount of blowback from people who find offense in the tradition. "You can do promotions about sex, drugs, and rock 'n' roll, but be careful what you wish for if you get religion involved," Whaley said. (Just to be sure they were okay, the team checked with Charlie Ruud, the team's all-time winningest pitcher and a Lutheran pastor, and Sister Rosalind, a Roman Catholic nun who gives massages at the ballpark, both of whom gave their blessing to the promotion.)

The promotion generates even more controversy than the team's "bobblefoot" giveaway in 2008 did. The team announced the bathroom-stall themed promotion shortly after a much-publicized scandal involving US Senator Larry Craig getting arrested for lewd conduct in a restroom in the Minneapolis-St. Paul airport. ("There was an unfortunate incident with a US Senator at the airport in Minneapolis," Whaley said.)

"We caught a lot of flak for that," Whaley said, "but it was nothing compared to what we got when we did A Night of Unbelievable Fun. We got letters from all over the world on that one."

The Saints have two traditional logos—no cartoon animal required—that have remained essentially the same since 1993, and they don't worry too much about marketing to the world outside their hometown. (That said, Bill Murray did wear a Saints cap in Space Jam, which gave the team some publicity.)

However, the Saints' conservative visual identity belies their willingness to embrace controversy and push the envelope, something independent baseball teams can get away with even more than affiliated minor league teams can. The team's classic look makes its outrageous promotions that much funnier, like the quiet kid in class who turns out to be a great practical joker. Like their unassuming hometown of St. Paul, home to such cultural contributors as Charles Schulz, F. Scott Fitzgerald, and Mitch Hedberg, there's a lot more to the Saints than first meets the eye.

Stockton Ports

Stockton Ports
2002–present
1946–2000

Current Team Data

Class
High A

Parent
Oakland A's

League
California

Stockton, California, is the asparagus capital of the world. The stinky green stalk is one of the San Joaquin Valley's major crops, and the city of Stockton is home to the San Joaquin Asparagus Festival, which celebrates all things asparagussy. The problem is, Hadley Massachusetts; Oceana County, Michigan; and Isleton, California, also lay claim to the title asparagus capital of the world—and those are just asparagus capitals of the world in the USA. The crop was cultivated by the Greeks and Romans, so who knows how many international asparagus capitals of the world there are?

Stockton, California, also lays claim to being the inspiration for the fictional town of Mudville in Ernest Thayer's classic 1888 poem, "Casey at the Bat." Stockton went by the nickname Mudville in the 1800s, and Ernest Thayer was known to have attended games there, covering baseball for the *San Francisco Examiner* in 1887.

The only problem is, Thayer grew up in Worcester, Massachusetts, very close to a town called Holliston, which has a well-known neighborhood called Mudville. In fact, the pro-Holliston faction points out, Thayer's family owned a mill about a mile from Mudville. Thayer himself was noncommittal on the subject, saying only that the poem was fiction.

One thing that no one can take away from Stockton is that it's home to the largest inland seaport in California. The Port of Stockton, roughly 80 miles east of San Francisco Bay on the San Joaquin River, officially opened in 1932, but the city has played host to seafaring vessels since the 1860s. It's because of this incontrovertible fact that the High-A California League Oakland A's affiliate in town has its name.

"The big thing about Stockton is the fact that we have this massive port, which actually runs into the San Francisco Bay," said the team's director of marketing Taylor McCarthy. "Being that we're right on the port, it was just kind of a natural fit."

Stockton was a charter member of the current iteration of the California League, when the team debuted as the Stockton Fliers in 1941. After the league shut down operations for World War II, the team came back as the Stockton Ports in 1946.

They've gone by that name every year since, except for a two-year stint in 2000–2001, when they were formally known as the Mudville Nine (basically a stick in the eye to those weasels in Holliston, Massachusetts).

Since 2005, the Ports have played in Banner Island Ballpark, located right on the banks of the river in an area known as Mudville. So, take that, Holliston.

The team's identity is classic and conservative, with a red, white, and blue color scheme and a traditional feel that's been a staple since 2002.

"The primary logo that we've had for a long time now is that one with the baseball and the bats in the background, and it has the Ports script around it," McCarthy said. "On our home uniform, we use a red cap, and that's with an S and the anchor with the baseball—the anchor going with the delta theme and we're right on the water.... Then when we're on the road, we have a P-anchor hat, you know, P for Ports."

So everything to do with the Ports is classic and traditional, except...

In 2013, the Ports brought in the guys from Brandiose, and flying in the face of those posers from Hadley Massachusetts; Oceana County, Michigan; and Isleton, California, the Ports speared their city's claim to chief asparagus-dom.

"Stockton is the asparagus capital of the world," said Jason Klein of Brandiose. "They have an asparagus festival every year. They also wanted to incorporate a new character, so we dreamed up a tattooed stevedore named '5 O'Clock Dock.'"

Every Friday home game, the Ports take to the field in asparagus-themed uniforms, with caps that feature 5 O'Clock Dock, meant to represent not just the agriculture of the area, but the local population.

"The term Five O'Clock Dock is 5:00, you're punching out, and he's a dock worker," McCarthy said. "It was a very good way to relate to the blue collar city, the every-day, 9-to-5 workers that are a big part of the Stockton community."

The asparagus theme continues with the team's kids club logo, Running Gus. (Get it?) On a side note, we can only hope that Running Gus and the Wilmington Blue Rocks' Mr. Celery never meet in a dark alley. Imagine the carnage.

Of course, the new look was not immediately beloved. "When they introduced it, it was definitely different, maybe took people a little bit of a while to get used to it," McCarthy said. "But now people, they love the logo."

Having an alternate identity that's completely different from a primary is not unheard of in minor league baseball—the Reading Fightin Phils' "Baseballtown" alternates are the poster child for that sort of thing. But the disparate identities of the Ports seem to present a unique challenge. The team's primary logo is from 2002, but it feels older, an homage to a team that dates back to the 1940s, and a city whose baseball history extends to almost mythical status in the 1860s. The asparagus-based alternate, on the other hand, is certainly the product (produce?) of minor league baseball's new era, where unique and fun take precedence over classic and traditional.

The Ports make it work, though, and the team's identities—both of them—are well received. "In fact," McCarthy said, "we're usually one of the top 60, 65 caps in minor league baseball, when they do the fan vote." Not bad for a Single-A team competing against 159 other teams.

So while there is no joy in Mudville—whether it be in California or Massachusetts—there is asparagus, and there is a giant inland seaport in Stockton, and more than a century's worth of baseball tradition is carried forward on the shoulders of a vegetable named Gus.

Toledo Mud Hens

Toledo Mud Hens
1965–present
1919–1952
1902–1913

Current Team Data

Class
Triple-A

Parent
Detroit Tigers

League
International

The original Mortimer logo

The Toledo Mud Hens, Triple-A affiliate of the Detroit Tigers, are perhaps the most iconic of all the teams in minor league baseball. If you were going to create a time capsule to tell our distant future descendants about the sport, is there another team you would pick?

The name dates back to 1896, when a gentleman named Charles Strobel purchased the Toledo Swamp Angels midway through the season. "The new owner wanted to play Sunday baseball games, and those were forbidden by blue laws in the city," said John Husman, the Mud Hens' team historian and author of the book *Baseball in Toledo*. "He made arrangements with the street car company to run a line north of the city to an area that's now called Bay View Park."

Bay View Park was the natural habitat to the animal that would become one of the most famous namesakes in sports. "The swamp on the edge of the lake was inhabited by what I understand were just literally thousands of American coots, which were commonly known as mud hens," Husman said.

And while there are many majestic, beautiful birds in North America, the American coot is not necessarily one of them. "Have you ever seen one?" Husman asked. "Oh, they're ugly. An ugly black duck. Spindly legs. You ought to look one up. They're just terrible."

To say that the name has stuck would be an understatement. Toledo has been home to the Mud Hens for more than a century with only a few gaps—the most notable of which was from 1953 to 1955, when the Milwaukee Braves owned the team and called them the Toledo Sox, which was followed by a nine-year period when there was no baseball in Toledo.

When baseball came back in 1965, "there was just no question that it was going to be Mud Hens," Husman said. "It's just part of the history of the city and I don't think people want to let go of that anymore."

The visual history of the team can be divided into two main eras: pre-Mortimer and post-Mortimer. "We didn't have a logo that I know of until 1949, and we had the first Mud Hen kind of as we know it," Husman said. "The Tigers bought the franchise in 1949 and made a lot of changes, and one of them was they developed this logo through a Toledo artist by the name of Robert Parsil."

The original Mortimer was only around for a few years before the team became the Sox and then went away altogether. When they came back in 1965, Mortimer was redesigned by an artist named Gabe Pinciotti. "He was a spindly legged thing we've got now with no pants on," Husman said (referring to the mascot, not the artist). "That's been modified a little bit, and now it's kind of the fierce-looking mud hen." (Note that the current primary logo is set against the backdrop of an egg.)

While the team's current mascots are Muddy and Muddonna, in 2012, the Mud Hens introduced a historic Mortimer-based uniform in 2013 to celebrate their team's visual history.

That said, the cartoon bird might not be the only logo the team has known. Husman provided the photo at right from 1933, '34, or '35. "I've been on the lookout for this for a long time," Husman said, "a jacket worn by our manager … that had a different logo that was a mud hen in flight that had a T on it. That's the only other one I've seen prior to 1949."

COURTESY JOHN HUSMAN

Of course, it's impossible to tell the story of the Toledo Mud Hens without telling the story of Max Klinger, the iconic character played by Toledo native Jamie Farr in the show MASH. When he wasn't wearing dresses, Klinger famously exposed millions of the show's fans to the Mud Hens by wearing the team's gear on the show.

I reached out to Farr, who was gracious and eager to speak about his role in popularizing his hometown's quirky team, which has been part of his entire life. He grew up watching the Mud Hens through knot holes in the fence at Swayne Field, then many decades later, there he was throwing out the first pitch at a beautiful new stadium—a stadium he helped make a reality by starring in commercials to garner public support for its construction.

The short version of the story of how Max Klinger became the Toledo Mud Hens' most famous fan is that Jamie Farr is from Toledo and was a fan of the team, so they made his character a fan of the team, too. Farr told me a much longer version of the story, which went like this: MASH's legendary producer Larry Gelbart grew up in the Hollywood area, and his father Harry was a barber in Beverly Hills—"he was the barber for all the comedians," Farr said. Harry the barber convinced one of these comedians, Danny Thomas, a Toledo native, to buy jokes from Larry, at the time an aspiring writer. When Larry became a producer on the mega-hit MASH, he saw an opportunity.

"To make Klinger from Toledo was sort of a payback from Larry Gelbart to Danny Thomas for buying his first jokes," Farr said.

Two of the show's writers, the legendary David Isaacs and Ken Levine, were also fans of minor league baseball, and played up this part of Klinger's character. "They thought about this character that Larry Gelbart created, this bizarre character Klinger. What team naturally would this character like but a team called the Mud Hens coming from Toledo, Ohio?" Farr said. "It brought in a team that, first of all, was very unusual in name," he said. "Mud Hens is just a strange, strange name."

Of course, the team loved this exposure, and Gene Cook, the Mud Hens general manager from 1978 to 1998, wanted to make the most of it—which raised a challenge in the show's efforts to be historically accurate to the period of the Korean War.

"Once the Mud Hens people found out what we were doing, they were sending us stuff," Farr said. "We wanted to make sure that we had things that were reminiscent of the '50s, although our show obviously was being done in the '70s. The logos changed."

1949 and 1965 program covers from John Husman's collection

This raised a couple challenges for Farr. First, he needed to be sure that he was wearing the appropriate team's gear ("A lot of people when they first saw me wearing that thought it was a Texas Ranger cap that I had on," he said) and he needed to keep the peace on set.

"Loretta Switt [Hot Lips Houlihan] used to get mad at me because I had better outfits than she did," he said. "Klinger brought color into the camp because everybody had to wear their olive drab things, with the exception of Alan Alda's purple robe. Klinger would wear these outrageous outfits and then also bring in Mud Hen caps and shirts and all kinds of stuff. It would just change the whole atmosphere of the camp."

The show, still in syndication worldwide, draws global attention to the team and helps keep the Mud Hens in the annual list of minor league baseball's best merchandise sales—once fans of the show realize the team is a real thing. "They thought it was a mythical team until they did some research and found, oh, there really is a Mud Hens team," Farr said. "Then they started ordering things from them. I'll be places around the world and somebody will come up to me and say, 'Hey, Mud Hens!'"

Farr does not get paid for of his involvement with the team—at least in cash— but that's not to say he doesn't benefit. "I don't think I've ever paid for a ticket since I was a kid," he said. "I get in free and they give me free pizza and popcorn and hot dogs and things."

Of course, photos of Farr are all over the stadium, and his likeness shows up other ways, too. The team once gave away a series of three Jamie Farr bobbleheads to fans. They sent the first two in the series to Farr, but there's a gaping hole on the mantle where the third one should be. Before we hung up in our conversation, Farr laughingly said to me, "If you can pull any strings, see if you can get me my final bobblehead."

The Mud Hens have had some of everything a minor league team needs to achieve success—a quirky name with a local connection, longevity in a brand, a loyal fan base, and a stroke of absolute dumb luck. Their brand was already positioned for success by the time MASH came around, but suddenly finding themselves on full display in a TV show that averaged 17 to 20 million viewers thrust them into stardom. They rode that wave masterfully, and now a team that was named for ugly swamp birds in the late 1800s finds itself as the most iconic in the minors.

The Mud Hens are right to treat Jamie Farr like a hero when he comes to town, putting his photo up all over the stadium and lavishing him and his guests with tickets and concessions. But still, who knows where they'd be without him, so the least they can do is get that last bobblehead to him, right?

Renaissance

THE MINORS REBORN

The chapters in this book are not broken down strictly chronologically, but it's fair to say that in the 1990s, the idea really caught on that it was a good idea to market minor league baseball teams as unique, community-based entities rather than lesser versions of their Major League counterparts. Teams started looking at what made their hometown unique and using that as the foundation of an identity. In many instances, teams abandoned simply using their parent club's nickname in favor of establishing their own brand.

Blue Rocks Stadium in Wilmington, Delaware, home of the High-A Wilmington Blue Rocks

Altoona Curve

Altoona Curve
1999–present

Current Team Data

Parent
Pittsburgh Pirates

Class
Double-A

League
Eastern

There's a 2,375-foot stretch of railroad tracks in central Pennsylvania that spins trains 180 degrees in a hairpin turn on their way over and across the Allegheny mountains. The so-called Horseshoe Curve, built from 1851 to 1854, is the tightest train track turn in the country. It's been traveled by presidents from Abraham Lincoln to Jimmy Carter, is a U.S. National Historic Landmark, and is listed on the U.S. National Register of Historic Places. Because of its importance as an access point to the heartland of the country, it was one of a handful of strategic sites targeted by Nazi saboteurs during the failed Operation Pastorius in World War II.

In its heyday in the 1940s, the Horseshoe Curve saw 50 passenger trains a day. The track is still in use today for freight rather than people, but human visitors can still explore the area at the Railroaders Memorial Museum.

The Horseshoe Curve's importance to the area is reflected in another cultural institution: It's the namesake of the Eastern League's Altoona Curve, Double-A affiliate of the nearby Pittsburgh Pirates. In 1998, when the new team held a vote to decide on a name, fans were given five options to choose from—and Curve was not one of them.

"Interestingly enough, it was a write-in candidate that came in with the Altoona Curve," said Rob Egan, the team's general manager. "It so perfectly fit with both the Horseshoe Curve and the curve ball in baseball, the double meaning, that was the one we selected.... It's one of those names where it came up and you're like, of course, that makes so much sense."

When the team debuted its first logo featuring a baseball train zooming through the Allegheny mountains, it became part of what seems to be something of a tradition for Pennsylvania minor league baseball teams. The Reading Phillies, Scranton-Wilkes Barre RailRiders, and State College Spikes have all included railroad themes or imagery in their identities.

"The rail history in our state is so huge that all of us have little hints of that in our franchises," Egan said. "Certainly, Altoona and Reading, because we've been in the same league, and they've had such a long history with the Phillies, we've had such a long history with the Pirates, it kind of ties that Major League rivalry into a minor league rivalry."

The ties between the area and the railroad industry are so strong that when the Curve rebranded in 2011, they unveiled their new look, designed by Brandiose, at the Railroaders Memorial Museum in Altoona.

"When we did the rebrand, it was very important to us to be as authentic as we could be to our name and to the history of the area," Egan said. "We used rail type colors with the reds and the bronzes, things like that in our new logo, because we felt that was really important."

As Brandiose's Jason Klein puts it, "They were red and green, and we felt that the brick red was more railroady, and copper for the rails."

The new look features an engineer ("We thought that might be appealing to younger fans," Egan said), a railroad track C, and another hallmark of Pennsylvania sports identities, a keystone. Pennsylvania's nickname is the Keystone State, because it was in the middle of the 13 original colonies, and, according to the state song, it is the "birthplace of a mighty nation, Keystone of the land." Tying the Keystone state and trains together, the Pennsylvania Railroad, which built the Horseshoe Curve, features a keystone in its logo.

But perhaps the biggest innovation introduced by Brandiose is the Curve's specially designed reversible rally cap. The hat, which features a lining designed to look like Curve mascot Al Tuna (get it?) is believed, according to MiLB.com, "to be the first in Minor League Baseball to feature a specially-designed, rally cap lining."

According to Klein, the idea came from a game that he and his Brandiose partner Casey White attended in Altoona, in which Al Tuna appeared and "did a crazy dance" when the home team scored. They first noticed a special edge to the crowd when the Curve got a runner to third base, and fans and players alike turned their caps inside out in the rally cap tradition.

"We started thinking about the rally cap concept, where players were sort of summoning Al the Tuna," Klein said. "We called up New Era, and it had never been done before, and it took a lot of wrangling, but we said, 'We want to create the first on-field rally cap design in the history of baseball.'"

The rally caps generated a lot of publicity, but more importantly, they create a scenario at Peoples Natural Gas Field (which, much to the delight of the seventh-graders in all of us, is the actual name of the stadium where the Curve play), in which fans and players alike become part of a sea of tuna fish eyes whenever the Curve threaten to score. (The Altoona Curve's identity dates back to a technological marvel from the 1850s, so it stands to reason that the tradition of engineering innovation would continue to this day with the very hats players and fans wear at the ballpark.)

The significance behind the Curve's name takes a little digging to understand if you're not from the area, but once you learn how important the Horseshoe Curve was—and is—not only to central Pennsylvania but to the nation, it makes perfect sense, and it seems like one of the better nicknames in all of the minors.

Augusta GreenJackets

Augusta GreenJackets
1994–present

Current Team Data

Parent
San Francisco Giants

Class
Single-A

League
South Atlantic

Augusta National Golf Club in Georgia has hosted The Masters since 1934. It's the only of golf's four major championships to be held at the same location every year, and it is home to arguably the most famous ugly piece of clothing in sports.

In 1937, officials at Augusta asked their members to wear green jackets during the Masters so that guests would recognize who was a member and who was not. Twelve years later in 1949, when Sam Snead won the famous tournament, he was the first Masters champion to be awarded a green jacket as a de facto trophy, a tradition that has continued ever since.

More than four decades later, Augusta's Single-A baseball team adopted the name GreenJackets as an homage to their town's sports heritage. Their logo, which has been a yellow jacket in a green jacket and more recently, an actual green yellow jacket, is a simple play on words, and completes the unusual cross-pollination (as it were) between golf and baseball.

"Obviously, it's touching on the history of golf in this area and what it is renowned for, and then obviously with a touch of minor league flair," said Tom Denlinger, the Augusta GreenJackets' general manager. "It's a moniker. Just like any of the names across the country. It does tie in with that history and the pageantry of The Masters, but puts our little own spin on it."

"The Super Bowl of golf, to coin that phrase, happens here," Denlinger continued. "If you think of the Augusta area, everyone thinks of the Masters. I think that's probably nationally and maybe even globally so."

While Augusta might be known for golf, the history of baseball in the city dates back to 1885, when the city played host to the Augusta Browns. Since then, teams called the Electricians, Tourists, Dollies, Georgians, Tygers, Tigers, Wolves, Rams, Yankees, and Pirates have called Augusta home. The Georgia Peach himself, Ty Cobb, played his first professional season as an Augusta Tourist in 1904.

"Baseball in Augusta, there's over a 100-year history," Denlinger said. "The Yankees used to way back when have their Spring Training here before it moved down to Florida. There's a wealth of baseball history in this area."

The GreenJackets and Augusta National do not have a formal relationship, though the golf club does hold season tickets for the baseball team. "They're a sports entity here in town. We're a sports entity in town," Denlinger said. "We're fortunate to be able to kind of resemble the name of the Augusta National, but at the same time we have to stay clear of them a little bit because they're their own entity."

"It's our job to create our own identity," Denlinger continued. "We do that through 70 home games offered through a three-hour experience that we like to think is unlike any other, similar to when you go to The Masters, but there you're only there for a week."

The cartoon, bee-themed logo creates a substantial amount of distance between the fancy golf tournament and the baseball team. The GreenJackets' first logo, which was used from 1994 to 2005, featured a yellow jacket with oddly feminine legs and pink wings wearing a green jacket. In 2006, a major rebrand initiated by the team's new owners at the time, the Ripken Baseball Group, introduced actual golf clubs into the team's visual identity, making it unique in minor league baseball. The current logo was introduced before the 2018 season.

The original logo

The GreenJackets' yellow jacket mascot was also introduced in 2006. "Auggie is the face of our franchise," Denlinger said. "Those are his golfing clothes. He wears plaid pants and a green jersey."

Obviously, the major difference between minor league baseball and golf is that the former goes out of its way not to take itself too seriously, whereas in golf, let's just say that's less the case. Even though they are paying homage to a major golf tournament, the GreenJackets, with their punny name and plaid-wearing mascot, are no different. "It's a minor league moniker, so we're trying to create something fun."

Speaking of fun, the team plays up its connection to golf with a wink and a nod to another of the sport's iconic traditions. "We started a *Caddyshack* race last year with our own *Caddyshack* figures," Denlinger said. "It's similar to the presidents' race in DC or the sausage race with the Milwaukee Brewers, something of that concept. But we wanted to kind of tie in, to bring in some of the golf levity, if you will, to the ballpark."

The 2006 rebrand

The GreenJackets, a South Atlantic League affiliate of the San Francisco Giants, have been around for more than 20 years and do not show signs of going anywhere anytime soon. If any rebranding does happen in the future, Denlinger said, it would most likely be in the form of additional alternate logos rather than a name change.

"The name is entrenched. It is one of those iconic names," he said. "It's catchy and unique, and that's what minor league baseball is all about."

Like most successful minor league teams, the GreenJackets have seized on something unique and interesting about the place where they play. Unlike most minor league teams, the GreenJackets reference a completely different sport in their visual identity. They succeed by making it their own, having fun with it, and not taking any of it too seriously.

Beloit Snappers

Beloit Snappers
1995–present

Current Team Data

Parent
Oakland Athletics

Class
Single-A

League
Midwest

When I first contacted the Beloit Snappers to talk about the reasons for their nickname, their director of media relations and marketing Bobby Coon told me exactly what I expected to hear: "There are a lot of snapping turtles in the Rock River that runs through Beloit."

The end! There are a lot of snapping turtles here and we're the Snappers. Right?

Turns out there's a little more to it than that. The Snappers, Single-A affiliate of the Oakland A's in the Midwest League, play in the southern Wisconsin town of Beloit, which has something of a longstanding obsession with turtles.

"There's just a kind of theme of turtles around here," Coon said. And that's putting it lightly.

The town's association with turtles goes back possibly as far as the year 400, when Native Americans built an effigy mound ostensibly shaped like a turtle. Turtle Mound is one of 20 mounds still found on Beloit College's campus, but it's the one that seems to have caught the area's imagination. In the early 1800s, according to an article by William Green in *Nature at the Confluence,* there was a Native American Ho-Chunk village called Ke-Chunk (Turtle Village) at the mouth of Turtle Creek.

According to a *Beloit College Magazine* article by Marlo Amelia Buzzell, turtles have long been the unofficial mascot of Beloit College, where there was from 1901 to the mid-1970s a secret organization called the Turtle Mound Society (whose secret members wore secret gold pins so members could recognize each other), there was a synchronized swim team called the Terrapins in the 1930s and 1940s, and major donors have been given lapel pins shaped like turtle shells since 1969.

"Also, next to Beloit is a town called the town of Turtle," Coon said. "I actually had the privilege of getting a speeding ticket in that town." (Guess the town of Turtle likes to take life at a slower pace! Hello? Is this thing on?)

Of course, the natural progression from an ancient, turtle-shaped effigy mound to a present-day town-wide affinity for turtles is best summed up in the *Beloit College Magazine* article by Marlo Amelia Buzzell: "Beloiters abroad take photos of turtles or turtle objects and post them to their Facebook pages, often with captions along the lines of, 'Beloit!'"

In 1995, the Beloit Brewers switched parent clubs from Milwaukee to Minnesota, and the team decided it was time for a unique identity that paid homage to their town's turtle

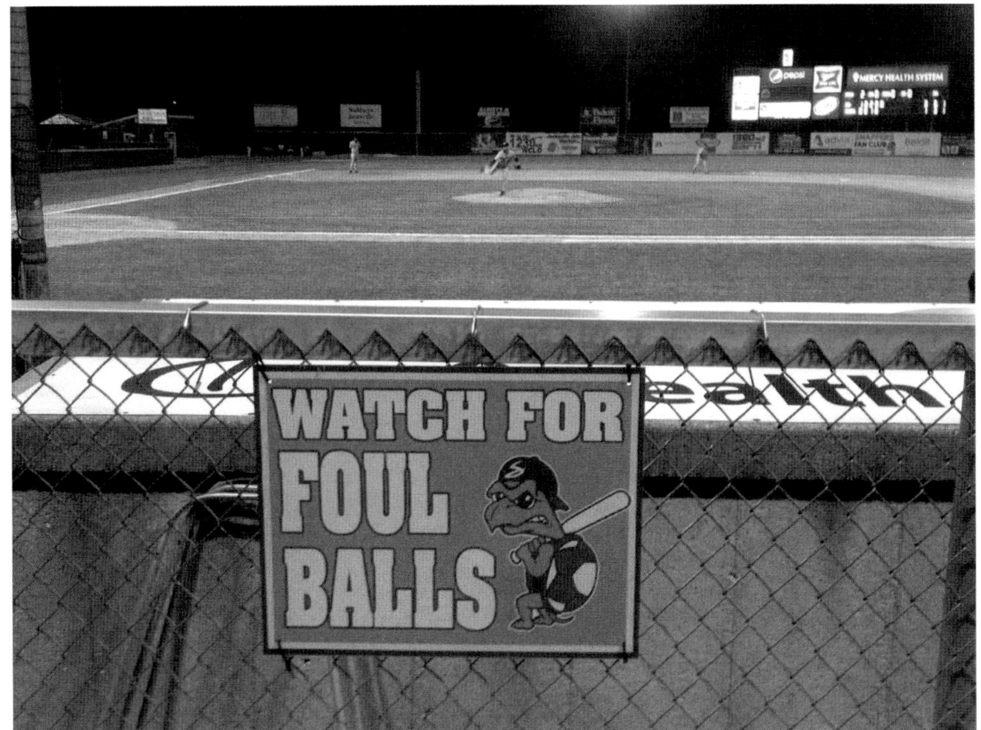

love. Not prepared to shell out (get it?) a ton of money for the new look, the team took a different approach.

"From what I was told it was a former general manager's cousin that designed it," Coon said. "And he didn't even do it for any money or anything. He just wanted some of the merchandise that we put the logo on."

The general manager in question was Steve Kretz, and indeed it was his cousin, Chris Kretz, who designed the logo. "I did get paid, although not much," Chris Kretz said, "but the experience and now 20+ years of following a creation through my love of baseball made it all worth it."

Of course, the modern era of the wacky minor league baseball logo was still in its infancy at the time, so Snappy the turtle was all the rave.

"At that time, in 1995, that was cutting edge. That was unique," Coon said. "There's little bit stranger names nowadays, and more cutting edge, and those teams are obviously selling tons of merchandise just because of their uniqueness."

In the face of new and increasingly wacky logos in minor league baseball, the Snappers have discussed the possibility of updating their look, but in this day and age of advanced marketing in minor league baseball, funding is an issue.

"We're a not-for-profit organization and community owned, and we just don't have the staff or the money," Coon said. "You know, we can't hire a company and say, 'We want you to design our new logo and we'll give you this amount,' because chances are we don't have that amount."

The logo features Snappy holding a yellow bat (which Coon assured me was not a whiffle bat, but a real wooden bat colored yellow because of the team colors). Notable about Snappy—apart from the fact that he's a turtle who has teeth—is his facial expression.

"Snappy's got his game face on," Coon said. "He's kind of PO'd at the pitcher and he's stepping up to the plate and he's going to hit a bomb. He looks kind of angry."

While Snappy has remained almost entirely unchanged for more than two decades, there has been one small update. In the team's early years when they were affiliated with the Brewers, Snappy's hat had a B on the front. That B became an S when the team became a Twins affiliate in 2005.

After eight seasons with the Twins, the Snappers switched parent clubs again in 2013 to Oakland, which led to something of a happy branding accident with the team's colors roughly matching. More than that, though, even though the new parent club is two time zones away, the team's fans feel a certain affinity for the A's. "The Oakland A's, they're kind of a small market team, they're the Major League version of the Beloit Snappers in the Midwest League."

That said, when the team was affiliated with closer-by parent clubs, it was more likely for fans to come to games just to see their team's future stars. That's not to say it still doesn't happen, though.

"I see people that are going on road trips or something like that, and they'll come into the office or come through the gates and they'll say, 'Yeah, I'm super excited to be here. I'm a huge Oakland A's fan.' And I'll say, 'Really?'" Coon said. And not only that, "I'm not even kidding you, I go to the Qdoba down the street in Beloit. The manager has an Oakland A's tattoo on his forearm."

Baseball fans talk about *what minor league baseball should be.* I attended a Snappers game on a frigid April opening day in 2014, and with the team's small park, diehard fans, and folksy logo, I felt I had stumbled on what minor league baseball should be. (I ended up leading the crowd in "Take Me Out to the Ballgame" that night because I was hanging out in the media box when they discovered moments before they needed it that the computer with the audio file they were going to play over the PA had been moved to another location.) The Snappers logo may not win any of Minor League Baseball's clash of the caps (or whatever) contests—those will go to the flashier new ones but it's kitschy, and it's just right for this small-town team.

Carolina Mudcats

Carolina Mudcats
1991–present

Current Team Data

Parent
Milwaukee Brewers

Class
High-A

League
Carolina

The scene that Steve Bryant describes the night he purchased the Columbus Astros before the 1989 season sounds like a cliché from a cheesy movie. "I bought it from four doctors in Columbus, Georgia, on a Saturday night," Bryant said. "They pulled out a fifth of Jack Daniels on the negotiating table, and at the end of the night, I bought a baseball team."

He continued, "The first time I went to the ballpark for a game, I actually owned the team. I bought it Saturday night, and I went to Sunday's game."

As you might imagine, there can be problems with an alcohol-fueled impulse purchase of a Double-A baseball team. That Sunday afternoon's game was at 1:00, and because it was summer in Georgia, it was stiflingly hot. One glance around the stadium gave Bryant cause for concern. "There were more players on the field warming up than there were fans in the stadium," he said. "What scared me the most was that a foul ball went in the stands, and no one went after it. It just sat there. I thought, what have I done?"

So Bryant, whose background is in advertising, knew that changes needed to be made. First, he knew that the team would be moving to Raleigh, North Carolina, as soon as a stadium was built. Second, he knew that naming a team after its Major League affiliate was boring, and a missed opportunity, so a complete rebranding was in order.

He had several requirements for a new logo, including that it appeal to kids (because it's minor league baseball and that's the law), that it be unique ("If you have the Chicago Bulls and the Durham Bulls, then that's not unique," he said), and that it have both local significance and national appeal.

Also, he didn't want it to be like those dumb new mass-noun soccer teams. "We wanted to kind of poke fun at the establishment, because all the hockey and the new soccer teams, they were called the Rage and the Fury," Bryant said. "How do you get your arms around that? What is tangible about that? How do you do a mascot with Rage?"

Names that were rejected included references to the Civil War, like Cannons, and one based on a delicacy found in a drug store in Columbus—Scrambled Dogs, a reference to hot dogs chopped up into cole slaw with onions, pickles, beans, and oyster crackers, developed by local World War II hero Charles Stevens for the Dinglewood Pharmacy more than 50 years ago.

The name the team settled on, Mudcats, which they used for their final two years in Columbus and their quarter century in North Carolina since, was one of the early wacky minor league nicknames. "We were sort of noted as the first team to really start the logo

NIKOLAUS JOHNSON

The original Mudcats logo illustration by artist Frank Harrod.

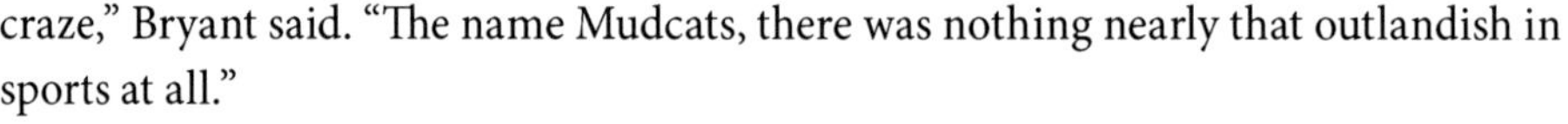

craze," Bryant said. "The name Mudcats, there was nothing nearly that outlandish in sports at all."

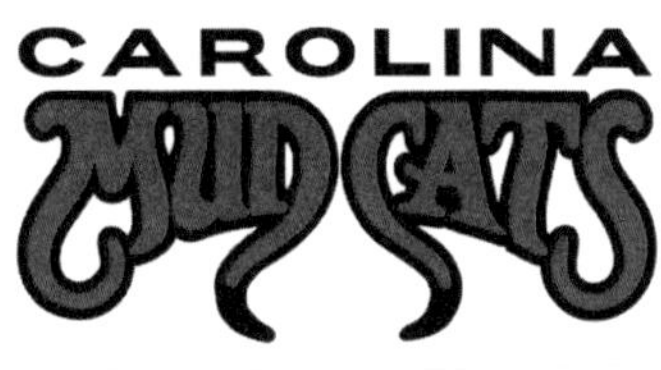

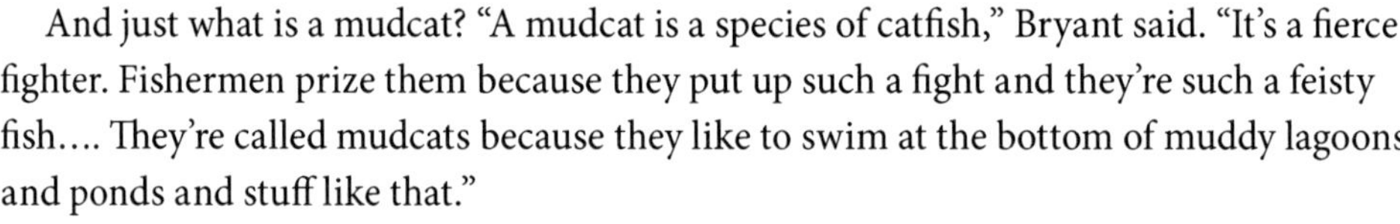

And just what is a mudcat? "A mudcat is a species of catfish," Bryant said. "It's a fierce fighter. Fishermen prize them because they put up such a fight and they're such a feisty fish.... They're called mudcats because they like to swim at the bottom of muddy lagoons and ponds and stuff like that."

The primary logo features a catfish swimming through the letter C, which stood for Columbus in 1989 and 1990, then for Carolina ever since. A wordmark logo features catfish whiskers hanging from the letters D and C. The logo was drawn by artist Frank Harrod, who according to a 1991 article in *The Times-News* of Henderson, North Carolina, was paid $500—nearly twice his normal rate. The team got a pretty good deal, too, though.

"For the first four or five years, we were the number one team in the country in sales, which was good because we weren't doing that well at the gate," Bryant said. "The logo sort of helped propel us."

In fact, the logo became a nationwide phenomenon. First came early success at home: They sold out of hats in their first season almost immediately, as fans went to games just to buy souvenirs. Then, a local newspaper promotion that offered a Mudcats hat with a renewed subscription sold out of 1,000 hats in less than a week, according to Bryant. The team started advertising in publications like *Baseball Weekly* and *Baseball America* (these were the days before the internet). Then after a photo of a kid in a Mudcats hat from the *Atlanta Journal* went national, sales really took off, and they haven't slowed down.

"Even though virtually every team in America has changed their name since we have, we're still in the top 10 sales in minor league baseball every year," Bryant said.

While the logo was developed quickly, one important tweak early on made a big difference.

"The first rendition just had the catfish head and the C," Bryant said. "When we added the tail, it gave that whole logo some movement, so it looked like the catfish, which tend to swim side to side, was sort of meandering through the C."

The Carolina Mudcats are currently a High-A affiliate of the Milwaukee Brewers, and were previously with the Atlanta Braves and Cleveland Indians. Prior to the existence of the Single-A Mudcats, a Double-A iteration of the team was affiliated with the Pirates (1991–1998), Rockies (1999–2002), Marlins (2003–2008), and Reds (2009–2011). While affiliations and classification have changed, the logo has remained constant. Their devotion to the logo is a simply a question of running a good campaign—in more ways than one. "When Bill Clinton was running for office the first time, there was a sign in his campaign headquarters, 'It's the economy, stupid,' In other words, don't talk about anything else," Bryant said. "The sign in our office is, 'It's the fish, stupid.' You don't screw around with the fish."

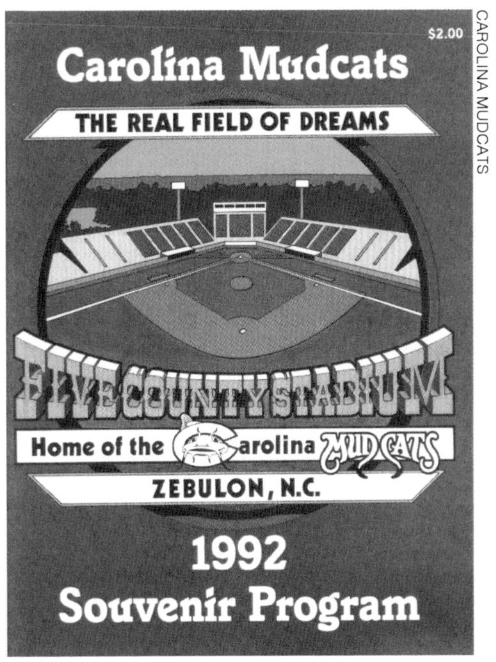

CAROLINA MUDCATS

A program guide from 1992 accentuates a connection to Field of Dreams.

That said, for a team that doesn't screw around with the fish, Bryant offers this tidbit: "You know, we serve catfish sandwiches, so we're one of the few people that eat their mascot."

Bryant compares the longevity of his team's logo to another nearby organization. "It's like, would Duke University change their logo?" he asked. "It's a standard."

Speaking of sports teams in the Raleigh-Durham area, the Mudcats have a friendly rivalry with the nearby Durham Bulls, just 25 miles away.

"We're one of the few teams that share a market with another team," Bryant said. "The owner of the other team is a billionaire and I'm a thousandaire. He owns a couple of TV and video stations and I own a station wagon."

And while the Bulls were buoyed by a certain classic baseball movie, the Mudcats claim a film of their own. The Mudcats' playing field was built in a plowed-under tobacco field, just like a certain field in Iowa was built on a plowed-under corn field. To accentuate that connection, they flew in Don Lansing, who owns the house from the *Field of Dreams* movie and who had never left Iowa, to throw out the ceremonial first pitch of their first game in Raleigh. The event was so popular that they sold out, and it created a familiar scene.

"We turned 4,000 cars away, and in all directions you saw headlights," Bryant said. "We said, this is so much like the movie it's scary."

A lot has changed in minor league baseball since Steve Bryant purchased a baseball team over what he describes as a very expensive bottle of Jack Daniels—but that feisty catfish meandering through a big, bold, sans serif C is not one of them.

Cedar Rapids Kernels

Cedar Rapids Kernels
1993–present

Current Team Data

Parent
Minnesota Twins

Class
Single-A

League
Midwest

At first, it seems like a cliché that a baseball team in Iowa would be named for corn. The city of Cedar Rapids has so much more going for it than just corn, right? It's the second-largest city in Iowa, home to a significant art museum, historical sites like the famous Paramount Theatre and Roosevelt Hotel, and museums that feature Czech and Slovak culture and African-American history. It's an important city economically speaking, and it's home to industry other than corn, like avionics giant Rockwell Collins and the US headquarters of multinational insurance company Aegon N.V.

"Iowans tend to get the fact that everyone thinks of Iowa as being a flyover state and nothing but corn and farms," said Andy Pantini, communications manager for the Cedar Rapids Kernels, who has been with the team in one form or another for more than 20 seasons. "I think that we know that we've got a lot more to offer. You can be in Cedar Rapids and drive forever and not see a cornfield."

However, with all of that being said, "It's something that the community's embraced," Pantini said. "Whenever somebody says, 'You should come up with something other than corn,' we say, 'Okay, what?' And a lot of times we really don't get a response."

Indeed, according to IowaCorn.org, the state's climate is perfectly suited for growing corn in terms of the length of the growing season, the amount of rain, and the particular qualities of its soil. Corn has been the state's dominant crop for more than a century and a half, and Iowa's corn crop has been larger than any other state's for 20 years. According to Iowa Corn, "In an average year, Iowa produces more corn than most countries. For example, Iowa grows about three times as much corn as a country like Mexico."

So ever since 1993, the Single-A baseball team in Cedar Rapids, currently a Midwest League affiliate of the Minnesota Twins, has chosen to embrace corn and base its identity on the important crop. But it hasn't always been that way. Baseball in Cedar Rapids dates back to 1890, when the city was home to a team called the Canaries. Then from 1896 to 1903, there were the Cedar Rapids Rabbits, which led to the Cedar Rapids Bunnies, who played until 1932.

Subsequent teams included the Raiders (a couple of times), Red Raiders, and Rockets, and a laundry list of teams named after their Major League affiliates, beginning with the Cedar Rapids Indians in 1950, then transitioning through the Braves, Cardinals, Astros, Giants, and finally, the Reds.

In 1992, the Cedar Rapids Reds won the Midwest League championship. "They received a congratulatory letter from the Cincinnati Reds," Pantini said. "Also in that letter, it said that they were going to move their affiliation to a different area."

Tired of having to rebrand every time they changed affiliates, the team signed on with the Anaheim Angels in 1993 and held a name-the-team contest. "We really didn't want to be the Cedar Rapids Angels," Pantini said.

The name Kernels won out, and in 1993, the team adopted a logo created by a local artist and used through the 2006 season. In 2007, the team decided to refresh its logo. They went to Dan Simon of Studio Simon in Louisville, Kentucky, who came up with the character in the current logo, who I am distraught to tell you does not have a name. (The team's mascot is Mr. Shucks, who is distinct from the logo guy and has nothing to do with corn.)

The original logo from 1993

The logo features a baseball bat standing in for an ear of corn with an expression that I think can best be described as mob boss disdain. "I think what they were trying to do was create a little bit of toughness," Pantini said. "It's not trying to be menacing or inspire fear, but it's just kind of showing a little bit of toughness within the logo, and hopefully it reflects a little bit on the toughness of the players on the field and what we try and do."

The team's cap logo features the corn-bat guy (he really needs a name) with the corn husks peeling away to create the letter K.

In a state that was the setting for the seminal baseball movie *Field of Dreams*, in which a corn field was unceremoniously plowed under to make way for a baseball diamond, the Cedar Rapids Kernels have proven that baseball and corn can coexist in harmony. The Kernels' nickname and logo embrace the most obvious aspect of the area—the thing you can see most clearly from the airplane window as you're flying over Iowa. Even if corn is not the most exciting foundation for a visual identity, the Kernels current logo is just quirky enough to be fun and make it work.

Charleston RiverDogs

Charleston RiverDogs
1994–present

Current Team Data

Parent
New York Yankees

Class
Single-A

League
South Atlantic

There's a whimsical anecdote on a Wikipedia page dedicated to the Charleston RiverDogs about how the team's owners, the Goldklangs, had a chocolate lab named Taco, or possibly Chazz, and how the neighbors called Taco/Chazz a "RiverDog." The story goes that the Goldklangs took a liking to the phrase "RiverDog" and decided to name their baseball team after it. The thing about Wikipedia, though, is that it also says Rob Lowe was raised by wolves in the Siberian tundra, that the *Minions* movie is a documentary, and that the government is controlling our brains through microwave ovens.

Okay, maybe not, but those are the sort of things you might see on Wikipedia, because Wikipedia itself tells you, "please do not use Wikipedia to make critical decisions" because "some articles may contain errors." Given that the citation for the Taco/Chazz story is (no joke!) a text message to the author, I thought I'd ask about it to confirm its veracity.

Noel Blaha, the team's director of marketing and new media, who has been with the team for almost a decade, told me this: "This story was new to me when I first noticed it in 2014 suddenly appearing on the RiverDogs Wikipedia page. I won't completely discount it but not one that I've ever been told first hand."

The real story is much, much less cute: The team was likely named for huge rats.

The city of Charleston, South Carolina, is situated on a peninsula at the convergence of two rivers, the Cooper and the Ashley, near the east coast. As such, it's a natural location for a port, and the shipping industry has played a significant role in the city's history dating back to the late 1800s.

The original RiverDogs logo

"The urban legend I was told when arriving in Charleston in 2006," Blaha said, "was that the sailors would notice large rats scuttling along the banks of the rivers and colloquially nicknamed them river dogs." Blaha is quick to point out that this story could be "hogwash," but I'm thinking if someone would just text it to a Wikipedia editor, we could get it chiseled in internet stone.

The RiverDogs nickname was chosen from a name-the-team contest conducted in 1993 by the Piggly Wiggly grocery store, "with the winning submission winning a jon boat," Blaha said. Since their debut, the RiverDogs have had conceptually the same logo (featuring a dog rather than a rat), but before the 2015 season, the team unveiled an updated look and a suite of new alternates designed by Studio Simon.

One issue that comes up repeatedly in minor league baseball names is the phenomenon of mashing two capitalized words into one word. Blaha, who worked for the Toledo Mud Hens

SCOTT CASTIGLIA

(two words) prior to his tenure with the Charleston RiverDogs (one word, two capital letters), had some thoughts on the matter. The RiverDogs are a Yankees affiliate in the Single-A South Atlantic League, where the practice is on full display.

"In our league we have the Augusta GreenJackets, Lakewood BlueClaws, and the now-defunct Savannah Sand Gnats," he said. "Why aren't we the Riverdogs or the River Dogs? Is it to balance the typeset? To look more intimidating? Why wasn't Savannah the SandGnats? Blue claw crabs are separate words, like sand gnats. How come they joined together, yet Sand Gnats didn't?" (These are all rhetorical questions, unfortunately, as for now, it's a mystery that has not been solved.)

The RiverDogs franchise debuted in 1980 as an affiliate of the Kansas City Royals. They were the Charleston Royals for five seasons before switching parent clubs to the San Diego Padres and becoming the awesomely named Charleston Rainbows in 1985, which they remained until 1993. After switching to the RiverDogs nickname for the 1994 season, the team basically pretended that the whole Rainbows thing never happened, until fans started making their voices heard.

"For quite some time the feeling was to forget this now-laughable nickname and chalk it up to silly '80s fad marketing like New Coke and jelly shoes," Blaha said. "But around 2009 or so, we began to get more and more people asking for throwback merchandise, and subsequently in 2011 we brought in snapbacks that sold very well, which then led to an expanded lineup of T-shirts and more hats."

Merchandise sales went so well, in fact, that the team had throwback nights each of the last two seasons where they took the field in Rainbows uniforms.

"I think that name resonates with so many people locally because it brings them back to their youth and the days of seeing Carlos Baerga and Roberto Alomar play at the old

College Park," Blaha said. "When we have the merchandise on display or if I'm wearing the gear around town it really elicits two responses—one of bemusement or confusion that a pro ball team actually had that name, but those that remember the Rainbows get really excited to see the old logo and wordmark."

Before the Rainbows and the RiverDogs, the city of Charleston already had a rich baseball tradition dating back more than 125 years. "In fact," Blaha said, "Abner Doubleday was a Union soldier stationed at Fort Sumter in Charleston Harbor."

In the late 1800s and early 1900s, the city's team was the Seagulls, Sea Gulls, or Gulls (note the lack of a "SeaGulls" permutation). For a brief period in the 1920s, the team in Charleston was called the Palmettos, later shortened to the Pals. There was no baseball in Charleston for almost two decades, then in the 1940s and early '50s, the Charleston Rebels were born, winning a couple South Atlantic League championships before closing up shop in 1953.

Looking back over the decades, all of these historical Charleston teams have one thing in common with the Rainbows and the RiverDogs. "What I've found so interesting," Blaha said, "is that long before brand identities and marketing and, shoot, even merchandise sales, Charleston baseball teams had really cool nicknames."

Even the ill-fated ChaSox (a White Sox affiliate who played the 1959 season before becoming the Charleston White Sox) and the Charleston Patriots (a Pittsburgh affiliate who went by that name in 1976 and '77 to celebrate the nation's bicentennial) bucked the trend of boring names for minor league teams.

The RiverDogs, whether they are named for disease-infested vermin or an adorable family pet, are carrying on a long and varied tradition of interesting baseball team nicknames in their hometown—a city that has hosted everything from Rebels to Rainbows. With a polished new take on one of minor league baseball's classic logos, the RiverDogs are writing their own chapter in Charleston's lengthy baseball lure.

Charlotte Knights

The city of Charlotte, North Carolina, was named for Queen Charlotte of Mecklenburg-Strelitz, wife of King George III of the United Kingdom, who held a career 0–1 record in American Revolutionary Wars. And where there are kings and queens, there are knights. So it is that the Triple-A minor league baseball team in Charlotte, one of the many American cities that go by the nickname "Queen City," is the Charlotte Knights.

"The symbolism there is we're defending the Queen City," said the team's general manager Scott Brown. "If you look at the knight's helmet, the top of it is adorned with the Queen City crown. You see that crown in different forms throughout the city, on signage. The Queen City moniker is really something that is used here as a pretty common synonym for the city of Charlotte."

The Knights had a big year in 2014, not only moving from a dumpy old stadium that was technically in a different state (Knights Stadium in Fort Mill, South Carolina) to a beautiful new stadium in downtown Charlotte, but brandishing a new identity that's unlike anything else in their league.

"We knew the ballpark was going to transform our identity in the market—create a Renaissance, so to speak," Brown said. "Our location was a bit of an Achilles heel for us previously. We just thought this was the time. Everything was new with the ballpark, let's create a new look.... The new logo was the next step."

In a growing city with lots of new residents, the buzz around the new stadium created the perfect opportunity to rebrand. "The city, it's really just taken to our location, but also the new look," Brown said. "For the first time in probably a long time, you're seeing a lot of Knights garb on heads and backs."

The new logos were designed by the prolific firm Brandiose, responsible for such wackiness as the El Paso Chihuahuas and the Lehigh Valley IronPigs, among many others. But the team had a specific vision in mind.

"They're known for telling a story, but they're also known for the more way-out, far-out type of look," Brown said. "Very early on, we said that's not what we're after. We were interested in keeping things classic, big league, crisp, clean."

In a city that thinks of itself in terms of the big leagues, it was important for the Knights to embrace a certain type of identity. "Charlotte's a major league city, with the NFL and the NBA," Brown said. "We wanted to keep that minor league affordability, but at the same time appeal to the major league fans who were looking for that classic look."

Charlotte Knights
1989–present

Current Team Data

Parent
Chicago White Sox

Class
Triple-A

League
International

RICK CURTI

The first question was whether the team would choose a new name or stick with the Knights, which they had been since 1989. One option was to go way back in the city's substantial baseball history to a team that appeared first in 1892 as an independent team and then in various iterations until the early 1970s, when they were an affiliate of the Washington Senators.

"Hornets was one of those nicknames that we considered as we were making the move uptown," Brown said. "Just about that time is when New Orleans gave up the name and things started to percolate around the NBA circles here that they were going to reclaim Hornets."

So the city's baseball team stayed with the Knights, but went away from the green and blue chess piece logo that they had used since 1999 to a color palette unique to the International League.

"When you look at our league, it's dominated by red, white, and blue," Brown said. "So we kind of skewed away from that."

The current logo features silver, an obvious reference to a knight's armor, but even more prominent is gold, which is not just a reference to the riches of the Queen City.

"Gold was discovered here back in the 1830s," Brown said. "It's why Charlotte is a banking hub for the southeast. It's in large part due to the discovery of gold and the need for banking." (That discovery of gold is why UNC-Charlotte goes by the name 49ers.)

Finally, the team's scheme features black and white. "We thought black and white, when you look at baseball, was classic, whether it's the Yankees, or in our case, the parent club being the White Sox," Brown said.

The team's cap logo features a knight's helmet and a letter C that references something not completely obvious to the casual observer. "The C itself is emblematic of the horse's tail wrapped around the knight's helmet," Brown said.

I asked how often he has to explain that the C in the team's logo is a horse's tail and Brown did not hesitate: "Pretty much every day."

The Knights nickname does create something of a conflict with their longtime mascot, a dragon named Homer. "Naturally, a dragon's main enemy is a knight, who's charged with slaying it," Brown said.

In fact, one of the team's alternate logos might be particularly alarming to Homer. "If you look at our alternate cap, it's the shape of a K with the sword going through the breast of the dragon," Brown said.

But Homer should breathe easy, as the Knights rely on him to be the face of the team. "In the minor leagues, players come and go, so it's hard to market around them," Brown said. "Homer is the most iconic symbol of the franchise.... Homer is the friendly dragon and a member of the team."

In a city named for a queen from 200 years ago with a baseball team named for warriors from Medieval times, it feels surprisingly like a brand new day for the Charlotte Knights. With a new stadium and a classic-feeling identity, the minor league Knights have staked a claim to their place in a major league city.

Clinton LumberKings

Clinton LumberKings
1994–present

Current Team Data

Parent
Seattle Mariners

Class
Single-A

League
Midwest

The sawmills along the banks of the mighty Mississippi River in Clinton, Iowa, were the centerpiece of a booming industry that, in its heyday, made royalty of its patricians.

"From the late 1800s, basically from about 1859 to about 1900, Clinton was known as the sawmill capital of the world," said Brad Seward, the Clinton LumberKings' public address announcer.

The city's riverfront was home not only to sawmills, but also the businesses that relied on that industry, like furniture vendors and companies that made materials and machinery for the sawmills.

"Eventually," Seward said, "the people that were in charge of the sawmills in this town were known as lumber barons, or lumber kings."

Of course, the economic influence of the lumber industry fell off significantly over the course of the 20th century, but it's still very much a part of the culture of the American Midwest. So when the Clinton Giants rebranded as the Clinton LumberKings in 1994, baseball fans got it.

"This is a community that has, unfortunately, not had the greatest of luck as far as economic development in the past, since the '80s," Seward said. "I think people really like that we harken back to the really fond days of our community—for lack of a better term, the glory days."

He explained, "At one point in time, Clinton had the most millionaires per capita in the world. Think about the population in the 1800s—you had 13 millionaires in the city of Clinton."

Baseball in Clinton started back in the days when the lumber industry was still in full swing, the late 1800s and early 1900s. "We actually were called the Orphans at one time," Seward said. "We were a team that had moved from another community and originally didn't have a home, so they settled in Clinton and they were called the Orphans."

The LumberKings franchise, established in 1956, is the last of the Midwest League's charter teams, and has gone by the names Pirates, C-Sox, Pilots, Dodgers, and Giants. When the Clinton Giants announced plans to change their name in 1993, a name-the-team contest generated references to the town's casinos, like Blackjacks and Gamblers; its river, like Captains, River Commanders, and River Pilots; and, of course, its lumber history, like Lumber, Lumber Barons, Lumber Company, Lumberjacks, Timber Crew, and Timber Barons, to name a few.

The reference to the lumber industry is not just appropriate to the town of Clinton in general, but specifically to the very spot where the players play the game—Ashford University Field, which first hosted the Clinton Owls in 1937.

"That ballpark is built where some of those sawmills were," Seward said. "A lot of the riverfront is on an old sawdust landfill. Literally, the home of the LumberKings is where the lumber kings, the people, were."

And as with many clever nicknames, Clinton's is a double entendre. "It harkens back to the past, but it also goes well with baseball and the use of wood bats," Seward said.

Seward has been the LumberKings' public address announcer since 1996 and is enough of a fixture that he was featured in the 2013 book *Class A: Baseball in the Middle of Everywhere.* ("Chapter 16 starts out with me being pretty emotional about losing the championship series," he said.) But his involvement with the team goes well beyond his professional role. He was a fan as a child, and had the same questions about the team's identity when the impending change was announced.

"I've been going to games since I was very young," Seward said. "I went through 1993 going, well why are they changing the name from the Giants to a different team?"

Little did he know at the time that maintaining the parent club's name would have resulted in even more change.

"At the time we were entering about our 12th or 13th year with the San Francisco Giants affiliation, and there were a lot of folks that really liked having that notoriety of being a minor league team and having the name of the parent club," Seward said. "After the 1994 season, as fate would have it, the Giants actually did leave to reaffiliate and we would have been known as the Clinton Padres at that point. And then we went through several different organizations. We would have had a different name every two to four years."

Louie circa 1994 (above) and updated for the 2000s (below)

Instead, the LumberKings, who have been affiliated with the Padres, Reds, Expos, Rangers, and now the Mariners, have had the same name and, essentially, the same identity for more than two decades.

"The one thing that has remained a constant since 1994 has been the LumberKing name," Seward said.

The team's mascot, Louie the LumberKing, originally designed by Todd Steffens of Sullivan and Steffens Marketing and Design, did undergo a fairly significant update in the mid-2000s. He grew his mustache out to a goatee, traded out his board with a nail for a real baseball bat, and made a wardrobe change wrought with significance.

"We had gone to the playoffs several times, and I think as part of the success we finally said, let's change this crown from silver to gold," Seward said. "So we put some gold into our logo, and it changed things."

It's also hard not to notice that at a time when many of baseball's stars were suddenly inflating like balloons, Louie was also looking a bit ripped.

"There were a few people who poked fun at the time because we were in the middle of the potential steroid controversy," Seward said. "And they're all, 'Oh, what happened to Louie?'"

Seward laughed about the connection, but it's something the team takes seriously. "We were actually the franchise that had a steroid awareness night and handed out sampling cups to folks," Seward said. "It was poking fun at those on the steroids, but at the same point in time it was bringing a lot of attention to a really critical juncture at that point in the game of baseball."

The LumberKings' alternate logos include a wood-grained C with a gold crown and a CL that features actual lumber.

While the primary logo itself is a cartoon with a fun backstory, the team's uniforms are fiercely traditional, following baseball custom to the letter, as it were. "The home uniforms have been white with script since 1994—that script LumberKings," Seward said. "The road uniforms have always been the grey with the green Clinton across the front of them."

The cartoon logo is not featured prominently when the team is on the field—for now. "The only time Louie ever shows up in our uniforms are on our hats and on our batting practice tops that we occasionally wear during games," Seward said. However, "there has been talk of incorporating Louie maybe more into a different set of uniforms."

Sports offer fans an opportunity for escapism, a service the Clinton LumberKings perform for the entire community by paying homage to better times, to an era in the city when the lumber industry made stars of its citizens (the Timberatti?). The LumberKings have a fun nickname and a likeable mascot, but the name is much more than that. It's the manifestation of a collective memory, a community's longing for the days that it was on top, when business was booming and industry made men kings.

Colorado Springs Sky Sox

Colorado Springs Sky Sox
1988–present

Current Team Data

Parent
Milwaukee Brewers

Class
Triple-A

League
Pacific Coast

The majestic Pikes Peak, one of 53 mountains in the state of Colorado that ascend above 14,000 feet, was named for Zebulon Pike, who led an 1806 expedition to the base of the mountain. The mountain has been called a lot of names, including the Arapaho *Heey-otoyoo* (Long Mountain), *El Capitán* (by Spanish explorers in the 1700s), Highest Peak (by Zebulon Pike himself), James Peak (after Edwin James, the first American to actually summit the mountain), Pike's Peak (by people who appreciate proper grammar), and Pikes Peak (by the apostrophe-hating US Board on Geographic Names in 1890). For the record, as a resident of Colorado, I would like the name officially changed to Zebulon's Peak, because Zebulon is kind of an awesome name.

At 14,114 feet, Pikes Peak is not the tallest mountain in Colorado—in fact, it's only the 20th tallest in the whole state—but it's the only "fourteener" for roughly 50 miles in any direction, so its height is accentuated. The mountain is one of the main attractions near Colorado Springs, Colorado's second-biggest city.

Colorado Springs is also home to another attraction, the Colorado Springs Sky Sox, Triple-A affiliate of the Milwaukee Brewers. The current version of the Sky Sox debuted in 1988 as an affiliate of the Cleveland Indians, then partnered with the nearby Colorado Rockies from 1993 to 2014. However, their name derives from a Major League team that this particular franchise has never been affiliated with. The first Sky Sox franchise played in a tiny Single-A league that existed for about a decade after World War II, and their name was an homage to their parent club.

STEVE & TAMMIE STILES

"Our name came about because of the affiliation with the White Sox back in the '50s in the earliest iteration of the Sky Sox here in Colorado Springs," said Nick Debroff, the team's director of public relations. "That team was part of the old Western League from 1950 to 1958."

The good news is that those Sky Sox won the Western League championship in the league's final season in 1958 and are the league's reigning champions for all eternity. The bad news is that the team drew only 61,000 fans for the entire season that year. The city would go three decades before being home to a baseball team again, and when that finally happened, the new franchise reprised the name of the city's former team.

The current franchise's nickname pays homage to the Western League's Sky Sox from the 1950s.

COURTESY COLORADO SPRINGS SKY SOX

"When that league folded, there was no baseball in Colorado Springs until 1988," Debroff said. "When they brought the team back, they used the same name that had been used with that White Sox affiliate."

So that's where the Sox part of the name comes from. But most baseball teams who adopt the archaic pluralization of "Socks" amend it with a color—be it Red, White, Blue, or Aqua. So where do the Sky Sox come from?

"The Sky is really just sort of a nod to being at the highest elevation of any ballpark in North America," Debroff said.

To elaborate, the Sky Sox play in America's highest-elevation professional baseball stadium, Security Service Field, which sits at 6,531 feet. So think about all of the problems that the Colorado Rockies deal with—batted balls that fly about 10 percent farther than at sea level, pitched balls that won't break or slide because of the lack of friction in the thin air, and baseballs that actually shrink and lose weight unless they're stored in a humidor. Then add about 1,000 feet to Denver's elevation and you'll see why Colorado Springs is the poster child for why the Pacific Coast League has a reputation as a hitter's league.

The original identity of this new Sky Sox franchise featured green script with Pikes Peak and the city's skyline illustrated in an underlining swash. Fans were reacquainted with this identity in 2015 when the team gave out bobblehead likenesses of Craig Counsell, who wore the Sky Sox green and interlocking CS from 1995 to 1997, and who was named manager of the Brewers, the team's parent club, in 2015.

The Sky Sox updated their look in 2009, abandoning the green script in favor of an ominous mountain, presumably Zebulon's—er, Pikes Peak—with a glowering expression complete with cloud eyebrows. Part of the inspiration for the new look can be found in Colorado Springs' culture itself—the top four employers in the city are Fort

Carson, Peterson Air Force Base, Schriever Air Force Base, and the US Air Force Academy.

"The reason for the rebrand was to put a fresh new spin on the Sky Sox logo," Debroff said. "Because of the military presence in Colorado Springs, red, white, and blue was a natural color scheme to move to."

The new logos, designed by Dan Simon of Studio Simon, don't just feature red, white, and blue, but also sky blue, a wink and a nod to the team's name and to Colorado's frequent sunny weather. The logo set includes an interlocking CS, which the team features prominently on its cap and in its merchandise, and an alternate Pikes Peak without the eyes.

The Sky Sox play in a state where baseball fans loudly cheer the line "From the mountains..." in God Bless America, and that hosts the Mountain Time Zone's only Major League team. (I don't count the Diamondbacks because Arizona doesn't observe daylight savings time, so they're aligned with the Pacific Time Zone during baseball season.) The Sky Sox name has its roots in a parent club-affiliate relationship that ended almost 60 years ago, but with a visual identity that embrace Pikes Peak as its centerpiece, the name still fits.

Erie SeaWolves

Erie SeaWolves
1995–present

Current Team Data

Parent
Detroit Tigers

Class
Double-A

League
Eastern

The Double-A Erie SeaWolves have all the qualities you'd expect from a loyal affiliate of the Pittsburgh Pirates. They play just under two hours north of the Bucs on the coast of Lake Erie, their nickname derives from a slang term for pirate, and their logo evokes Pittsburgh's erstwhile primary mark from 1997 to 2013.

The problem is, the SeaWolves haven't been a Pirates affiliate since 1998, when they were a short-season Single-A team in the New York–Penn League. After a short stint in the Anaheim Angels' farm system from 1999 to 2000 when they first moved to the Double-A Eastern League, the SeaWolves have been a Detroit Tigers affiliate since 2001.

It's not an accident that the SeaWolves' identity draws from their Big League neighbors to the south. The team is well aware that their brand ties them visually to their former parent club, but it's all part of the club's history. The nickname derives from their original affiliation, in addition to another important factor.

"The combination of the fact that the team was a Pirates affiliate and was just 10 short blocks from Lake Erie made for kind of a natural fit," said SeaWolves president Greg Coleman. "One could debate the geographic description of being near the sea, but it was kind of a nice play on the Pirates affiliation at the time."

The SeaWolves had the chance to put some visual distance between themselves and the Pirates when they rebranded in 2013, but chose to double down on the pirate theme instead. The team briefly considered changing the name of the team altogether during the rebranding process, but decided against it. Then they considered keeping the name but changing the backstory, and decided against that too.

"It became, well, should SeaWolves continue to mean what it meant?" Coleman said. "There's some history with the Battle of Lake Erie in the War of 1812.... So there was kind of a question of whether we should stick with the pirate or lean kind of more towards the War of 1812."

The local history Coleman references is specific to the *Flagship Niagara,* the official state ship of Pennsylvania, which is docked in Lake Erie. The *Niagara* was commanded by Commodore Oliver Hazard Perry, who earned the nickname the "Hero of Lake Erie" for his decisive victory over the British in the Battle of Lake Erie. Perry famously flew a battle flag that read "Don't Give Up the Ship," which Coleman says is the reason there's a flag logo in the SeaWolves' identity system.

Ultimately, though, the War of 1812 just wasn't as much fun as the pirate theme as a primary inspiration for an identity.

"While the War of 1812 has a lot of great relevance locally," Coleman said, "it's a little tough to build a brand around."

Another concept the team explored was to take the idea of the sea wolf to a scary pirate extreme. Dan Simon of Studio Simon, who created the current brand, proposed an identity based on a skull of a sea wolf, but the team wanted a friendlier look.

So the SeaWolves stuck with their current name and its accompanying backstory, as well as the color palette that had been in place since the team's inception. While they toyed with a blue version of the logo to tie in to their parent club in Detroit, the SeaWolves stuck with their original black, yellow, and red.

"They had a lot of equity built up in those colors, and those are colors that fans and the community associated with the SeaWolves," Simon said. "They wanted to maintain some connection to their existing identity."

That said, the SeaWolves decided to emphasize one of those colors more than others.

"We didn't want to mimic the Pirates exactly," Coleman said, "which is why red is a much more dominant color in our palette than the gold is."

The skull identity proposed by Simon was too extreme

The new identity unveiled in 2013 replaced one that, frankly, was not very good. In fact, the logo used from 1999 to 2012 was listed in Bleacher Report's 50 Worst Logos in Baseball History. Dan Simon, who is a kind person and does not like to say negative things, went through great contortions to find a nice way to say that he was glad to give the SeaWolves a new look.

"The main thing we were trying to do was give this identity, the execution of the identity, the professionalism it warranted," he said. (Later in our conversation, Simon told me that he has instructed his wife and children that he wants the epitaph "Life is too short for bad design" engraved on his tombstone.)

1999 to 2012

Coleman, who had worked with Studio Simon on projects with other teams before he joined the SeaWolves in 2011, approached the rebrand with a simple goal. "Our objective was to do something that had local relevance but also would be widely accepted on a national scale," Coleman said.

The SeaWolves are an interesting case. Their 2013 rebrand looks to the casual observer to have been simply an upgrade to the visual brand (and a huge upgrade, at that). But the process was much more than that. It was an affirmation of the team's brand—everything from the team's name, the backstory behind it, the colors, and the logo were questioned, and in the end, only the logo changed. Even the spelling of the name was in question—in the end, the traditional SeaWolves, "one word, two capital letters, in that old-fashioned minor league baseball charm," as Coleman puts it, won the day.

It's the story of a team whose rebrand was successful without resorting to change for change's sake, and in this day and age in minor league baseball, that's saying something.

Everett Aquasox

Everett Aquasox
1995–present

Current Team Data

Parent
Seattle Mariners

Class
Short Season A

League
Northwest

The city of Everett, Washington, about 25 miles north of Seattle, gets roughly 49 inches of rain per year—a good 30 percent more than the national average. That's almost an entire Danny Devito of rain each year. And when it's not raining there, it's just about to rain. When you're in Everett, you know that misty, Pacific Coast drizzle is on its way at any moment.

So in 1995, when it came time to come up with an identity for the local short-season Single-A Northwest League team, a newly minted Mariners affiliate, there was one animal that leapt to mind.

"The frog I think was appropriate and chosen because, you know, we're here in the Northwest and we've got a lot of rain and moisture," said Pat Dillon, the team's radio broadcaster for almost 20 seasons. "Frogs are amphibians and spend time in water and on land."

So the AquaSox baseball team is represented by a frog, but it's not just any frog.

According to Dillon, "The frog is a cross between a Pacific tree frog and a Central American red-eyed tree frog—and Brooks Robinson," And if that sounds just a touch oddly specific, Dillon has his sources. "I'm looking at the official release that we put out back in early 1995."

The frog has another defining characteristic: It looks like it's on a constant, bug-eyed, LSD high, perhaps induced by licking its own hallucinogenic skin. It's this look that likely inspired one of the team's annual traditions.

"Once a year—we've been doing this since 1996—we have a promotion called Frogstock, where it's a salute to the 1960s," Dillon said. "I don't know if you ever played any Grateful Dead music," he trailed off, the implication lingering for a moment, then continued, "The players wear tie-dyed uniform tops."

If you come from a relatively dry part of North America, like my home state of Colorado, you might wonder just what an aqua sock is. While an internet search of the term turns up a footwear item that companies will sell you to wear when you're walking in water, the Everett AquaSox are merely walking in the footsteps of their predecessors, carrying on the baseball tradition of adopting an archaic pluralization of socks (sox) and ascribing a team color to it.

One of the AquaSox's alternate logos pays specific tribute to that tradition. "The Chicago White Sox, one of their logos is just a white sock, and then the Red Sox's primary logo is a pair of red socks positioned a certain way," Dillon said. "We wanted not to duplicate that, but to have something play off the color of our socks."

And this being minor league baseball, "To put our own spin on it, we put the frog toes in there," Dillon said.

All of that being said, there's this: "We don't actually wear aqua socks," Dillon said. "Aqua is one of the colors in our scheme." (Of course, with a logo that features multiple gradient blends and many of the 10 million distinct colors visible to the human eye, it's hard to find a color not in their scheme.)

When the team introduced its new identity in 1995, it was coming off a decade as the Everett Giants, named for its parent club in San Francisco, and a new relationship with the Mariners was beginning.

"I don't know if there was any passing thought of calling us the Everett Mariners, but it was a perfect opportunity," Dillon said, "At that time, 20 years ago in minor league baseball merchandise, crazy logos and colors were just coming into vogue."

But this logo was a bit crazier than some people were prepared for. "It was kind of out there," Dillon said. "People, it takes a while for them to warm up to it. A frog? What is this? After a relatively short period of time, really after the first season, people took to it really well. Right after it was introduced, our hat through New Era was one of the top-selling hats in minor league baseball."

In 2010, the team's relationship with its parent club gave rise to one of the more clever elements in minor league baseball logos. An update to the team's identity took the Mariners' trident M from the 1970s and 1980s and upended it—or at least turned it on its side. Rotated one turn counterclockwise, the M for Mariners works perfectly as an E for Everett, and while the Mariners have moved on to a tepid compass logo, the AquaSox have revived one of Major League Baseball's more popular retro logos.

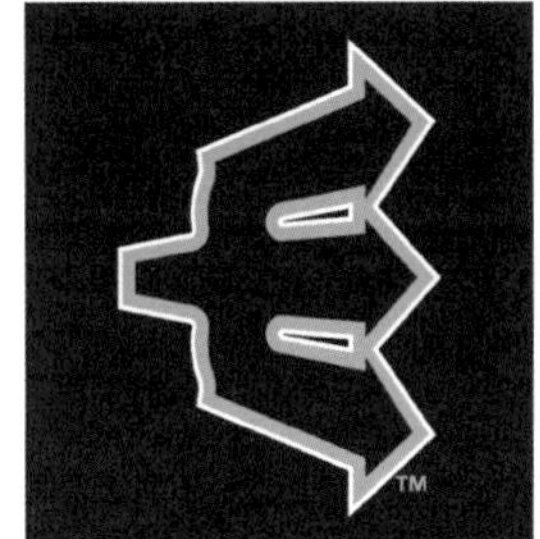

The 2010 update to the logo (pictured at the beginning of this article) included another wink and a nod to the parent club. The new logo moved away from a generic copperplate typeface and incorporated a font similar to the one the Mariners used on their jerseys in the early 1980s.

The old Copperplate pictured here was replaced in 2010.

While much of the AquaSox's identity is out of the ordinary, their origin story shares one important element with basically every other minor league team's—the fraudulent name-the-team contest.

"There was a name-the-team contest, and I can't really speak to the validity of these things, because a lot of times teams will have a name-the-team contest and they'll know exactly what they want to call the team," Dillon said. "You know, they'll say that they chose one of the thousands of entries."

The most important thing about the Everett AquaSox's identity is that it accomplishes what it set out to accomplish. "I think people look at it and they just think fun," Dillon said. "Here's an organization that doesn't take itself too seriously. It's creative and I think it's disarming for folks."

The AquaSox's logo pays tribute to the fact that they play in a town where it's soggy and gray much of the time, but at the same, they've introduced a burst of much-needed color. It's unashamedly wacky, and doesn't try to be anything other than fun. And sometimes, if you're tired of getting rained on all the time, that's just what you need.

Frederick Keys

Frederick Keys
1989–present

Current Team Data

Parent
Baltimore Orioles

Class
High A

League
Carolina

Fort McHenry, a star-shaped military facility in Baltimore, Maryland, was built in 1798. It's been a national park since 1925, but before that, it featured prominently in a handful of wars, including World Wars I and II, and, most notably, the War of 1812. It was during a battle in September of 1814 when US forces at Fort McHenry famously fended off the invading British Navy—with an American flag waving in the sky day and night—that the fort really made a name for itself.

So important was this battle that it inspired a 25-year-old lawyer and amateur poet at the time to write "Defence of Fort McHenry," a poem that tells the harrowing tale of the fort's flag, with its broad stripes and bright stars, illuminated by rockets' red glare, and also bombs bursting in air. The poem was later set to the tune of "To Anacreon in Heaven," the official song of the British Anacreontic Society, an 18th-century group of amateur musicians, and widely used as a patriotic (and difficult to sing) ditty.

With its patriotic message and repurposed tune, the song was titled "The Star Spangled Banner." It would be adopted by the US Navy in 1889, then recognized by President Woodrow Wilson for official use in 1916, and finally, some 88 years after the death of the part-time poet who wrote the lyrics, Congress would adopt the song as the American national anthem in 1931.

The poet who gave us the words to the American national anthem, Francis Scott Key, is buried 50 miles west of Baltimore in the Mount Olivet Cemetery in a town called Frederick, Maryland. Just across the street from Mount Olivet Cemetery lies another institution of American culture, a minor league baseball stadium. The Frederick Keys, high-A affiliate of the Baltimore Orioles, certainly have a unique origin story for their nickname.

"Francis Scott Key is buried across the street. The Keys is kind of a natural name to go there," said Geoff Arnold, the team's broadcasting and public relations manager. "It really kind of captures what minor league baseball is all about, and that is figuring out a name for the city where you are in that helps connect with the historical elements of where you are."

Without this key (ha!) bit of historical information, the reasoning behind Keys' nickname is not immediately evident based on their visual identity. The team's current primary logo does not reference music, and the color scheme has more to do with the Keys' parent club than the red, white, and blue you might expect from a team name for the creator of the American national anthem. (When I first encountered the Keys, I thought they were based in Florida—the orange logo, the F on their cap logo, and the fact that there's a string of islands called the Florida Keys led me astray.)

Once you do know the reason for the nickname, though, everything falls into place. The solid block of text feels like Fort McHenry's ramparts (o'er which we are watching) and the exploding baseballs are actually bombs bursting in air.

While those outside the area might not immediately make the connection between the national anthem and the Keys' nickname, the team has been around for more than a quarter-century and they know their audience.

"We have a pretty dedicated base of fans that have been coming to Keys games for a long time," Arnold said. "I get a lot of different questions, but very few ask me why we're called the Keys."

Not only that, but people who live in the state are inclined to get the reference because of something they see every day. The "bombs bursting in air" in the Keys' logo are also featured on Maryland's official license plate, which depicts the Battle of Baltimore at Fort McHenry (and not, as I had previously thought, Fourth of July fireworks over that Ikea on Interstate 95).

Minor league baseball is full of change. There are 160 affiliated teams (not to mention countless independent ones), and every year, more than a few of them change their parent club, logo, nickname, or location. With almost three decades under their belts, though, the Frederick Keys feel like a stalwart.

"I don't think it's a name that would ever change because of what it represents, and just how fans have embraced it," Arnold said.

A lot of teams have nicknames that derive from their local natural or cultural heritage, but the Keys are the only one I can think where the team's namesake is so specific that it's right across the street. They're not expecting to rebrand anytime soon, but I hope the next time that option comes around, that the only changes they make have to do with the logo and color scheme, and that they leave that name in place as long as they're playing within a baseball's throw of Mount Olivet Cemetery.

Fresno Grizzlies

Fresno Grizzles
1998–present

Current Team Data

Parent
Houston Astros

Class
Triple-A

League
Pacific Coast

The first time a bear appeared on a California flag was in 1846 during the Bear Flag Revolt, a precursor to the Mexican-American War, which ultimately led to California becoming the 31st state of the United States in 1850. Granted, the bear on that flag looks more like the American black bear (or possibly a capybara) than it does the iconic California grizzly that graces the current state flag, but it set the standard for California being represented visually by a bear.

The California grizzly, an extinct subspecies since the 1920s, is the official state animal. It appeared on California's first state seal, designed in 1849, and continues to hang out on the current version, designed in 1937, eating grapes at the feet of Greek goddess Minerva on the banks of the Sacramento River with the Sierra Nevada mountains looming in the background.

The current California state flag, officially adopted in 1911, features Monarch the bear, the last specimen of captive California grizzly, who died in 1911 and whose taxidermied corpse currently resides in the Academy of Sciences at Golden Gate Park in San Francisco. This 169-year history of bears representing the state of California has led to this moment, where Monarch the grizzly's likeness graces the souvenir mug that I am drinking coffee from as I write this article.

It also brings us to the Pacific Coast League's Fresno Grizzlies, Triple-A affiliate of the Houston Astros. Fresno, located in the center of the state, due east of the Monterey Bay and just south of Yosemite National Park in the San Joaquin Valley, seemed like a natural fit for a bear logo.

"Our original thought on the team name was the California grizzly," said Derek Franks, the Grizzlies' general manager, who has been with the team in varying capacities for 12 years. "That was the thing, the tie to Yosemite, the Valley and all that, the California state flag. They chose Grizzlies way back in 1998 when they were putting this thing together. We've stuck with it ever since."

For their first seven seasons, the Grizzlies wore purple and yellow and featured a bear throwing a baseball as their logo. In 2004, Franks' first season with the team, the Grizzlies were ready for a change.

"There was a change in management that led to a change in ownership," Franks said. "I think that at that time there were some thoughts that it was time to refresh and do something different."

"Something different" turned out to be a somewhat ill-fated attempt to cram too many ideas into one brand.

"When they were sort of trying to figure out what's Fresno's thing, there was a lot of talk about agriculture," Franks said. "In some of the polling that they did, there was a lot of mention of the Yosemite National Park, so their goal was to take the agriculture and the sunshine and the warm weather and Yosemite and some of the stuff that people associated with our area and tie it all in to one brand."

The short-lived identity, which was used from 2005 to 2007, featured an unfamiliar color palette, a shield with the letters FG, and a bear possibly eating an exploding baseball.

The new look never really caught on, so it was back to the drawing board. Fan sentiment seemed split in two directions: those who wanted the team to reprise their purple and yellow days, and those who wanted the team to adopt the colors of the only parent club they had ever known, the San Francisco Giants.

Enter the team's current identity, which was designed by the Connecticut-based Silverman Group and has been in use since 2008.

"When we made that switch to that identity, the day we announced it, we did say that we were adopting the orange and black of our parent club," Franks said.

After 17 years together, the Grizzlies and the Giants split up before the 2015 season. The Giants signed on with Sacramento RiverCats, which has led to hilarious but possibly only semi-joking public feuds between the Grizzlies and the RiverCats over such topics as which team has more of a right to wear the California flag as a uniform and which team has a logo that looks like that grumpy cat meme.

Luckily for the Grizzlies, their new parent club, the Astros, not only has a much better farm system, but it also features orange as its primary color.

"We looked at it and said, we do share the color orange as the common color between us and Houston," Franks said, "and that's going to help make this first year work out and be a little bit easier of a transition. It sort of softened the blow that there are some familiar colors there."

The Grizzlies considered a rebrand, but didn't want to rush a new look for the 2015 season, even with a 60-day extension the league grants to teams who change parent clubs.

"Our goal this year has been to change our look and our marketing efforts to reflect an evolving brand without actually changing the primary logo and the colors," Franks said.

This has led to the more prominent use of what Franks calls the G-Paw logo, which had been a secondary logo used only for merchandise purposes, but which has found its way onto the team's new home uniforms and caps this season. (One aspect of the G-Paw logo that warrants pointing out is that the G is shaped like a baseball diamond. "That's one thing that people see at first shot and other people you point it out to them and they say, 'Oh man, that's great,'" Franks said.)

The Grizzlies' identity is decidedly serious and intimidating rather than cartoonish and fun, but the team balances that with attention-grabbing, wacky promotions.

One such promotion has been the team's alternate Fresno Tacos identity. The uniforms were wildly well received, and even resulted in the promise from one prominent company of free tacos for everyone if the team changed their name permanently.

The Grizzlies are unlikely to change their name any time soon, but the fun promotions will be part of the team's identity.

"We feel that the Grizzlies marks are, for 17 years, going on 18 years now, that's been a tradition here in Fresno that we like that we've kept," Franks said. "But we're making up for being kind of a ferocious by doing as much fun and wacky stuff on the marketing side that we can."

There are likely some changes ahead for the Grizzlies as they experiment with fun promotions, but the name Grizzlies, which has roots that date back almost 170 years, will be a fixture in the Pacific Coast League for the foreseeable future.

Hudson Valley Renegades

Hudson Valley Renegades
1994–present

Current Team Data

Parent
Tampa Bay Rays

Class
Short Season A

League
New York–Penn

If you were to get on a boat in New York City and travel north for about 75 miles along the Hudson River, you would arrive at a tiny town of Wappingers Falls, New York. On your way there, you would pass countless historical sites related to the American Revolutionary War. The Hudson Valley played a crucial role in the British goal to divide the New England states, and as a result, lots of important battles were fought there. So important to American history is the Hudson Valley that fortifications built there during the Revolutionary War have since become the United States Military Academy at West Point—just about 25 miles from Wappingers Falls.

So in 1994, when a short-season Single-A team called the Erie Sailors moved from Pennsylvania to Wappingers Falls, they adopted the name Renegades, which reflects the spirit of those plucky Revolutionary Americans, who, in the words of President Thomas Whitmore, declared in one voice, "We will not go quietly into the night! We will not vanish without a fight!"

"We're in the hotbed of the Revolutionary War, West Point, a lot of battles were fought here, and Washington's encampment is in this area," said the team's vice president Rick Zolzer, who has been with the team since its inception. "There are so many things that we thought the name Renegades linked back to, that it just seemed like a natural."

Of course, as with any team name, there were dissenters when the team was announced, but given that this was 1994, before the onslaught of wacky nicknames we see now, it wasn't too bad.

"You're never going to please everybody," Zolzer said. "It's just impossible. There's always going to be somebody who wanted them to be called the Hudson River Sea Monsters." (Hudson River Sea Monsters would have been cool, but if I had been around, I would have advocated for the name Wappingers Falls Honkers, an homage to the area's onetime occupation by the Dutch, who call baseball *Honkbal.)*

"If there were naysayers," Zolzer continued, "they shut up pretty quick, because I think after the sixth or seventh game that year, they started the sellout streak that went for like four or five years."

All of that said, the Revolutionary inspiration for the team name has never been evident in the team's visual identity. Instead, there have been several iterations of a raccoon-based logo. They debuted in green and burgundy, then switched to blue and red a few years later, and then two different shades of cyan.

Selections from the 2017 suite of logos created by Dan Simon

"They thought that you could make a raccoon cute," Zolzer said, "and doing an actual renegade, like a minuteman, just didn't seem to have the same caché."

Raccoons do seem to fit naturally with the term *renegade*—they're smart and curious and they're not afraid to eat your garbage if they have to. Not only that, the Hudson Valley is full of them.

"It is an animal that is all over this area," Zolzer said. "You can't go through Hudson Valley and not see raccoons on the side of the road. They're everywhere."

1994

I asked Zolzer if he gets a lot of questions about the disparity between the origins of the team name and the raccoon-based visual identity.

"I don't think anyone's asked me other than you in the last ten years," he said. (That's why I'm here, folks!)

The original Renegades logo and updated versions a few years later were created by prolific designer Dan Simon of Studio Simon. While those logos were successful (and just the right amount of adorable for a short-season Single-A team), in 2013 the Renegades took the unusual step of having amateur designers on staff create an entirely new brand.

That 2013 current identity was designed by Eben Yager, the team's general manager, who is still with the team, and Corrine Adams, who was involved with the Renegades marketing at the time.

2004

"They spent hours and hours and hours going over concepts and color schemes," Zolzer said. "They got to it. Bunker mentality, and they got it done."

There are aspects of the 2013 logo that a professional designer would have done differently (I'm pretty sure that the word "Renegades" is set in a free font called "Super Hero"), but the result was popular with fans. In particular, a cap logo featuring the eyes of Rascal the raccoon was the team's best-selling merchandise item during that era.

After the 2017 season, the team went back to Simon to update the look. The updated look maintains the color palette that the team adopted in 2013, and refines the centerpiece of the team's identity, Rascal the raccoon. New to the brand are a custom typeface and several new marks.

2013

Every time I research a team, I learn something unexpected. The Renegades have played more than 25 seasons, and are one of the longer-tenured teams in the New York-Penn League. Having seen their logos for years, I never would have guessed that the inspiration for their team name was the Revolutionary War. It's yet another example of what our team's nicknames say about what matters to us about the places we live.

French-born philosopher Jacques Barzun famously wrote, "Whoever wants to know the heart and mind of America had better learn baseball." I might be biased, but I'd argue that if you want to know North America even better, you'd better learn the stories behind minor league baseball nicknames.

Lake Elsinore Storm

Lake Elsinore Storm
1994–present

Current Team Data

Parent
San Diego Padres

Class
High A

League
California

In 2001, the Lake Elsinore Storm, Single-A affiliate of the San Diego Padres, took their unremarkable storm cloud logo and made a terrific decision: They scrapped most of it.

But they didn't scrap all of it. They ditched the cloud and the breezy type and the lightning bolt and even the words "Professional Baseball Team," but they kept one thing—the eyes—the eyes of the storm, as it were.

If brevity is the soul of narrative and a picture is worth a thousand words, then the Lake Elsinore Storm's logo tells a powerful, soulful story. The Storm play in southern California, roughly an hour from San Diego and Los Angeles—a part of the country where it does not rain much—so the shift away from a literal storm cloud to a more figurative storm was appropriate.

"We don't get a lot of weather other than sun and heat," said the Storm's director of media relations Eric Theiss. "It is warmer than most places and a little bit drier than most. When it comes to storms, people might chuckle about that."

So why are they called the Storm? And what's the thinking behind a spooky logo that looks like eyeballs in a haunted Scooby Doo painting that follow you while you walk? Well, start with the city of Lake Elsinore:

"Their logo here is Dream Extreme," Theiss said. "They pride themselves on being this action sports capital of our country or of the world, and I think our logo kind of fits that bill of being a little more extreme logo."

Given that the city of Lake Elsinore is known for extreme sports like motocross and sky diving, the typical minor league baseball approach of appealing to families and children with adorable cartoon logos was not going to work.

"It's a little bit edgy and it's a little bit dark," Theiss said. "We pride ourselves on the edginess and the coolness of it. Our area is that kind of way. It's that edgy motocross new-age guy who is getting tattoos, and we kind of fit right in." (Now that he mentions it, the Storm's full logo has a kind-of tattoo-ish quality about it.)

Original Storm Logo

The Storm's logo is so edgy and cool that the team sells gear to people who have no idea that it's connected to a baseball team. If you visit the team's StormThredz store, it's filled with the team's brand, but no mention at all of any sort of team sport.

"Those guys who are motocross guys are not into baseball or football," Theiss said. "They're into bikes, and even they are the ones who say how cool our logo is."

The Storm's edgy approach extends beyond their nickname and logo. The team pushes

Mascot Thunder (left) with the author

the limits with in-game promotions like its famous "Charlie Sheen-Co de Mayo" in 2011, which included a Charlie Sheen bobblehead, "Tiger Blood" cocktails, a taco-eating contest, and two-for-one Ho-Hos. The promotion garnered national attention and earned the team the Larry MacPhail Award for the top promotional effort in minor league baseball.

This focus on edginess probably explains why the Storm are the only team I've seen that has hosted a World Fighting Championship (WFC) event.

Though it does not explain why the Storm's mascot is a lovable, kid-friendly green dog named Thunder. According to the team's website, Thunder "has a beautiful coat of green fur and wears one of the world's largest pair of shoes." And, "As anyone can see he loves his food, just look at his belly." Not exactly dark.

Lake Elsinore's uniform features the primary logo on the chest, and the famous eyes on the cap (and even the batting helmet). The team has stripped down its logo even further on social media, where their avatar is simply one eye against a red background. (Any graphic designer will tell you that this is basically cheating, as red and black logos almost always look good. To take an already-popular logo and go red and black with it is almost too easy.)

As a brand, the Storm landed on the map in the 2002 season. Their decision to ditch their storm cloud logo after the 2001 season in favor of a minimalist manifestation of an edgy attitude has paid huge dividends.

If the sport of baseball were to tragically disappear from our collective consciousness one day, the Storm are one of the few teams out there that could still exist and even thrive in that horrible dystopian future simply as a cool brand.

Lansing Lugnuts

Lansing Lugnuts
1996–present

Current Team Data

Parent
Toronto Blue Jays

Class
Single-A

League
Midwest

Lansing, Michigan, is known for being an industrial center, home for more than 100 years to Oldsmobile, which was founded as Olds Motor Vehicle Company in 1897 and produced more than 14 million cars at its Lansing factory before production ceased in 2004. The state capital, Lansing is located in mid-Michigan, or for those familiar with local geography, right on the ball of the thumb of the mitten.

Even after the closing of Oldsmobile's doors and recent economic struggles that have hit Michigan particularly hard, the city of Lansing still strongly identifies with its industrial past. So when a Single-A Midwest League baseball team moved to the city before the 1996 season, the inspiration for its new name was easy to spot.

"The automotive industry, pure and simple," said Jesse Goldberg-Strassler, the team's radio broadcaster and author of the book *The Baseball Thesaurus*. "It is the history of Michigan and it's the history based right in Lansing dealing with the automotive industry."

And what, precisely, is a lugnut and what does it have to do with the automotive industry? "Lugnuts are what keep your tires on your car," said Goldberg-Strassler.

From their debut, the Lansing Lugnuts were so tied to the automotive industry that their stadium, now Cooley Law School Stadium, was initially called Oldsmobile Park. Fans of the team were so taken with the name that they permanently altered the city's skyline.

"We're located directly downtown, and right across the street, catty-corner … there's a smokestack, which I believe belongs to the Lansing Board of Water and Light," Goldberg-Strassler said. "And in 1996, the inaugural season, the booster club for the Lansing Lugnuts paid to have an enormous lugnut placed atop. So if you come, you're like, 'There's the biggest lugnut I've ever seen.'" (It's important to note here, as MiLB.com's Ben Hill points out, that the team's logo is technically a bolt, not a lugnut.)

The logo itself features Luggy the Lugnut, who can best be described as dizzy. I asked Goldberg-Strassler whether the team incorporates a lot of spinning-related activities into between-inning entertainment. He said they do not, except for the dizzy bat races, which every team does. I think this is a missed opportunity for the Lugnuts, because while a lot of teams have friendly, cartoonish logos, the Lugnuts are the only team I can think of where the mascot looks as though he might be about to be physically ill.

The non-threatening logo is part of the team's approach to the minor league baseball experience. "We don't need to scare anybody," Goldberg-Strassler said. "If you name your team the Lugnuts, you have that great, goofy Luggy the Lugnut logo. It appeals to all ages.

There's just this idea, look, you come here, you're going to have a good time."

In their more than two decades, the Lugnuts' identity has remained relatively unchanged, with only minimal changes along the way.

"Over the years, heck yeah, the font might be updated, or jerseys might be changed a little bit," Goldberg-Strassler said. "The logo did receive a change, I believe it was in 2004, in terms of the L, which was a very block L, suddenly became a much more fun L."

But the name itself? "The name will not be changed," Goldberg-Strassler said. "The name is a favorite. We're a proud partner with the Toronto Blue Jays, but we're not going to become the Lansing Blue Jays."

The Lugnuts were one of the early adopters in the current wave of wacky minor league nicknames. While some give the Lugnuts credit for helping to usher in the current logo Renaissance, Goldberg-Strassler sees the team as part of a long progression of baseball entertainment that traces back to early personalities like Germany Schaefer and Max Patkin—"people who want to make sure that people who come to the ballpark are engaged and entertained"—and continues today with new and crazier minor league team names each year.

As with recent teams who announce new identities, the reaction to the Lugnuts was predictably mixed when it was first unveiled.

"I think it's the same sort of reaction that we saw [in 2014] with the Akron RubberDucks or the El Paso Chihuahuas or [in 2015] with the Daytona Tortugas, where everyone goes, 'Whoa whoa whoa!'" Goldberg-Strassler said. "And then you give it two years, three years, and now something else has replaced it, and you just take it for granted, and you go, 'Okay, so they're the Hillsboro Hops, they're named after beer.'"

While the Lugnuts have been around for two decades, an eternity for a minor league baseball team these days, they still appear on the list of the top 25 teams in terms of merchandise sales each year, holding their own against an army of newcomers. Goldberg-Strassler attributes this to the logo's timelessness. "One thing I'm proud of, I don't feel that the nickname has been dated over time," he said. "I'm glad that Lansing Lugnuts are still as fresh as ever."

A fun L (above) replaced an older, blocky L (below).

The Lugnuts have accomplished exactly what they set out to accomplish with their identity. Their team name pays homage to an important aspect of their local community while still being light and fun. Even after just 20 years, they're firmly entrenched not just in their own community, but as one of the patriarchs in the current movement of wacky, family-friendly minor league logos.

Lowell Spinners

It's a safe guess that the Lowell Spinners, a short-season class-A Red Sox affiliate in the New York–Penn League, are the only sports team whose identity is based on yarn.

In the early 1800s, the city of Lowell, Massachusetts, rose to prominence as the cradle of the Industrial Revolution. The foundation of the thriving city was water-powered textile mills, which took raw cotton and turned it into cloth or yarn. The main innovation of Lowell's mills, invented by the town's namesake, Francis Cabot Lowell, was integrating machines and human employees in one building for the first time. With new technology powered by the nearby Merrimack River and operated at first by the "Lowell Mill Girls" and later by Irish immigrants, the city was transformed from a farming community to one of the most important in the New World.

With cotton production eventually moving to Southern states, Lowell fell into decline in the early 1900s and was fairly depressed until a slow rebound began in the 1970s. While the city found a new identity as a trendy destination for arts and culture, many mills were converted to apartments or office buildings. One of the innovations that has contributed to the city's rebirth was a new minor league baseball stadium, Edward E. LeLacheur Park, which opened in 1996 in the shadow of Lawrence Mills, now a residential building, just over half a mile from Lowell National Historical Park.

The ballpark plays host to the short-season class-A Lowell Spinners, named for the process of cotton spinning.

"If you come to Lowell," said Spinners Assistant General Manager Jon Boswell, "when you're at the ballpark, when you're sitting in the seats in the stands, you look out and you see the smokestacks, you see the old mill buildings, and that's really where the name the Spinners comes from."

What you'll notice first in the team's current logos, designed before the 2017 season by Francis Santaquilani of FS Design, is a smirking alligator wielding a baseball bat and entangled in yarn spun from those aforementioned mills. The team's longtime mascot, named Canaligator for Lowell's extensive system of canals, takes center stage in the identity. As with nearly every rebrand, the new gator-centric look has raised some eyebrows.

"The feedback has been interesting," said Brian Radle, the team's

Lowell Spinners
1996–present

Current Team Data

Parent
Boston Red Sox

Class
Short Season A

League
New York–Penn

assistant general manager. "It's funny how some people ask us about the alligator."

He understands the questions, but Radle says the team is unapologetic about taking a fun approach to their new look.

"Alligators don't necessarily exist in Massachusetts," Radle admits. "But that's something about us, if it gets people talking about us, then great. It's a fun side of our product."

The Spinners' previous logos, created by Single Source Marketing, feature the product most commonly associated with the mills. "When you look at the logo, you see the yarn, you see thread, you see the spindle," Boswell said. "And that's really what we wanted to encompass when we came up with the logo."

The team's most commonly used marks are the primary wordmark with a baseball bat spindle as the letter I and a cap logo that features the spindle with the yarn form the letter S for Spinners, all of this in colors that are almost (but not exactly) those of the only parent club the team has known, the Red Sox.

The Spinners logos might seem understated now, but they've been through their fair share of cartoony, kid-friendly logos. The team featured a dizzy baseball named Stitch from their inception in 1996 until a rebrand in 2008. But Stitch, too, didn't quite fit the bill, as it were.

"He always had a little bit of aggression in his face there," Boswell said. "When we were sitting down for the logo rebrand, as we got talking, and as we got to spitballing, Stitch kind of became, 'Is it family friendly?' We pride ourselves on family as one of the first things we do, and when you see this angry baseball, does that really fit that message?"

While the Spinners have a distinct identity and a deep back story, the team is aware that it's competing for kids' attention in an increasingly crowded minor league marketplace. They participate in the Little League uniform program, but how could they get kids interested in a logo based on the Industrial Revolution and buildings that have been around for 200 years?

"You look around, Boswell said, "and you see all these funny team names like the Biscuits and the RubberDucks and those are the ones that all the Little League teams are named, even in your local community, and we were like, 'How do we change that?'"

By playing on your community's hate for their biggest rival, that's how. The Spinners play just 25 miles from Boston, so their fans are likely to have specific feelings about a certain team to the south. Thus was born the Yankees Elimination Project, which not only did away with a lot of Little League Yankee gear, but was a great way to promote the Spinners.

"If your Little League team in the market was named the Yankees, we would allow you to become the Spinners," Boswell said. "We would provide hats and a stipend to get T-shirts or jerseys or whatever the league happened to make. We had kids who would say, 'I don't want to be a Yankee,' so we didn't want anyone to have to be a Yankee either."

The Spinners have a logo based on a cartoon alligator and a team named for a serious aspect of their community's past. They play at the lowest level of the affiliated minor leagues, so you're not likely to see them topping any merchandise sales charts. But they are beloved by the local community and have a loyal fan base—the team sold out 413 straight games from 1999 to 2010. The Spinners accomplish exactly what they hope to with their identity. What they lack in pizzazz (what I think of as "the Chihuahua effect") they make up for in consistency and sincerity, maintaining the same name for two decades and relying heavily on just a couple logos for most of their branding.

Memphis Redbirds

Memphis Redbirds
1998–present

Current Team Data

Parent
St. Louis Cardinals

Class
Triple-A

League
Pacific Coast

In a minor league baseball landscape of increasingly outrageous logos and team names, the St. Louis Cardinals farm system is unusual. Three of the Cardinals' six affiliates are named directly for their parent club, including Double-A Springfield, High-A Palm Beach, and Rookie League Johnson City. Two of the three Cardinal affiliates with unique names are the Low-A Peoria Chiefs and the Short-Season Class-A State College Spikes.

The third is the Triple-A Memphis Redbirds, who, of course, are indirectly named for their parent club. The nickname Redbirds has long been an unofficial moniker for the St. Louis Cardinals—in fact, the big league club sells a membership to a fan club called Redbird Nation, which has nothing to do with the minor league team in Memphis.

The Memphis Redbirds have been the Triple-A affiliate of the Cardinals since the franchise's inception in 1998. But minor league baseball in the city dates back to 1877, featuring team names over the years of Reds, Grays, Browns, Giants, Fever Germs (!), Lambs, Egyptians, Turtles, Chickasaws, Blues, and Chicks.

The Redbirds rebranded before the 2017 season with logos designed by Dan Simon of Studio Simon. While the Redbirds were working on their new look, other teams were upping the ante on the already considerable stakes of minor league baseball's wacky nicknames—teams like the New Orleans Baby Cakes, Binghamton Rumble Ponies, and Jacksonville Jumbo Shrimp, to name a few, would unveil new identities during the same offseason.

But the Redbirds were content to remove themselves from that discussion.

"We could have gone several different routes, and I always use the Memphis Mudbugs as an example," said Peter Freund, the team's owner since March of 2016. "You've got the Mississippi River, you've got the crawfish. We could have just done a total rebrand. That would be what has become more typical in minor league baseball."

In staying with their traditional name and not adopting an overtly outrageous logo, the Redbirds were bucking a trend.

"I almost feel like we were the outlier," Freund said. "We were the one that was unique as opposed to the other teams that were attempting to be unique."

Prior to the rebrand, the Redbirds played two seasons with a primary mark that reflected their parent club, which at that time owned the Triple-A club. Peter Freund knows something about classic brands—he's a minority owner of the New York Yankees, as well as several other minor league clubs. So when he purchased the Redbirds, switching away from a successful logo was not a decision made lightly.

"The birds on the bat is probably my favorite logo in sports. You've got to be careful taking that away," Freund said. "In the end, that's the Cardinals logo, it's not ours. It doesn't reflect the city of Memphis."

That focus on the city of Memphis guided the thinking behind the new logos.

"We didn't think of it in a context of minor league baseball, we thought of it in a context of Memphis," Freund said. "What was intentional was that we created a unique brand for Memphis but remained loyal to the Cardinals identity."

The new logos incorporate neon lights found on the city's famous Beale Street; the team's mascot, Rockey the Redbird; and a musical note that evokes Memphis's considerable musical heritage.

One mark in particular has been popular not just with baseball fans, but fans of the city's music. During a recent music festival in Memphis, caps and shirts featuring a letter M made of neon musical notes was flying off the shelf at the team's store. The mark achieves the team's goal of being iconic and simple.

"Our music note M—which is basically just an M, but it's got the neon tubing and it's shaped like a music note—that M is identifiable with Memphis," Freund said. "I think it's fabulous, and I think that it's timeless, and I think 20 years from, that music note M will always be associated with the Memphis minor league baseball team."

While the new suite of logos focuses on the local community, the Redbirds wanted to be sure that they maintained a close tie to their parent club's brand.

"I just think it's something you want to celebrate," Freund said. "We're four hours away from St. Louis, we're in Cardinals country. Why take away the power of the Cardinals brand, which is one of the great brands in all of sports anywhere in the world?"

To that end, one of the most popular new looks in the new suite has been the "dirty bird" logo on alternate powder blue jerseys, the idea for which Freund credits to Dan Simon. The Cardinals are among a handful of teams that wore powder blue in the 1970s, '80s, and into the '90s, and that retro look has become a sentimental favorite among baseball fans.

The Redbirds are walking a couple fine lines, and doing a fairly good job of it. The first fine line is between a classic look and the wackiness that defines the minors now. Their brand is simple and classic, but the cartoon dirty bird is a little more fun than the identities you'd find in the Majors (Baltimore's cartoon Oriole notwithstanding). The second fine line is the one between adopting their parent club's identity and creating something unique to their local home. The team name is an overt wink and a nod to the Cardinals, but the focus on neon and music in the branding is distinctly Memphis.

Midland RockHounds

Midland RockHounds
1999–present

Current Team Data

Parent
Oakland Athletics

Class
Double-A

League
Texas

The Double-A Oakland A's affiliate in the Texas League is called the Midland RockHounds because it sounds better than the Midland Geologists. And Rocky the RockHound is definitely a better mascot than some guy named Ted (or whatever) in a white lab coat. When I spoke with Brian Smith, Midland's director of public relations, he said that the first thing people want to know about the team is just what a RockHound is.

"It's simply just a nickname for a geologist," he said. "Out here in west Texas, the oil and gas industry has been the way of life for years, for a century. And so, when we were coming up with the new nickname in 1999, we wanted to have a name that would honor our local tradition, and be unique, so we went with RockHounds."

The logo features a dog named Rocky wearing a hard hat and holding a bat and a baseball-shaped rock. The word "RockHounds" is set in a cracked-rock typeface, while the name of the town, Midland, is set in a stretched-out approximation of the typeface from Jurassic Park. With all that going on, you might not notice the oil rigs over Rocky's shoulder, but locals recognize them right away.

"If you were ever out here in west Texas," Smith said, "that's what you would see. You would see the rigs everywhere, the pump jacks and the gushers. That's definitely a ubiquitous symbol for us."

Another detail that casual observers might overlook is a subtle homage to the RockHounds' home state worked into the logo. "If you look on the hound's arm that's holding the baseball," Smith said, "he has the sundial, the old-fashioned geologist's watch. And then the two shapes on the band are actually a rough outline of the state of Texas."

Because my journalistic integrity compels me to ask the tough questions, I had to follow up on a hunch I had about this logo. The first time I saw Rocky the RockHound, I immediately thought that he was the older, burlier brother of Poochie the Dog from the Simpsons. Poochie first appeared on the Simpsons on February 9, 1997—two years before the RockHounds arrived on the scene—in an episode called "The Itchy and Scratchy and Poochie Show," and it's my professional opinion that they look like they might be related.

I asked Brian Smith if there was a connection. He laughed, and said, "No, I've actually never heard that."

So that answers that.

At home, the RockHounds wear an "RH" logo with the "RockHounds" wordmark emblazoned on the front, but on the road, they like to show off their city.

"The 'M' is our away logo," Smith said. "When we're outside of our market, it's just a way to promote Midland and promote west Texas and show our city off. Our away jerseys say 'Midland' across the front. It's just a natural tie-in there."

The RockHounds are the western-most Double-A franchise in baseball, so while they are not close to their Major League affiliate in Oakland, they're closer than any other Double-A team is. When they were affiliated with the Cubs (1972–1984) and Angels (1985–1998), they adopted the identities of their parent clubs. Some minor league teams that are close to their parent clubs, like the San Jose Giants, can get away with that. But when the RockHounds switched affiliations to the A's in 1999, they saw an opportunity—and the need—to rebrand with something more appropriate to the local community.

"Although the A's are a fantastic organization, they're just very far away from here. It's tough for our casual fans to keep that connection," Smith said. "When your parent club is too far away, then having your local brand is really what drives your casual baseball fan and your entertainment fan."

With that in mind the RockHounds became one of the early adopters in the current wave of fun, kid-friendly, location-specific minor league nicknames. Recent years have seen a growing wave of teams taking a similar approach. Rather than feeling threatened by the competition, the team feels a certain amount of pride in seeing the increasingly wacky logo landscape.

"We had our chance to create our own brand and become very unique and have a very distinct identity, and it was something we were very excited about," Smith said. "Now, you see a lot of other teams that are trying to come off of that. You've got teams like the Chihuahuas, the RubberDucks—the Storm have been fantastic. You see a lot of new creativity there. If you look back over the last 15 years, you see that ours has been consistent, because it was so bold at the beginning."

They've been around for almost two decades, but the Midland RockHounds are still regularly included on minor league baseball's annual list of the top 25 top merchandise sellers. This requires not only support from the local community—which they have, setting attendance records the last three seasons—but nationwide. One of the ways this national support manifests itself is in little league teams that adopt the RockHounds nickname and logo from as far away as California and Vermont.

"All the post cards we get from kids all over the country wearing their RockHounds gear and being part of the team," Smith said, "it's just fun. Because you know, even if they never set foot in west Texas, you've made a RockHounds fan, you've made a baseball fan."

You don't necessarily think of west Texas when you go looking for fashion makers, but the Midland RockHounds are the poster team for the location-appropriate, kid-friendly, cartoonish logo that you see everywhere now. It's not unusual to see a Rock Hounds cap (or a whole bunch of them on a little league team) at Major League or minor league games anywhere in the country—and it's a pretty safe bet that that was not the case when they were the Midland Angels or the Midland Cubs. They took a deliberate approach to their branding and their success has exceeded even their own expectations.

Ogden Raptors

Ogden Raptors
1994–present

Current Team Data

Parent
Los Angeles Dodgers

Class
Rookie

League
Pioneer

The Ogden Raptors, advanced rookie level affiliate of the Los Angeles Dodgers, were never meant to be. In 1993, Dave Baggott, who describes himself as the founder, president, owner, and janitor of the team, went to the mayor of Ogden, Utah, with the idea of bringing a minor league team to town, and the mayor was quick to respond.

"He said, 'That's great, but it has to be called the Trappers,'" Baggott said.

The Trappers were a popular team, owned in part by noted baseball executive Bill Murray, that played about 40 miles to the south in Salt Lake City in the late 1980s and early 1990s. The idea was that adopting that nickname would give the new Ogden team a head start in the marketing department.

"We had every intention of calling it the Ogden Trappers, until we did a name-the-team contest with the local newspaper," Baggott said. "We had no intention of changing the name, but it's a good way of getting some free publicity and get off the snide in getting some marketing done."

If they had gone with the popular vote, the team in Ogden would definitely have been called the Trappers, but something funny happened along the way. A 10-year-old girl named Tracy submitted the name Raptors to the contest.

"We did a little research and obviously the popularity of the *Jurassic Park* movies had just hit the country," Baggott said. "We have a dinosaur park right here in Ogden, and Utah is world-renowned for its archaeological finds of dinosaur fossils, and I thought, this would be a great way to give ourselves our own identity instead of playing off of somebody else's."

The rest, as it were, is prehistoric history. Tracy is in her 30s now, and has taken full advantage of her prize of lifetime season tickets. According to Baggott, she's never missed a game.

"Now she's got a husband and two kids that come to the game, too," Baggott said. "She gets hers for free and she pays for the others, and it works out."

The team's original logo, which was created in house in 1993, is modeled after a utahraptor found at the George S. Eccles Dinosaur Park in Ogden. The utahraptor, Baggott is quick to point out, is quite a bit larger than the fearsome velociraptors found in the *Jurassic Park* movies.

The team's colors, which were determined through informal market research, are shared with a Major League club that the team has never had a relationship with.

"Our original concept colors from day one were basically the same as the Seattle

Mariners," Baggott said. "The surveys we did before we chose our team colors—we did surveys of men and women—and the majority of the folks voted for the color scheme that was basically the Seattle Mariners at the time."

On the last day of the 2015 season, the Raptors unveiled a new look for the first time since their founding. The updated identity features a leaner, sleaker Oggie the raptor.

"We wanted to change the look of the logo, but we didn't want to change the identity of the logo," Baggott said. "After 22 years, we just gave him a makeover. So now, instead of posing upright, he's on the move and he's heading somewhere. The kids like to think he's on the hunt."

The new logo set, designed by Jeremy Maxwell of New Era, includes a primary mark featuring an updated rendering of the raptor itself, as well as cap logos that feature the letter O encircling Oggie and Oggie's claw.

With more than two decades of hindsight in his back pocket, Baggott sees that the decision to forego the name Trappers in favor of Raptors was a good one.

"It turned out to be the best thing we ever did," he said. "So far, of the 160 minor league baseball teams nationwide, other than ours, there is no other dinosaur-themed team, so hopefully we have a little bit of a niche with the kids' market in regards to wanting to wear something dinosaur related."

Of course, as with all successful minor league baseball logos, the team's brand has appeal beyond the sport. The *Jurassic Park* movies are back in favor, and dinosaurs are on the forefront of the popular imagination again. (To wit: You know those wacky inflatable T-Rex costumes you see everywhere these days? The Raptors will have four people wearing those to drag the infield after the sixth inning next season.)

Most importantly, if it's an attractive logo featuring popular subject matter, it's going to be well received.

As Baggott explains, "You don't have to be a baseball fan to have a dinosaur on your hat."

Portland Sea Dogs

Portland Sea Dogs
1994–present

Current Team Data

Parent
Boston Red Sox

Class
Double-A

League
Eastern

The Portland Sea Dogs are among the most consistently popular teams in all of minor league baseball. They have been a fixture in New England since the 1993 expansion of Major League Baseball required the minor leagues to expand as well, first as the Double-A affiliate of the Florida Marlins, and more recently with the Boston Red Sox. The design of their logo is the result of a simple equation that goes like this: Chicago Bulls plus San Jose Sharks plus Nancy and Sluggo equals Portland Sea Dogs.

In case that equation is not entirely self explanatory, I spoke with Chris Cameron, the team's assistant general manager and director of media relations, who explained. "The logo's actually created by Guy Gilchrist. He's the guy who does the Nancy comic strip," he said. "He told us he took the eyes from the old Chicago Bulls, and got the bat-in-the-mouth idea from the San Jose Sharks."

Guy Gilchrist not only draws the world-famous Nancy comic strip, but he worked on the Muppets, Looney Tunes, Tom & Jerry, Fraggle Rock, and The Pink Panther. Not only that, he's a huge baseball fan—specifically of the Red Sox. In a recent phone conversation, he regaled me with stories of growing up on baseball, then raising his own children in minor league parks all around New England.

The Portland Sea Dogs were the first minor league baseball logo he designed, followed by the Norwich Navigators, New Britain Rock Cats, and Binghamton Mets. And about that equation above?

"At the time that I did the Sea Dogs, the biggest-selling logos were the San Jose Sharks and the [Chicago] Bulls," he said. "And so, I mean, duh. I took Slugger and instead of him having a hockey stick in his mouth, I put a bat in his mouth. And I had him looking straight at us, just like a bull."

The Sea Dogs' arrival on the scene ended a 45-year baseball void in Portland, Maine. Their logo, in its original Marlins teal (required by law of all 1990s expansion sports teams) was popular during the early years, but it became even more popular when the Sea Dogs switched affiliations (and team colors) to the nearby Boston Red Sox in 2003.

"When we became a Red Sox affiliate, we took a good thing and made it even better," Cameron said. "Obviously, New England is the heart of Red Sox Nation. Everyone up here, for the most part, is a diehard Red Sox fan, and so the fact that you can now see the future of your favorite Major League Baseball team right here in your back yard has just really increased the popularity of the team."

The original Marlins teal Sea Dogs logo

One of these diehard Red Sox fans was Guy Gilchrist, whose feelings were pretty clear when the team made the switch. "Oh, my gosh, I went crazy. Are you kidding me?" And as for Slugger's new colors? "He does look good in red, white, and blue. He really does."

As is the case with nearly every new logo in minor league baseball, however, fans didn't buy in right away. "One person called the local radio station and complained, Who's going to like this? Women and children are the only ones who are going to like this," Cameron said. "And our owners were like, yup. Jackpot. We want the women and children to like it and we'll have success with that because we've already got the sports fans." (One woman who liked the logo was Guy Gilchrist's future wife: "When I met my wife," he said, "she had one of the Sea Dogs caps in teal. She's a Marlins fan.")

Guy Gilchrist put the team's early marketing strategy a little more bluntly: "I think many people, when they try to create a character or create a logo, they're trying to sell products to fans of the organization. And that's not the right way to do things. Fans of the organization will buy anything. If they're fans, they'll buy it. It could be the ugliest thing you've ever seen in your life. What you're trying to do is create something that's appealing to somebody who doesn't even know what it is."

Obviously, this formula (which the rest of the baseball world seems to have caught on to in recent years) has been successful for the Sea Dogs. Minor League Baseball's annual list of the top 25 teams in terms of merchandise sales has included the Sea Dogs every year since their inception. "Only one other team can say that for the same amount of time that we've been on it and that's the Durham Bulls," Cameron said. "Of course, they had a major Hollywood motion picture made about them, so it's pretty good company to be in."

Slugger, who is featured in the primary logo as well as a secondary logo, got his name from a cracked Carl Yastremski bat that cup-of-coffee Major Leaguer Roger LaFrancois gave to Gilchrist in the early 1980s. Gilchrist was doing an interview with *Baseball Weekly* about the early success of the logo, when the interviewer asked what the mascot's name was. Gilchrist looked around his studio and came up with an answer on the spot. "His name was either going to be Louisville or Slugger," he said.

So the logo has been popular, the team draws more than 5,500 fans per home game (above average for an Eastern League team), and it can't be lost on the notoriously superstitious Red Sox Nation that their big league team has won three World Series titles since Portland became an affiliate. But it's not all been smooth sailing for the Sea Dogs. One persistent problem has been a misconception about Slugger.

"A lot of people think that a sea dog is a dog, and that is incorrect," Cameron said. "A sea dog is just another name for the common harbor seal, which is found right off the coast of Maine.... If you look at our mascot, he doesn't have paws, he actually has flippers. So he is indeed a seal and not a dog."

Ultimately, if the price you pay for having a wildly successful logo and selling a bunch of merchandise every year is that you have to explain the difference between a dog and a seal every once in a while, that's not such a bad deal.

Rancho Cucamonga Quakes

Rancho Cucamonga Quakes
1993–present

Current Team Data

Parent
Los Angeles Dodgers

Class
High A

League
California

The Rancho Cucamonga Quakes have had the same team name and, conceptually, the same logo since their inception in 1993. In minor league baseball terms, this puts the team's identity roughly on par with prehistoric cave paintings and Betty White—attractive, but really old. In a logo landscape that shifts and changes constantly, it's refreshing to see a team that has stood by its identity and been embraced by the community.

"We don't change our look or name and everything that goes along with it just for the sake of doing so," said Voice of the Quakes Mike Lindskog. "If we were stuck with something that wasn't synonymous with our community and wasn't catchy and cool and neat, maybe we would be driven to try to upgrade."

The Quakes, a Dodgers affiliate in the Single-A California League, are among many sports teams named for horrific natural disasters that might affect a specific area—see the Colorado Avalanche, Miami Hurricanes, Iowa State Cyclones, and San Jose Earthquakes, to name a few. They play about 40 miles east of Los Angeles, not terribly far, geologically speaking, from San Andreas Fault, which threatens to wreak devastating havoc pretty much any day.

In fact, I attended a Quakes game August 23 of 2014, just hours before the South Napa earthquake rattled the state. It raises the question of what the team's response would be should an earthquake hit southern California.

"I imagine that would cause some conversation," Lindskog said. "We want to be respectful in those situations.... I don't think it would necessarily require an identity change if that were the case. Hopefully, we'll never have to cross that bridge."

If anything, the Quakes are doubling down on their identity. The cracked-font logo type appears on pretty much anything they produce—including their caps, which feature a stand-alone cracked Q logo. Beginning in 2014, fans at Quakes games saw the cracked type more than ever before, with a major branding initiative to feature the typeface not just on players' uniforms, but on all signage.

"There are like 350 signs in this ballpark," Lindskog said, "and each and every one of them now is going to have a cracked font."

The earthquake-based identity does not come in to play during promotions or in-game activities, Lindskog said. (When I asked about this, I'm not sure what I was thinking the response would be. I may have been secretly hoping for some promotional theme night where the field splits in half during the seventh-inning stretch and swallows the opposing team into the depths of the Earth.)

The game experience itself in Rancho Cucamonga is intensely family friendly. "This is a huge family environment.... We're not real big envelope pushers as far as the racy stuff," Lindskog said. "We know we live in southern California, but we try to keep it as classy as possible, too."

Much of the in-game experience focuses on the team's mascots, Tremor, who is not an underground, Kevin Bacon-eating monster, but rather a big, green dinosaur—a "Rallysaurus," to be precise. Tremor not only dances and delights fans during the game, but he's a regular at community parades, ribbon-cuttings, and, according to Lindskog, "everywhere you would expect a player in the community to be."

"When you think Rancho Cucamonga," Lindskog said, "I think there's no greater ambassador than Tremor."

The longevity of the team's nickname reflects the attitude of the team towards its community. Just as the Quakes are a fixture in Rancho Cucamonga, the strength of their visual identity has been in consistency. While other teams rebrand and adopt increasingly wacky logos and nicknames, the Quakes have had more than two decades with essentially the same look—with that cracked font appearing everywhere from stadium bathroom signs to the players' jerseys.

In a place where the ground might shift under your feet at any moment, the Quakes are the picture of stability.

Salem-Keizer Volcanoes

Salem-Keizer Volcanoes
1997–present

Current Team Data

Parent
San Francisco Giants

Class
Short Season A

League
Northwest

The year 1997 saw the movies *Titanic* and *Men in Black* take Hollywood by storm. The TV shows *Buffy the Vampire Slayer, Teletubbies,* and *South Park* premiered. Hanson was singing "Mmm Bop," the Back Street Boys were making their United States debut, and the first *Harry Potter* book was published.

And in a small town in western Oregon, a short-season Single-A baseball team in the Northwest League debuted, wearing simple logos created in a world that had yet to witness the likes of the El Paso Chihuahuas, Lehigh Valley IronPigs, or New Orleans Baby Cakes. Today, the Salem-Keizer Volcanoes still play in the Northwest League, they still play in the same stadium, quaintly called Volcanoes Stadium, they've had only one parent club (the Giants), and they still wear the same logos that they wore when they first debuted.

The Volcanoes technically play in the town of Keizer, but they incorporate the larger, adjacent Salem into their geographic identifier to tap into that town's rich baseball history. Salem has played host to minor league baseball since 1940, including teams like the Salem Senators and Salem Dodgers. Before their debut as the Volcanoes, the franchise had played as the Bellingham Giants for two seasons, but moved after having the Northwest League's lowest attendance both years.

The logos rely on type as image, including a primary that features a volcano with lava forming the letter S and a wordmark with a volcano forming the letter A. The team's cap logo takes a slightly less subtle approach, with a baseball literally blowing its top, volcano style.

The team's name, submitted to a name-the-team-contest by Keizer resident Bill Lien, derives from the significance of volcanoes in the region.

"Team ownership selected that name based on how it identifies with Oregon with its large number of Volcanoes," said Jerry Walker, who owned the team in 1997 and continues to do so now, "including Mount Jefferson that is clearly visible over the stadium's centerfield wall."

In addition, the team plays just an hour and a half away from one of the world's most famous volcanoes, and at the time the team was named, that volcano was still fresh in the public's mind.

"Back in 1996, it was only 16 years after the 1980 eruption of Mt. St. Helens," Walker said, "an event that left an indelible mark on many in the region."

And three hours to the south of Salem (and Keizer) lies another volcano-based attraction that defines the state of Oregon.

"Crater Lake, one of the most popular tourist attractions in the state, was created as a result of a volcanic eruption of Mount Mazama," Walker said.

With the preponderance of volcanoes in the area and the impact they've had on Oregon's geography, culture, and economy, it's no wonder that they became the namesake of the local ballclub. But it was the nature of the geological feature itself that made it perfect.

"The name seemed a perfect fit for a sports team as it denotes grandeur and explosiveness," Walker said.

With a nickname and brand that's been in place basically unchanged for two decades, the Volcanoes' uniform is bound to have seen its fair share of eventual big leaguers. Sure enough, the likes of Joe Panik, Buster Posey, Pablo Sandoval, Tim Lincecum, and Sergio Romo have sported the same Volcanoes' red, orange, and yellow that this year's team of wide-eyed, freshly drafted youngsters will wear when short-season Single-A games start later this month.

Mount Jefferson, the one that can be seen beyond the outfield wall from Volcanoes Stadium, is the second-tallest mountain in Oregon. It hasn't had an "eruptive episode" for roughly 15,000 years, which is the geological equivalent of the amount of time the baseball team's brand has remained unaltered. So it seems that Mount Jefferson and the Salem-Keizer Volcanoes are in a battle of wills, waiting to see which will see significant changes first. My money is on the mountain.

Tacoma Rainiers

Tacoma Rainiers
1995–present

Current Team Data

Parent
Seattle Mariners

Class
Triple-A

League
Pacific Coast

If you're not familiar with the history of minor league baseball, and, more importantly, beer in the Pacific Northwest, then the nickname for the Triple-A franchise in Tacoma, Washington, seems to be about as straightforward as they come. The Rainiers' name is obviously inspired by Mount Rainier, the tallest mountain in the state of Washington.

When the weather is clear, fans on the third-base side of the Rainiers' Cheney Stadium get a spectacular view of the mountain, which was named in honor of British naval officer Peter Rainier by fellow naval officer George Vancouver. But to say that the team is named for the mountain and that's the end of the story is a vast oversimplification.

The city of Tacoma, Washington, has had a team in the Pacific Coast League every year since 1960, the longest such streak of any city. Those teams have been called the Giants (1960–65), Cubs (1966–71), Twins (1972–77), Yankees (1978), Tugs (as in tug boats, 1979), Tigers (1980–94), and since 1995, Rainiers.

Before that 1995 season, the franchise switched parent clubs from the Oakland A's to the Seattle Mariners, their neighbors just 35 miles to the north. In the midst of updating their A's-colored Tigers logo to a Mariners-colored Tigers logo, brand-new general manager Dave Bean saw the opportunity for a bigger change. His idea was not well received at first.

Rainiers Media Relations Coordinator Brett Gleason explains:

> He just kind of was offhandedly like, you know maybe this is a perfect opportunity with the new affiliation and all the changes in the front office, the perfect time to rebrand and move on from the Tacoma Tigers—which wasn't a very popular thing at the time because the city had come to like the Tacoma Tigers name and the logo and everything.

In order to sway a skeptical public, the new team name had to really land, so the team turned to two surefire ways to secure the hearts and minds of baseball fans: nostalgia and beer. The Rainiers nickname was first used in the area by the Seattle Rainiers, a Pacific Coast League team from 1938 to 1964 and a short-season class A team from 1972 to 1976.

The Seattle Rainiers took their name from the company that purchased them in 1938, the Rainier Brewing Company, a now-defunct institution that traces its origins back to 1878. In fact, that script R, which should look familiar to those familiar with baseball in Tacoma, once sat atop the brewery in Seattle emblazoned with red light bulbs. The sign was such an icon of the city that it now sits in Seattle's Museum of History and Industry.

When the team announced that a name change was coming after the 1994 season, they

The R Bar down the left field line in Cheney Stadium

let it be known right away what that name would be. Fans who had grown attached to the Tigers nickname were swayed by the new name.

"They figured it might be a good way to grease the wheels on the new name, they started to design some very basic hats and T-shirts with that Rainiers logo," Gleason said. "They put together some really basic hats and T-shirts and they sold like crazy. According to one of our old PR guys who was around at the time, he said they couldn't keep them in stock."

It's probably not by accident that the first Tacoma Rainiers logo looked like it could be a vintage beer ad in Mariners colors.

JARED HAM

In 2009, the Rainiers went through a major rebrand in which they adopted a compass logo to match their parent club, but changed color schemes to red and blue, which do not at all match their parent club. Before the 2015 season, the team's creative director Tony Canepa refined the old script, which had been through countless permutations if you trace it back through the Tacoma Rainiers' first logo, the Seattle Rainiers' logos, and beer labels since the late 1800s.

The Rainiers' brand has been around in one form or another for more than 125 years, so while many teams in baseball are pushing the boundaries with edgy and unique identities, the Rainiers are happy to have a traditional, classic baseball feel.

"It's nice to get some national attention, but we really, really like to serve Tacoma and the south sounds," Gleason said, "and we think we can do that best by just being a recognizable brand that hasn't changed for a long time."

In the end, the origins of the Tacoma Rainiers' name are not as simple as they seem. They're not just a team named for a mountain—they're a team named for another team named for a brewery named for a mountain named for a naval officer who died more than 200 years ago.

Tulsa Drillers

Tulsa Drillers
1977–present

Current Team Data

Parent
Los Angeles Dodgers

Class
Double-A

League
Texas

In 2002, when starry eyed recent college graduates Jason Klein and Casey White of Plan B Branding visited Tulsa, Oklahoma, on a research trip for one of their first projects, the spectacular view from their luxurious accommodations gave rise to a minor league baseball brand that has endured for more than a decade.

"We were staying at a Super 8 because we didn't have any money," Klein said. "On the outskirts of town, there were these great blue flames at night from the refineries as we were out on the more rural part of Tulsa."

Plan B Branding, of course, would become the prolific minor league baseball branding firm Brandiose, and those blue flames would become one of the marks in the suite of logos belonging to the Tulsa Drillers.

The reason for the Drillers' name is pretty obvious to anyone who knows the history of Tulsa. For most of the early 1900s, Tulsa laid claim to the title Oil Capital of the World, and was home to the industry's glitterati—oil giants like Howard Hughes, J. Paul Getty, and William Sinclair.

"It's basically what put Tulsa on the map, when they struck oil just south of Tulsa," said Drillers Director of Public/Media Relations Brian Carroll. "It's still very much an important part of the culture here in this city. As a professional sports team, we liked having that tie back to that era."

So when a Double-A team from Lafayette, Louisiana, moved to Tulsa before the 1977 season, the name Drillers seemed like a natural fit. Oddly enough, the Lafayette team, which had only been around for two seasons, was already called the Drillers, so that made the transition pretty easy. Those Lafayette Drillers, Texas League co-champions in 1975, featured the likes of eventual Major Leaguers Jack Clark and Gary Alexander.

The Drillers filled the baseball void left by another industry-themed team, the Triple-A Tulsa Oilers, who after 72 years in Tulsa, left Oklahoma in 1977 and are now the Louisville Bats, with stints as the New Orleans Pelicans and Springfield (Illinois) RedBirds along the way. (The name Tulsa Oilers lives on today in the form of a hockey team in the ECHL, founded in 1992.)

"It was very applicable to just keep the name Drillers when they moved here," Carroll said. "It worked out perfectly because the Oilers had left town, but obviously the oil industry was very important to people at that time still, so the name Drillers just slotted right in."

While big oil has declined in Tulsa, the name evokes the history of a city that, frankly, would likely not exist were it not for the industry. "It's really about history and what put Tulsa on the map. What changed the livelihood, what made it grow and prosper?" Klein said. "History allows us to provide a romantic angle to something like the oil industry that put you on the map."

The approach that Plan B took, as with all of their early work, was to focus on a narrative. "The story that we told, and all bought into collectively with the team, was this idea of the oil tycoon," Klein said. "Here you are heading west, and as a prospector, you only needed to find one single drop of oil for your life to change as you knew it."

For that reason, there's no oil rig spewing oil all over the place in this brand—the current look, in use since the 2004 season, focus on that micro level.

"This is not a greasy, sticky identity," Klein said. "It's a very regal, majestic identity, specifically designed to highlight that idea of the single drop that would change your life."

The Drillers' brand fits right in with their relatively new parent club, the Los Angeles Dodgers.

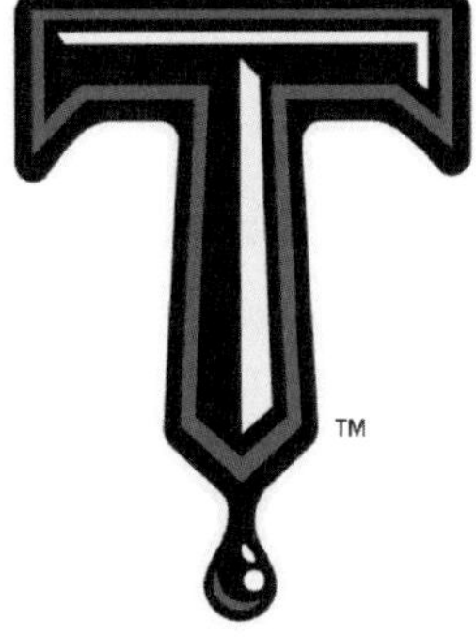

"Our colors match perfectly with the Dodgers, and I think that's helped with the interest there," Carroll said. "That relationship is starting to build and I think that will only get better and open up more doors in that area for us."

And while the Drillers are a Double-A team, when they unveiled their new look in 2004, they wanted a brand that reflected the Major League aspirations of their players.

"We knew you could probably sell more caps by going the cartoon character route, or something like that. We didn't want to go that direction," Carroll said. "I'm not trying to knock anyone else and what their look is, but we want people to know that we're a professional baseball team."

You won't find the Drillers on the list of minor league baseball's top merchandise sellers, as they lack the splash of the Isotopes or Chihuahuas, the market size of Louisville or Oklahoma City, or the historical cache of the Bulls or Mud Hens. But you will find in them a brand that is consistent, relevant, and clean, and that's an animal that's becoming more and more rare in the current landscape—a landscape that has a slightly different look when you see it from the front door of your motel room at the Super 8.

Williamsport Crosscutters

Williamsport Crosscutters
1999–present

Current Team Data

Parent
Philadelphia Phillies

Class
Short Season A

League
New York–Penn

In the late 1800s, Williamsport, Pennsylvania, was home to more millionaires per capita than any other town in the United States. The source of their income was a booming lumber industry that put the town on the map. So when a short-season Single-A baseball team started playing in Williamsport in 1994, the team's staff had some ideas about a potential name.

"When we first moved here in 1994, believe it or not, we wanted to be the Lumberjacks," said the team's general manger, Doug Estes. "Our ownership group here at the time, which was two gentlemen out of upstate New York, outvoted us two to two."

So the team took on the identity of its parent club and was called the Williamsport Cubs.

"We were like, that's boring and who wants that?" Estes said. "We had this crappy logo. We were like, geez. We really kind of missed the boat on that, to be honest."

A few years later, changes in ownership and affiliation (from Chicago to Pittsburgh) forced the team to adopt a new identity. In 1999, Estes and the staff got their wish and adopted an identity that paid homage to their town's storied history—appropriate for the baseball team, considering that the construction of the now almost 90-year-old facility that they play in was funded by lumber baron J. Walton Bowman.

Williamsport sits on the west branch of the Susquehanna River, which facilitated the transport of harvested logs to the town's many mills. The nickname itself comes from the tool those lumbermen used in their trade.

"The crosscut saw is what they used as their tool of choice to harvest the lumber," Estes said. "That's kind of the impetus of the name."

The first Crosscutters logo was drawn by a local artist and featured a character who would become the team's first mascot, Rusty Roughcut. The logo had to be developed quickly because the team was caught somewhat off guard by the affiliation change, but it lasted for seven seasons. (On the bright side, the necessity for a quick change meant that the team could forego the pageantry of a rigged name-the-team contest that every other minor league baseball team seems to go through.)

Before the 2007 season, the team would change affiliations again, this time to their current parent club, the Phillies. While they did not want to change names, it was time for an update. The Crosscutters brought in Plan B Branding, now, of course, known as Brandiose, and they had some ideas.

BRANDIOSE

"Williamsport was pretty early in our careers," said Brandiose partner Jason Klein. "We were still sort of figuring things out in the minor league baseball universe and where we could take design."

When the Brandiose guys visited Williamsport, they were struck by a particular aspect of the town's lumber history.

"All of these lumber barons had these mansions on a street still today named Millionaire's Row," said Brandiose's Jason Klein. "That's where we went first, we drove down Millionaire's Row and we looked at all these mansions."

Those long-ago residents of Millionaire's Row inspired a logo concept that Klein and his partner Casey White had to flesh out.

"We were really excited about the idea of playing off of the millionaires concept, and early on, we had lots of sketch concepts off the idea of the lumber barons," Klein said. "There was a character that looked sort of like a Monopoly man." (If it had come later, I would have been sure it was based on John Hodgman's deranged millionaire character from The Daily Show.)

Of course, the final product was more Brauny Man than Monopoly Man. This is in part because the lumber industry in Williamsport is practically nonexistent now, replaced in part by marcellus shale gas production, and the team wanted to focus more on the heritage of the lumbermen themselves rather than the financial peaks and valleys the town has experienced.

"I could conceivably see that we went more of the lumberjack route as opposed to the lumber baron route because, you know, there's no more lumber barons," Klein said.

"At that turn-of-the-century time, this place was just an amazing place to live," Estes said. "They say, and this is a couple of natives talking, that we had trolleys before Philadelphia did. We had electricity before Philadelphia did. This is the story."

But after decades of environmentally unsound logging practices and swings in the economics of the lumber industry, the town looks decidedly different now.

"Back in the day, they pretty much wreaked havoc with the trees here. I mean, they cut them all down," Estes said. "They cut so much, and they were not replanting. They cut themselves out of business."

So the team went with a more straightforward lumberjack approach to their identity. The logo suite reflects an early phase of Brandiose's strategy. As compared with their current approach, which Klein describes as creating a series of logos that contribute to a larger narrative from different angles, the Crosscutters logo set is more of a deconstruction of the primary logo.

"When we got started, gosh, 15 years ago, we were looking at what people were doing in the sports industry," Klein said. "It really started in the '90s with SME Branding. One of the things that we noticed with them and their design was not only did they have a primary logo and some secondary logos, but they had things called 'peel-ables,' where you could peel off different elements that would work by themselves independently."

For a team that plays a short season in an old stadium in a small market, the Crosscutters have a lot going on. From the first days of the franchise, team staff wanted to push the envelope with a unique team name as early as 1994, when that sort of thing was just starting to catch on, but couldn't convince ownership. Then, a quick-fix identity lasted seven seasons after a sudden affiliation change in 1999. And today, the team's current identity represents important early work from one of the giants in the field of minor league baseball branding.

Wilmington Blue Rocks

Wilmington Blue Rocks
1993–present

Current Team Data

Parent
Kansas City Royals

Class
High-A

League
Carolina

The Wilmington Blue Rocks' name derives from large chunks of rock found in Delaware's Christina River. How the team went from a name based on lumps of blue-ish granite to logos that feature a moose and a stalk of celery merits some explaining.

The first iteration of the Blue Rocks was a team that played in the Interstate League from 1940 to 1952. More than four decades later, when the Peninsula Pilots, a Single-A Carolina League affiliate of the Kansas City Royals, relocated to Wilmington, they decided to go with the city's old team name and a new logo.

"In 1993, we set up shop in January and had a game in April, so there wasn't a lot of time to do anything," said Chris Kemple, the team's general manager. "We spent maybe a day trying to figure out what this logo would be."

They went with a baseball stalwart, interlocking letters, knowing that they would make a change one day. The logo incorporated the state of Delaware with a diamond marking the location of Wilmington—a reference not only to baseball diamonds but also Delaware's unofficial nickname, the Diamond State. (Thomas Jefferson considered Delaware "a 'jewel' among states due to its strategic location on the Eastern Seaboard," according the state's website.) The Blue Rocks still use a version of the interlocking B-R as one of their secondary logos.

The current interlocking BR

It took the team a decade and a half to rebrand, and when they did, it was by incorporating their longtime mascot, a moose, into the primary logo. The new look, developed by Brandiose, was unveiled in 2010 and was immediately well received.

All of this begs the obvious question, why is the mascot of a team called the Blue Rocks a moose in the first place? Kemple credits Frank Bolton, the team's owner/president in 1993.

"I don't know how he came up with Rocky Bluewinkle," Kemple said. "I do remember him telling me it was after some bad Chinese food. I don't know if that's a joke or not. Obviously, it's a play on Rocky and Bullwinkle."

So there's a connection (albeit tenuous) between the moose and the team name—Rock leads to Rocky, Blue sounds vaguely like Bull, there's a famous moose in a show called Rocky & Bullwinkle, so Rocky Bluewinkle. (Not to be a stickler, but wasn't Rocky the flying squirrel on that show? Should he be Richmond's mascot?)

What about the team's most popular secondary logo, Mr. Celery? Kemple starts the story with, "In minor league baseball, there are no original ideas. I stole the concept from another team."

In 1999, Kemple was in Lake Elsinore, California, attending the all star game between the Carolina League and the California League. During the game, every time the California League scored, a pink bunny mascot came out to dance behind the wall in right field. "It was one of the funniest, one of the craziest things I had ever seen," Kemple said. "I thought, I gotta do something like that in Wilmington."

During the offseason, Kemple brought the idea to the team, and it was well received. But who would this character be who came out to dance—to *cel*-ebrate—when the Blue Rocks scored? Kemple wasn't sure the idea would stick, and the team didn't want to invest a lot of money in a new mascot costume for an idea that might be scrapped after a few weeks if it didn't work out. So they considered their options.

"We had this old beat-up celery costume that had been sitting in a warehouse for years," Kemple said. "Actually, it was the property of our food and beverage company, Centerplate.... We dusted it off, put a guy in it, called it Mr. Celery."

Mr. Celery

Initially, the idea was met with skepticism, but Mr. Celery was quickly embraced, and today, his image can be seen everywhere at the stadium, and the team store features an entire wall of Mr. Celery logo items. (Sadly, the Blue Rocks were shut out 1-0 the one and only time I've been to a game there, so there was no actual Mr. Celery sighting for me.)

With his unlikely origins, fans still look for a hidden meaning, some sort of connection. "To this day, people still ask us where it came from," Kemple said, "whether there's some sort of Da Vinci Code, matching numbers and letters and codes, why it's celery. Literally it's because we had the costume."

Kemple is grateful for Mr. Celery's success, even if it is something of a fluke. "It makes us in a way look like we're geniuses," he said, "but we didn't know what we were doing."

The team even tried to sell celery at concession stands, but that was pushing the envelope just a little too far. "People seemed to buy it more to throw it on the field or to use it as a prop with Mr. Celery than to actually eat it," Kemple said.

In 2014, the Blue Rocks (and Mr. Celery) hosted the Carolina League-California League All Star game for the second time (they previously hosted it in 2002). The All Star logo, predictably, featured Rocky and the Blue Rocks' color scheme, but the All Star festivities in June featured something most baseball fans had not seen before—a backwards home run contest, where batters stood in centerfield and hit into the stands behind home plate.

The Blue Rocks play in a stadium that is more than 20 years old (though it is still very nice) and just 25 miles down the road from the Philadelphia Phillies, so to succeed, they've had to be creative. Their willingness to embrace and run with quirky branding ideas—whether they're inspired by bad Chinese food or other teams' mascots—has been key to their popularity. Now I just need them to score some runs the next time I visit so I can actually see Mr. Celery.

Wisconsin Timber Rattlers

Wisconsin Timber Rattlers
1995–present

Current Team Data

Parent
Milwaukee Brewers

Class
Single-A

League
Midwest

The origin story of the Wisconsin Timber Rattlers' nickname is a short one. In the succinct words of Chris Mehring, the team's director of media relations and radio announcer, it goes like this: "A timber rattler is a snake in northern Wisconsin. It's indigenous to the area of northern Wisconsin."

I had surmised that perhaps the name was a double entendre that played on timber as a reference to a baseball bat—as in, their batters hit the ball so hard it makes the timber rattle. I posed the idea to Mehring, who told me, in short, *no*.

"It was just that's the species of snake," he said.

In 1995, when the Appleton Foxes moved from Goodland Field, their home since 1958, into their new stadium, now called Neuroscience Group Field at Fox Cities Stadium, the team felt the time was right to adopt a new identity. A vote by local schoolchildren selected the name Timber Rattlers over several other options, including the Fox River Current and the Fox River Phantoms (which is the only baseball logo concept I can recall seeing that incorporates a supernatural umpire).

The danger in putting an image of that snake front and center in your identity is that people with snake phobias have real and visceral reactions to seeing the reptiles, or even just images of them. I wondered if the team worried that having snake imagery at every turn in their ballpark might keep some ophidiophobic baseball fans away. Again, in short, the answer was *no*.

"We've never had an Indiana Jones Night, but I don't think that would prevent us from doing it," Mehring said.

In fact, the serpentine identity seems to have had the opposite effect. "Snakes, when it comes to sports brand identities in general, are normally well received," said Dan Simon of Studio Simon, the firm responsible for the team's rebrand after the 2010 season. "It's something that a lot of people do like even though a lot of people are creeped out by them."

This snake-based logo has been particularly successful. The Timber Rattlers have been on Minor League Baseball's list of top 25 teams in terms of merchandise sales for every season but one, according to Mehring.

Keeping in mind the menacing nature of the mascot and the target audience of minor league baseball at large, the current look created by Studio Simon walks the fine line between cartoonish and intimidating.

"Inherently, minor league baseball logos are designed to not be threatening," Simon said. “Given that minor league baseball is about, to a large degree, family entertainment first, baseball second, at least with the way these businesses are operated, the logos are meant to be a little less fierce than if they were closer representations of the actual animal and/or object.”

The team itself didn’t go into the redesign with a specific agenda regarding the tone of the new look.

“We just wanted to come up with the best logo possible,” Mehring said. “If it was going to look like a Looney Tune, if it still worked, we would have gone with that. But I think everyone is pretty happy with how it turned out.”

In today’s landscape, the Timber Rattlers name is not outlandish, but in the mid-’90s, the era of wacky minor league identities was just starting to take shape.

“Fans of minor league baseball associate minor league baseball with all of the fun and weird and disparate names. We’ve got Storm Chasers and IronPigs and Lugnuts and on and on and on, but 20 years ago, that was only just starting,” Simon said. “The Wisconsin Timber Rattlers were actually, if not in on the ground floor, they were like on the first or second floor before we reached the skyscraper heights of the crazy logos we have today.”

The Appleton Foxes logo

Of course, when the team changed from Foxes to Timber Rattlers in 1995, they didn’t just change the nickname. They changed their prefix from Appleton, the city where they continue to play, to Wisconsin. The change had an immediate effect on the range of their potential market.

“Appleton Foxes in their last year in their old stadium drew 70,000 fans,” Mehring said. “By going to the Wisconsin Timber Rattlers, the first year in the new stadium with the new logo and the regional kind of draw, drew over 200,000. The second year it was over 233,000 fans. By going from that one city to a region with a team name and a logo that went along with it, it really helped boost attendance.”

For two decades, the Timber Rattlers, a Single-A affiliate of the Brewers in the Midwest League, have quietly been one of the more successful identities in the minors. While the landscape has heaved and changed around them, the Timber Rattlers have stealthily held their ground, staying atop the charts as one of baseball’s most steadfast brands.

Rise of the Minors

THE 2000s

By the early 2000s, minor league baseball had come into its own. Executives had embraced the fact that most fans were not attending games to see their team win or even watch prospects develop. They were there for family entertainment, and part of that experience was a unique brand. The teams represented in this section took hold during a boom in the business of minor league baseball.

Smith's Ballpark in Salt Lake City, Utah, home of the Triple-A Salt Lake Bees

Bowling Green Hot Rods

Bowling Green Hot Rods
2009–Present

Current Team Data

Parent
Tampa Bay Rays

Class
Double-A

League
Midwest

The team's original logo, 2009–2015

The city of Bowling Green, Kentucky, has had a long love affair with all things automotive. First and foremost, it is home to the Bowling Green Assembly Plant, which produces Chevrolet's Corvette. The city's association with the iconic sports car is so close that the National Corvette Museum has been located there since 1981.

In 2009, the Columbus (Georgia) Catfish, a Single-A affiliate of the Tampa Bay Rays, moved to Bowling Green. Given the city's relationship with the famous car and the name of their baseball team's parent club, there was one obvious, slam-dunk name for the new team—the Bowling Green Stingrays. It's perfect, right? The Rays. The Corvette Stingray. Except one thing.

"Minor league baseball has a rule against naming a team after a corporation or a corporate association," said Jason Klein of the prolific design firm Brandiose, who created the logo the team's first logo. "So that got shot down."

But Bowling Green is about more than just Corvette. It's about all sort of automotive stuff. "There's a lot of companies here that are all hot-rod based," said Adam Nuse, the team's general manager. "There's a lot of industry here in Bowling Green centered around the race car."

That industry includes—to name a few examples—assembly plants for several auto makers, auto parts manufacturers, and an annual gathering of hot rod enthusiasts, which take place at the city's Beech Bend Raceway.

So fans in Bowling Green chose the name Hot Rods—a more generic (non-corporation specific) term for souped-up sports cars, some of them dating back to the 1930s, usually with red and yellow flames painted on them.

The Hot Rods' original logo featured a vehicle with accentuated features—a caricature of a fancy race car. "There are so many things—you think about big tires, you think about flames and a grill," Klein said. "Everything after that is really secondary."

The colors reflected the decorations on hot rod vehicles, with silver thrown in to reflect metallic tail pipes. The red was also a wink and a nod to nearby Western Kentucky University. The team's secondary logos included an interlocking BG represented as tail pipes with flames coming out of them, and a tire with a baseball hubcap taken directly from the vehicle in the primary logo.

Before the 2016 season, the Hot Rods rebranded with the current orange and blue logo designed by SME Branding. (The blue is a reference to Kentucky, the Bluegrass State, and the orange is meant to reflect the color a hot rod turns when it is heated.)

The Hot Rods are one of a handful of teams that play one sport but borrow their identity from another. They've had almost a decade to introduce their town to baseball, and they've taken full advantage of the opportunity. The team has won awards for promotions and marketing, and in 2014, their slogan, "It's just #FUNNER," while grammatically suspect, was a rallying call for the sport at large.

"The history of race cars and drag racing and certainly the Corvette has been here since the '80s," Nuse said. "We're fighting against history on that, but I think we're making some good strides to make baseball be the favorite."

One of the places where the team has made in roads is with children—and they didn't do it through the use of cartoon characters, but rather another path to kids' hearts.

"A lot of kids love that race car," Nuse said. "A lot of Little League teams have started naming their teams the Hot Rods, so we sell a lot of merchandise across the country to that youth sports market."

While Brandiose did not design the team's original logo with the specific intention of getting the Hot Rods into Little Leagues, the unique design ultimately had that effect.

"Every year Outdoor Cap and Majestic get together and they look at who the top-selling teams are, and put together 30 teams that they're going to offer in a national catalog," Klein said. "That can be a real source of revenue for some really small teams."

In 2009, when the Hot Rods debuted, they had a couple factors going for them that helped land them among those chosen few. "Up until that point, they didn't really have any good black and yellow teams in that catalog," Klein said, "and they also thought that cars would appeal to young kids as well."

The unique color palette and the souped up car have indeed gotten the attention of fans, and the nickname and logo seem like a natural fit for the town. That said, there are some who wonder to this day what might have been when it comes to the team's identity. While fans were participating in a name-the-team contest, Brandiose got a head start on concepts for some of the names in consideration, including the Grease Monkeys, whose sketch would become a Hot Rods mascot named Roscoe; the automotive-themed Sparkplugs; and the Bowling Green Mammoths, an homage to nearby Mammoth Cave.

But the name that wasn't that many still consider a sentimental favorite is the Cave Shrimp, which was narrowly edged out by the Hot Rods in the name-the-team contest.

"The story behind that is that Bowling Green has the largest underground cave system in North America," Klein said. "There's one spot where you can put an entire NFL stadium inside without touching the wall. It's huge. One of the animals that lives down there is a blind, translucent, prehistoric cave shrimp.

To that end, Brandiose developed a blind (note the thick glasses) caveman shrimp character. In their inagural season, the Cave Shrimp logo was featured on the Hot Rods' "What Could've Been Night," which won that season's promotion of the year award in minor league baseball.

In an alternate universe, the Midwest League affiliate of the Tampa Bay Rays is the Blind Cave Shrimp—and in another alternate universe, they were allowed to be the Stingrays. But in this reality, the Bowling Green Hot Rods have been doing a great job of carving out a niche for baseball in automobile-centric western Kentucky with a stylized, tricked-out race car for a logo.

Concept sketches courtesy of Brandiose

Brooklyn Cyclones

Brooklyn Cyclones
2001–Present

Current Team Data

Parent
New York Mets

Class
Short Season A

League
New York-Penn

More than four decades after the Dodgers broke the hearts of Brooklyn's baseball fans by moving to Los Angeles, the sport returned to the borough in the form of a short-season class A Mets affiliate located on Coney Island—with a rickety old roller coaster called the Cyclone looming just beyond the outfield wall.

The Cyclone roller coaster, which is roughly 90 years old, opened in 1927—thirty years before the Dodgers left Brooklyn for the west coast. The iconic roller coaster continues to run to this day, testing the limits of physical abuse its patrons are willing to endure—patrons like noted graphic designer Todd Radom, who rode the roller coaster a few years ago.

"It was an incredibly jarring ride—the kind that could rattle the fillings out of your teeth," Radom said. "Keep in mind that the Cyclone is made of wood and metal—and that it dates back to the 1920s."

For the uninitiated, Coney Island is basically a perpetual 4th of July celebration. If you could live on funnel cake and skee ball, you would never have to leave. Situated right on the shore, Coney Island is home to one of the nation's most famous boardwalks, complete with all the rickety amusements and deep-fried food you would expect, not to mention the annual Nathan's hot dog eating contest on Independence Day.

"Coney Island is such a historic part of Brooklyn," said Billy Harner, Director of Communications for the Brooklyn Cyclones. "Before there was Vegas, before there was Atlantic City, there was Coney Island."

Normally, a low-level minor league baseball team located in the middle of a bunch of kitschy boardwalk amusements would beg for a wacky cartoon logo.

"When we were choosing the name, people suggested Hot Dogs and things like that," Harner said.

But this team was special. It wasn't just that Brooklyn had loved and lost a Major League team, it's that the team they lost had such a storied history. These were the Dodgers of Jackie Robinson, Sandy Koufax, Pee Wee Reese, and Don Drysdale. When the minor league Brooklyn Cyclones debuted in 2001, there were people for whom the wounds left by the Dodgers' departure still felt fresh.

The Cyclones brought in designer Todd Radom, who is known to many baseball fans for his weekly appearances on Buster Olney's *Baseball Tonight* podcast, during which he tries to stump the host with a uniform and logo quiz.

The need for a serious identity for Brooklyn's new team was not lost on Radom, who started working on the project during the 2000 World Series between the Yankees and the Mets. "It was a real labor of love," he said. "I am a New Yorker, and I am big on history. The Cyclones brought pro baseball back to Brooklyn for the first time since the Dodgers left after the 1957 season, so this was a really special project for me to be involved with."

Obviously, the idea of a cartoon hot dog or something equally silly for a logo was kind of out the window. "This was intended to be a minor league logo for a Major League market," Radom said, "so it made sense to go with something refined and classy."

Brooklyn's baseball past isn't just about the Dodgers; the sport's historians attribute the first instances of such baseball mainstays as the box score and the curve ball to the borough. "The fact that Brooklyn has such a rich history with baseball is 100 percent the reason why we've maintained the more traditional kind of classic look," Harner said. "We kind of look at ourselves as the guardians of something that's much bigger than the Cyclones and goes back for over a century."

Photo by Todd Radom, a little woozy after getting knocked around by the Cyclone.

As a native New Yorker, Radom was well familiar with the rich visual vernacular of Coney Island's amusements. "The logo was inspired by things like old postcards and travel decals," Radom said, "punctuated by a vivid palette and big, bold letterforms."

The primary logo features the telltale cross-hatch pattern of the structure that holds up a roller coaster, and incorporates a baseball actually riding that coaster. With the Mets being the only parent club the Cyclones have ever known, the choice of blue as the main color was an easy one.

The cap logo includes a B that pays homage to the old Dodgers' B cap with an interlocking C for Cyclones. Though with the demographics of Brooklyn changing, Harner says, many younger residents do not recognize the reference to the Dodgers B. The interlocking BC logo has been mistaken for Boston College or even Red Sox logos.

"It's kind of mind-boggling for a kid who grew up in a house where my grandfather and father told me stories of Jackie Robinson and Pee Wee Reese with reverence normally held for Biblical characters," Harner said.

While the Cyclones' logo has remained unchanged for their more than 15-year existence, they introduced a new logo in 2015, which is featured on a cap and incorporated into the team's 15-year logo. The mark, created by the team's in-house designer Kevin Jimenez, features an outline of the Brooklyn Bridge, of note because it represents the entire borough rather than just Coney Island.

Of course, even though the team takes the responsibility of representing baseball in Brooklyn with a classic identity seriously, it's still minor league baseball, and minor league baseball is fun.

"We've kept our logo the same for forever and don't have any plans to change it," Harner said. "So where we've been able to show our creativity and uniqueness is through our promotions."

Among these promotions had been perhaps minor league baseball's most talked-about theme the last few seasons, Salute to Seinfeld Night, which draws fans from around the world. The team's ballpark is renamed Vandelay Industries Park, foul poles are called Festivus poles, and the team has given away such items as Keith Hernandez bobbleheads, technicolor Kramer jerseys, and a Little Jerry rooster "bobble-beak."

The Cyclones were the first professional sports team to call Brooklyn home since the departure of the Dodgers. Since then, the NBA's Nets and the NHL's Islanders have moved in to the revitalized borough. In reestablishing Brooklyn as a home for professional sports, the Cyclones walked a fine line between creating a unique identity specific to their very neighborhood, Coney Island, while still paying tribute to the rich baseball heritage of Brooklyn at large.

In a lot of ways, the Cyclones are like a child wearing a tailored three-piece suit. They have a sharp look and can mingle with the grown-ups, but underneath it all, they're just a little kid who wants to roll around in the dirt and have fun.

Clearwater Threshers

Clearwater Threshers
2004–Present

Current Team Data

Parent
Philadelphia Phillies

Class
High-A

League
Florida State

In late 2003, residents of Clearwater, Florida, were startled to see this billboard appear in their hometown without explanation:

And this one:

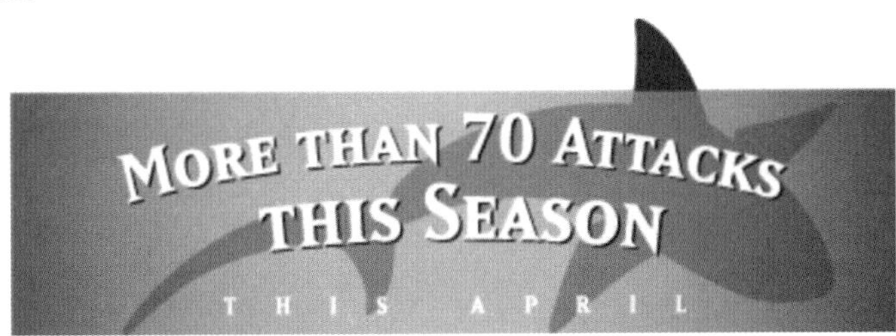

The cryptic message caused some concern.

"People started freaking out," said Jason Klein, co-founder of the baseball-centric design firm Brandiose. "They called Viacom, and they wanted Viacom to disclose who the client was."

Viacom had been sworn to secrecy, but when community leaders joined the freakout, they relented—the billboards were teasers for the new-look Clearwater Threshers, hitherto the Clearwater Phillies of the Single-A Florida State League.

"About four days go by and my phone starts ringing. I get a call from the county commission, I get a call from the city manager of Clearwater, and from the Clearwater Chamber of Commerce wanting to know what the hell are we doing," said John Timberlake, the team's general manager. "They got so much heat locally from politicians that they eventually gave in and had to tell them who was doing it."

By the time the team placed an ad in the *St. Petersburg Times* (now called the *Tampa Bay*

Times) designed to look like a news story about a fisherman who pulled a thresher shark out of the Gulf of Mexico and a baseball rolled out of its mouth, the gig was pretty much up.

All of this was in anticipation of the Phillies' High-A farm team ditching the name of its parent club for something more appropriate to the local community. The team had considered options like Barracudas, Beach Dogs, and Sand Sharks, all of which came up in a name-the-team contest.

"We definitely wanted something that branded us as Clearwater as a beach community," Timberlake said. "We kept coming back to the shark theme—sand sharks, variations of that, and toying around with the different types of sharks."

They enlisted the Brandiose guys Jason Klein and Casey White, who visited Clearwater and delved deep into the local community. "We literally went down to the docks in Clearwater and started asking people, 'Tell us about what are you pulling out of the gulf, tell us some stories,'" Klein said.

While the most common shark in the local waters was the sand shark, it felt too passive, a little too common, and maybe a little too obvious as a choice for the local team name. During their visit to Clearwater, one local fisherman's anecdote captured Jason and Casey's imagination.

"We latched on to one story a guy told us about the shark with the longest tail in the shark family, which is a thresher," Klein said. "It beats its tail against its prey, stuns them, then goes in for the kill."

The more the team and their designers learned about thresher sharks, the more they liked the idea. They liked the aggressive image of the shark disabling then circling its prey (like a baseball player circling the bases) before moving in to devour it, as well as the fact that as a deep-sea shark that hunts alone, threshers carried an air of mystery.

"It wasn't as common," Timberlake said. "It wasn't a hammerhead, something that every single person would have heard of."

And not only that, but it just had a good ring to it. "The name Thresher sounds like flash, it sounds like thrash," Klein said. "The sound of it was aggressive and good for a sports team."

The logo itself features the distinctive form of the thresher shark set in colors that Klein describes as a beachy take on the Phillies brand. The team debuted the new look the same year they moved into their new ballpark, Brighthouse Field, which is also home to their parent club's spring training. The new ballpark featured prominently in the team's branding in a unique way.

"The colors, we actually stole from the ballpark construction blueprints," Klein said. "We saw in the plans for constructions, the stands were going to be this smokey blue and navy and there was a little bit of Phillies red in there, and so we designed it right off the ballpark colors."

Klein describes a conversation between Timberlake and the Phillies president at the time. "When the Phillies came down that first year for spring training, David Montgomery said, 'John, why the hell would you paint the entire ballpark Threshers colors?' He said, 'No no no, they made the logo off the ballpark colors.'"

Another reason for the team color is pure pragmatism. As a Phillies affiliate (they've been owned by their big league club since their inception in 1985), there are financial reasons to have a certain palette.

"Quite honestly, if you're going to have a team full of players that are going to have red shoes, you're either going to buy them spikes and turf shoes and all of those things as part of your expense, or you're going to have your colors match up with their red shoes," Timberlake said. "It's kind of crazy, but it's something that played into the thought process."

The Threshers have two cap logos, both of which feature a shark forming the letter C, which serve two different purposes. They wear the shark chasing a ball when they are in the field, and the shark with the bat when they're at bat.

And in the wordmark, "they use a metallic peach glitter twill so that it looks like a Florida sunset on the jersey lettering," Klein said.

It would be impossible to discuss all of the particulars of the Threshers logos because, to put it lightly, there are a certain number of them. "Clearwater has been our biggest and most loyal client that we've worked with in our history," Klein said. "They have more logos than anybody we've ever worked with."

Collectively, these logos tell a larger story, which Klein describes: "One of the big stories behind this brand that Casey came up with was this idea that maybe the shark is a little mysterious, and let's not show all of our cards all of the time. So his idea was this relationship between adults, kids, and a shark that was similar to Captain Hook and the crocodile.... There would be times when you saw the effects of the shark—like the life preserver with the bite taken out of it—and that the adults were the ones who are actually scared of sharks. But kids aren't scared of sharks, so the kids club logo has this kid, looks sort of like Dennis the Menace riding the shark. He's got a fishing pole with a baseball dropped in front of the shark's mouth, sort of carroting the shark along."

While Timberlake says that the Threshers were admittedly late to the game in rebranding by the time they did so in 2003, the ultimate effect of adopting a name and logo with local appeal has been a boon.

"The first year that we had our logo, we sold almost a million dollars worth of merchandise," he said, "and that was compared with maybe selling $80 to $100,000 in merchandise in previous years."

And it's not just been a financial boon, but a boon in terms of building a unique brand. "People will ask, 'Who are you guys affiliated with?'" he said. "That is not a negative for me. That is really a positive of we have our own identity."

Corpus Christi Hooks

Corpus Christi Hooks
2005–Present

Current Team Data

Parent
Houston Astros

Class
Double-A

League
Texas

Corpus Christi, Texas, sits on the Gulf of Mexico, where recreational and commercial fishing are a big deal. So when you look at the identity for the Double-A Corpus Christi Hooks, the connection to fishing is obvious.

And indeed, if you call up the Hooks and ask them about the origin of their logo and nickname, they'll send you a statement that begins like this: "The Hooks name acknowledges Corpus Christi's association with both commercial and recreational fishing on the South Texas coast."

However, as is usually the case, the story runs deeper than that. In 2005, the city of Round Rock, Texas, 250 miles from Corpus Christi, went from having a Double-A franchise to having a Triple-A franchise. The Round Rock Express had been a Double-A Astros affiliate since 2000, but when the Triple-A Edmonton Trappers moved to Round Rock to assume the mantle of the Round Rock Express, the Double-A franchise moved to Corpus Christi to become the Hooks.

Both the Express and the Hooks are owned by Ryan-Sanders Baseball Inc., whose CEO is Reid Ryan, son of Hall of Famer Nolan Ryan. When it came time to name the new team in Corpus Christi, Reid Ryan knew what he wanted the team to be called, and his reasons went beyond a mere connection to the fishing industry.

"His dad had, in addition to his amazing fastball, a great curveball, which, in baseball parlance, is sometimes referred to as a hook," said Dan Simon of Studio Simon, who created the Hooks' logo. "Reid liked that tie-in."

The Hooks' logo is based on this sketch by Reid Ryan

This makes two teams named for Nolan Ryan's pitches, as the Round Rock Express's name comes from the nickname "The Ryan Express," inspired by his fastball.

Reid Ryan, who is now the president of the Hooks' parent club, the Houston Astros, even had an idea of what the logo might look like, and faxed a sketch to Dan Simon.

"It was the proverbial scribbles on a cocktail napkin, although it wasn't on a cocktail napkin, it was on some type of a piece of paper," Simon said. "It was the stick figure equivalent of an anthropomorphized fish hook."

Dan Simon turned Reid Ryan's cocktail-napkin doodles into his own sketches. In the interest of giving credit where credit is due, Simon notes that he is not a cartoonist, so he turned to character artist Kevin Bright, his former coworker from his days in the employ of the Los Angeles Dodgers, to help develop the body of the hook character.

With the character, named "Rusty Hook," fully developed, Dan Simon set about creating the rest of the identity for the Hooks. This process was a bit out of sequence for Simon, who usually does not begin developing a complete identity by creating a cap logo.

"Normally when I do an identity," he said, "I tend to do the primary logo first and then everything grows from there. The reason for that is the primary logo usually has a character in it, it has a typographic element in it, it's got all the colors that are going to be part of the system, and then really everything kind of grows out of there."

For the details of the Hooks' primary logo, which does not actually feature Rusty, we turn again to the formal statement provided by the team: "The Hooks' primary colors of navy blue and light blue represent the ocean and sky. There's a tip of the cap to the State of Texas on the lone star CORPUS CHRISTI banner, and of course the eyelets of the hooks serve as the O's in the Hooks name."

While the hooks serve as the double-O in the primary logo, Simon used those very same hooks to create an alternate CC logo. This logo not only serves as the road cap logo, but it's also used on the team's road jerseys. Simon suggested this deviation from baseball custom simply because "Corpus Christi" is an awful lot of letters to fit on a road jersey.

"What I told them was I don't recommend putting Corpus Christi on the road jersey," he said, "so let's just use the CC as the left chest logo on the road jersey."

The Hooks franchise has been around since 1968, playing with six names in five cities, but they've finally found a long-term home in Corpus Christi. Their identity has remained largely unchanged since 2005. And while the identity is superficially related to their hometown's connection with fishing, a peek beneath the surface reveals that there's a little more to the story behind their nickname. Just when you expect one right down the middle, you can count on the Ryan family to throw you a curve.

Dan Simon's sketches

Dayton Dragons

Dayton Dragons
2000–present

Current Team Data

Parent
Cincinnati Reds

Class
Single-A

League
Midwest

Dayton, Ohio, is inextricably linked with the history of aviation. The city was home to Orville (who was born there) and Wilbur Wright, who are credited with inventing manned flight. (They weren't the first to build a machine that could fly, but they were the first to invent a machine that could fly and also be steered, and that seems like a big deal.) Dayton Aviation Heritage National Historical Park is found there, and some of the city's sports teams—The University of Dayton Flyers, the Universal Basketball Association's Dayton Air Strikers, and the erstwhile Dayton Bombers of the ECHL—reflect Dayton's connection to the industry.

And there's another Dayton team that has a connection to flying.

"The history of the Dayton area is so rife with aviation themes," said Eric Deutsch, executive vice president of the Dayton Dragons, Single-A affiliate of the Cincinnati Reds. "We kind of went a different direction to change it up a little bit. Dragons are fun. They're a mythological creature."

So Dayton is all about flying and dragons fly, but there are reasons beyond a connection to aviation that the Dragons chose their name. For one, Deutsch explained, the team wanted to stand out from the crowd a bit. "Dragons had not been found in a lot of other teams in our sports landscape across North America," he said. "It was a different name."

The Dragons stand out particularly because they play in the Midwest League, where many of the other teams' identities are based on local industry or lore, like the Lansing Lugnuts, Cedar Rapids Kernels, and Clinton LumberKings, to name a few. It's easy to take note of a fantastical creature, specifically one that's artfully drawn rather than cartoonish, when they're playing against the Fort Wayne TinCaps or the Quad Cities River Bandits.

While the name Dragons is not terribly common, one of the reasons for it can be found throughout sports. "The alliteration of the letter D worked out very nicely," Deutsch said.

The Dragons' name was chosen by the team's ownership group—not by a name-the-team contest, as is so often the case with minor league baseball teams. As the team prepared to launch before the 2000 season (the Chinese year of the Dragon, coincidentally), time was running out to get all of the appropriate paperwork and approvals processed.

"Since we were on such a time crunch, the owners thought it might be good to get a name selected by themselves instead of a submit a name of the team process that the community would normally participate in," Deutsch said, "just to make sure that they had things ready to go with logos, marks, registration, uniforms, hat designs, etc., getting everything up on the short time frame."

However, in order to let fans participate in the process, the team came up with a creative solution after the fact. "When we did finally formally announce that baseball was to come to Dayton, we had a 'Guess the Name of the Team' contest for the fans to try to guess the name of the team that had been selected," Deutsch said.

For their logo, the Dragons turned to designer Terry Smith of Terry Smith Creations (TSC), a firm responsible for a number of sports logos, most notably the NHL's San Jose Sharks. TSC's website features a red version of the identity, one of the many colors the team considered before committing whole-heartedly to green.

"It's worked out very well," Deutsch said. "I think that it interjected a new color, a new look, a new brand for our Dayton community."

While the Dragons' logo has been consistent since the team's inception, featuring a three-quarter angle view of the dragon, the team did contract with Smith to create a front-facing version of the dragon, which is used on merchandise and on some the team's communications.

"We've kept our standard brand and marks and logos similar," Deutsch said, "but for other art pieces, ticket collaterals, merchandise, we're able to create some new looks from the original mark that have become very popular and very cool."

Smith also designed a custom typeface—one that looks like it could be featured on the cover of a fantasy novel as easily as it is on a minor league baseball team's jersey. The typeface is used in all of the team's branded items, from uniform numbers to the team's in-stadium store, the Dragon's Den.

"It was really kind of neat that, not only did we have that cap logo, the team-branded logo, the marks, the uniforms, we also had our own numbers and alphabet to use in terms of branding," Deutsch said.

When they debuted more than a decade and a half ago, there was no way the team could have known that dragons would be front and center on the cultural landscape, specifically with the popularity of *Game of Thrones*. But the team has never tried to play off the dragons of literature or gaming or other aspects of culture.

"There are just so many out there, from mythical cartoon lore to *Game of Thrones* to *Dungeons and Dragons* to the Chinese dragons, the year of the dragon on the Chinese calendar," Deutsch said. "They've come up but they've never really stuck. We've had our own brand and we've been consistent on the use and the marking of it. So I think in our community, the Dayton Dragon has stuck in regard to what people think about in terms of baseball and the Dragons."

Dragons merchandise has been a hot commodity since the team debuted, in part because they have an attractive, distinct identity, and in part because the Dragons hold the record for consecutive sellouts by a professional sports team in North America. The Dragons have sold out every game in their history—a streak that passed the 1,000 mark in 2014 and was still alive at the end of the 2017 season—and they frequently appear on the list of Minor League Baseball's top 25 teams in terms of merchandise sales. Dayton's path to success has been different from other minor league baseball teams', but a serious, artful logo and a fiercely loyal fan base have made the Dragons one of the most popular brands in the minors.

Fort Wayne TinCaps

Fort Wayne TinCaps
2009–Present

Current Team Data

Parent
San Diego Padres

Class
Double-A

League
Midwest

Fort Wayne, Indiana, has two notable claims to fame. First, in 1845, a noted American conservationist named John Chapman died and is buried there (more on him later). Second, on May 11, 1871, the first-ever professional baseball game was played in Fort Wayne, when the Fort Wayne Kekiongas beat the Cleveland Forest Citys 2-0.

With all that history, it was a little weird that the city's minor league baseball franchise took on the milquetoast and significance-free nickname Fort Wayne Wizards when it debuted in 1993.

"I think it was fairly obvious that it was kind of just the alliteration of the W," said the team's Broadcasting and Media Relations Manager John Nolan. "At the time, there was no other major professional sports team with the moniker of Wizards."

Since then, Major League Soccer's Kansas City Wizards have come and gone, and the Washington Bullets became the Wizards, so the team's one and only possible reason for its nickname went away. "All the sudden," Nolan said, "Wizards wasn't a very unique name."

In the mid-2000s, the team was purchased by Hardball Capital, and plans were launched to build a new downtown stadium, Parkview Field, which was named the #10 overall stadium experience in 2014 (first in minor league baseball) by the website Stadium Journey.

With the new ballpark, the organization wanted to get a fresh start, which included a rebranding effort. A name-the-team contest was announced, and participating fans were asked to keep certain factors in mind. "The emphasis at that point in time was for there to be something unique, creative, and local," Nolan said.

Before the 2009 season, the team announced a new name and unveiled a logo designed by Sky Design. According to Nolan:

> TinCaps is a reference to Johnny Appleseed. The legend of Johnny Appleseed is based off a real person, John Chapman, who is famous for helping to plant apple trees throughout the Midwest, including in Indiana, and John Chapman died in Fort Wayne, and is buried in Fort Wayne. There's a park named Johnny Appleseed Park in Fort Wayne, and every year there's a Johnny Appleseed festival, so there's strong roots between John Chapman, Johnny Appleseed, and the city of Fort Wayne.

The TinCaps' primary logo is an apple with a pot on its head, significant because Johnny Appleseed was famous for wearing a pot on his head. The team's alternate logo also features a tin cap, this one atop the letters FW for Fort Wayne. (I asked if the team ever considered a uniform that included an actual metal pot for a cap, and Nolan said that the team had not considered it. I can't imagine why.)

As with many logo changes, this change was initially not well received. "There were people who thought Wizards was a fine name and we should just keep it," Nolan said, "or weren't on board with TinCaps being so unique."

COURTESY FORT WAYNE TINCAPS

But by the time the first season rolled around, fans not only in Fort Wayne had come around, but all through baseball. The team was included on Minor League Baseball's list of the top 25 teams in terms of merchandise sales for the first seven years of its existence, pretty good for a Padres affiliate in the Single-A Midwest League.

"That first year right off the bat there was a record sale for merchandise that had never been matched during the Wizards days," Nolan said.

And it's not just fans who like the logo. "I've been here for two seasons, and every player I've talked to finds it pretty cool," Nolan said. "One guy who we had this past year, he was only 18 years old from the Dominican Republic, Franmil Reyes.... He told me that he was anxiously awaiting his chance to play for the TinCaps for a few reasons, but one of them was that he told me he thought the hat and the logo were cool."

As part of the branding effort, the team incorporates apples into the entire fan experience. The team store is called the Orchard, the kid's club is called the Apple Core, there's a seating area atop a parking garage called the Tree Tops (modeled after Wrigley's rooftop seats), and the stadium's Mexican food concession stand is called Manzana's (Spanish for apple).

"When you're here, you realize that there's an apple theme going on," Nolan said.

Of course, there are all sorts of apple-based concessions. The Apple Cart behind home plate sells everything from actual apples to apple wontons, apple streusel, and one particular item that has become the apple of baseball fans' eyes.

"The one that was just introduced during the 2014 season was named the best new food item in minor league baseball by *Ballpark Digest*. It's the BIG APPLE," Nolan said. "BIG APPLE, for what it's worth, is all capitals."

And no wonder: "It's got all those apple items I just mentioned, like sliced apples and the desserts, plus four scoops of ice cream, caramel, chocolate syrup, sprinkles," Nolan said. "It's really for a family of four. And that's all in a batting helmet."

When Fort Wayne's team made the switch from Wizards to TinCaps, the most significant decision it made was to seize on an identity with meaning to the local community. It's the hallmark of nearly every successful minor league brand—something that reinforces a connection between the team and the place. And if there's a way to tie in a gigantic helmet filled with apples and ice cream while they're at it, then that's even better.

Frisco RoughRiders

Frisco RoughRiders
2003–Present

Current Team Data

Parent
San Diego Padres

Class
Double-A

League
Texas

On July 1, 1898, the 1st United States Volunteer Cavalry charged alongside other military regiments (most notably the Buffalo Soldiers) into the bloody Battle of San Juan Hill in Cuba, helping to deliver a decisive blow in the Spanish-American War. With Spanish troops retreating and ultimately leaving Cuba shortly after the battle, the U.S. would declare victory in the war just weeks later.

The 1st United States Volunteer Cavalry, which was commonly referred to as the Rough Riders, was led by former Assistant Secretary of the Navy and future U.S. President Theodore Roosevelt. History remembers the volunteer cavalry as a hodgepodge band of outdoorsmen, ranchers, cowboys, Ivy League athletes, Texas Rangers, Native Americans, and others—many of them from Texas. They would see action in two other battles, but it was their role in the charge up San Juan Hill in support of Cuban independence from Spain that has become the stuff of legend.

More than a century after that battle, the world was reintroduced to the Rough Riders, this time in the form of the Double-A affiliate of the Texas Rangers, the Frisco RoughRiders. (I should point out here that the volunteer cavalry from 1898 is called the Rough Riders, with a space, and the 21st-century minor league baseball team is called the RoughRiders, with the words jammed together, because it's minor league baseball and that is how it's done.)

The RoughRiders, who had previously been the Shreveport Swamp Dragons, were relocated to northern Texas in 2003 by a new ownership group that included Tom Hicks, then part-owner of the Texas Rangers. The RoughRiders' name reflected the historical tradition of their Major League parent club, named for the law-enforcement agency, the Texas Ranger Division.

The original logo, 2003–2014

Before the 2015 season, the RoughRiders, ranked in 2012 by *Forbes* magazine as the fourth-most valuable franchise in minor league baseball, were sold to an ownership group led by Chuck Greenberg, who also owns the State College Spikes and the Myrtle Beach Pelicans. The new ownership group wanted to update the team's identity and reinforce its Roosevelt roots.

"We started with the premise that we loved the name but everything else was up for grabs," Greenberg said. "We thought that the current marks at that time, while being a little tired after a dozen years, were also more generic than we would like."

The new look was decidedly not generic. "What we decided to do was focus on the name,

RoughRiders, and in this instance, take it back to the true roots of the name," Greenberg said. "And the roots of the RoughRiders begins with Teddy Roosevelt."

Working with Brandiose, the RoughRiders came up with two Teddy Roosevelt-themed logos, which the team refers to internally as Smiling Teddy and Swinging Teddy. Those who follow minor league baseball logos know that one of Brandiose's signatures is the logo character awkwardly swinging something that is not a bat like a bat (see the Inland Empire 66ers' mechanic swinging a wrench, the Eugene Emeralds' sasquatch swinging a tree, and the El Paso Chihuahuas' chihuahua swinging a dog bone, to name a few). In the case of Swinging Teddy, who is swinging an actual baseball bat, there's a reason for the technically unsound swing.

"Teddy was not a baseball player, but he was a very gregarious, physically active fellow," Greenberg said, "and so he took a mighty, if not altogether skilled swing."

And not only that, but this, too: "He's taking his first step towards first base," Greenberg said. "He's going to charge down the first base line as though it was San Juan Hill."

One of the things that makes the new identity distinct is how easily caricatured Teddy Roosevelt is. "No doubt, if James K. Polk had founded the Rough Riders, it would have been a lot more challenging," Greenberg said, "but Teddy is such a larger-than-life figure in a magnitude of ways and so universally recognized."

To that end, the team immerses fans in a Teddy Roosevelt experience at the ballpark. Photo murals featuring Roosevelt in various stages of his life are featured throughout the stadium, such as in the team store and in lounges or restaurants, like the Bull Moose Saloon. The team colors and typeface, which are meant to evoke Roosevelt's era, are used consistently in the ballpark.

Speaking of the team colors, they might look like red, white, and blue, but they are in reality scorched red, cream, slate blue, and Texas navy. This is, of course, intentional.

"We didn't want it to be the same red, white, and blue that you see in a lot of uniforms, including our Major League affiliate, the Texas Rangers," Greenberg said. "We decided to have a red, white, and blue that would be more fitting for Teddy Roosevelt's era, and in that era, things were left out in the sun, they'd become baked, they'd become bleached, they'd become faded a little bit."

The RoughRiders play just 35 miles from their parent club, but that creates more opportunity than competition, according to Greenberg. "In every other market that's larger than this, there are two Major League teams, and here there's one," he said. "We think it's a perfect fit, it's a perfect complement."

That said, the proximity to the Rangers is all the more reason for the RoughRiders to cultivate a distinct, fun logo. "It did further our resolve to have a look that was completely unique," Greenberg said. "We wanted a look that didn't recall another college or another professional team or our Major League affiliate. We wanted it to be unique to the Frisco RoughRiders."

By featuring a well-known and easily identifiable historical figure in their logo, the RoughRiders have achieved that unique look. The new identity was well received by fans and critics alike in its first season, and more than a century after the 1st United States Volunteer Cavalry charged up San Juan Hill, Teddy is leading the charge to this day.

Great Falls Voyagers

Great Falls Voyagers
2008–Present

Current Team Data

Parent
Chicago White Sox

Class
High A

League
Pioneer

In 1950, two alien space crafts gliding over western Montana were caught on film by Nicholas Mariana, the general manager of a minor league baseball team called the Great Falls Electrics. The footage is conclusive evidence of the fact that aliens have visited us, even though the government has been placating us with half-truths and platitudes for decades to try to convince us otherwise.

"If anybody watches those crazy UFO shows on HBO, you've probably seen footage that was taken by the general manager here in the '50s with a handheld camera of a supposed UFO flying over centerfield," said Scott Reasoner, general manager of Great Falls' current minor league team. "It's considered one of the best UFO sightings of all time."

And check it out, if you use SportsLogos.net's proprietary UFO image-enhancement technology, developed by site founder Chris Creamer on his Texas Instruments TI-99/4A in 1997, you get a clear image of those shimmery orbs:

The so-called Mariana UFO Incident is the most famous in Montana's distinguished UFO-sighting history, but it's only one of thousands of reports that the government has documented in a thing called *Project Blue Book*. "If you talk to residents, one out of 10 will tell you that they've seen a sighting or some unusual movement in the skies at night," Reasoner said. "So it's definitely part of the community."

Before the 2008 season, the team that had been the Great Falls Giants, Great Falls Dodgers, and Great Falls White Sox in its almost 40 years in existence, made the long-overdue decision to adopt their own unique identity instead of that of their parent club. When it came time to choose a name, they focused on that important aspect of their local community.

"Great Falls is considered a hot spot for UFO-type sightings and activity here in the country," Reasoner said. (And in case there are any doubters, "I'm sure it has nothing to do with the fact that we have a large Air Force base about 15 blocks from the ballpark.")

One of the most famous UFO sightings ever was filmed from a ballpark right there in their hometown by a general manager of the local team. It seems that there was hardly any choice at all that the local team would pay homage to the preponderance of extraterrestrial visits with an alien-themed identity.

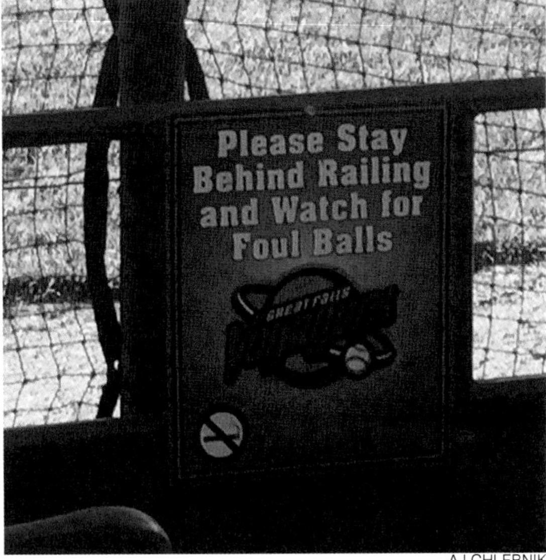

AJ CHLEBNIK

The team encourages fans to be on the lookout for flying objects of both the identified and unidentified variety.

The Great Falls Voyagers and their mascot Orbit—"the little alien who came to visit us and loved baseball so much he decided to stay," according to Reasoner—debuted in 2008. The identity, designed by Studio Simon, has received a fair amount of attention in the press and from fans. "We've been voted a couple times one of the best hats in minor league baseball," Reasoner said, "so you know the logos, the branding, when they put that all together, they did a really great job."

Of course, by the time the Voyagers came along, they were not the only alien in town. There was a team in Las Vegas named for a secret government facility where alien visitors are stored and/or questioned on the physics of intergalactic travel.

"Obviously there's been teams like the 51s that had already been there and kind of done that with the theme," Reasoner said. So Great Falls needed another angle that made them distinct.

It just so happens that Great Falls is home to another kind of voyager. Lewis and Clark traveled through Montana, and the Lewis and Clark Expedition included *voyageurs*—French-Canadian explorers and traders—who transported supplies for the expedition. And Great Falls is home to the Lewis and Clark Interpretive Center, one of the biggest Lewis and Clark museums out there.

"We're in kind of the heart of Lewis and Clark country here," Reasoner said. "So any time we can do anything with the voyaging theme like that, it goes over well with the people in the community, because there's a lot of history tied in with that."

For a wacky minor league logo to really work, it has to tap into something meaningful at the core of the local community—it's not enough just to be wacky for the sake of wackiness. With a visual reference to aliens in their logo and a name that conjures the Lewis and Clark expedition, the Voyagers are accessing two disparate and important aspects of Great Falls' heritage.

"I think minor league baseball does about as good as any industry in coming up with unique ways to use logos and branding," Reasoner said. "I think ours is up there with the best of them."

The Voyagers still play at Centene Stadium—the same place where Great Falls Electrics general manager Nicholas Mariana recorded that footage of those famous space aliens back in 1950. Those glowing lights may just have been reflections of planes from the nearby Air Force base, they may have been weather balloons, or maybe they really were little green guys buzzing the Earth on an interplanetary joy ride. Whatever they were, they gave rise to one of the more endearing identities in minor league baseball.

Idaho Falls Chukars

Idaho Falls Chukars
2004–Present

Current Team Data

Parent
Kansas City Royals

Class
Rookie Advanced

League
Pioneer

The Idaho Falls Chukars, a Kansas City Royals affiliate in the rookie-level Pioneer League, are not named for the most intimidating bird out there.

"No, in fact, it's essentially a little partridge," said the team's longtime president and general manager Kevin Greene. "It's a fat little bird. They're out in the countryside and they make little clucking noises."

But there's something about the Chukars nickname that has made it work for the team for almost a decade and a half.

For most of its history, the baseball team in Idaho Falls took the name of its parent club, as with the Idaho Falls Braves and Idaho Falls Padres. There have been two notable exceptions: The Idaho Falls Russets in the 1940s and '50s (awesomely named for potatoes), whose 1946 team featured Billy Martin, and an ill-fated attempt at branding in the early '90s.

"The year before I got here they had taken the name the Idaho Falls Gems," Greene said. "It was a miserable failure. It didn't work on any level." (That said, that 1992 Idaho Falls Gems team included future Major Leaguers Marty Malloy, Chris Brock, and Terrell Wade."

Before their current affiliation with the Kansas City Royals began in 2004, the team in Idaho Falls had basically been associated with all of the Major League teams, and, oddly, one minor league team. Their list of parent clubs over the years includes the New York Yankees (1940–41 and 1962–65), Brooklyn Dodgers (1948), New York Giants (1949–51), the Pacific Coast League Sacramento Solons (not sure how that works, but it was 1953–54), Detroit Tigers (1954–58), Pittsburgh Pirates (1959), Chicago White Sox (1960–61), California Angels (1966–81), Oakland Athletics (1982–84), Atlanta Braves (1986–94), and San Diego Padres (1995–2003). When the time came to switch parent clubs again, the team went looking for some more permanent branding.

"We were up for an affiliation change again, I guess it was in the fall of 2003," Greene said. "We looked like we were going to sign on with the Royals, but we didn't know how long that affiliation was going to last, so we knew it was time to really establish our own brand, our own identity."

So the team took on that time-honored tradition of conducting a name-the-team contest, then ignoring the results of the contest and going with something good instead.

"I put out a name-the-team contest that fall, and the most popular name was the Eagles," Greene said. "I didn't like the Eagles, only because you go to any county in the United States and there's a high school team called the Eagles. Just too common."

As the contest was winding down and there were not a lot of great names to choose from, the team's radio broadcaster John Balginy drew inspiration from a childhood memory that would change the team.

"The contest was citywide, and there were some wretched names," Balginy said, quoted in an article by Benjamin Hill on MiLB.com. "And Kevin Greene, our GM, he goes, 'I just want something unique.' So I start thinking, maybe something like the Toledo Mud Hens. And when I lived in Kansas, I remember that my dad used to go chukar hunting all the time.

"And you call a pitcher a 'chucker.' So I told Kevin, 'How about the Chukars? It's a bird that lives in the area and it's also a slang for a pitcher.' He goes, 'OK'—and that day we named the team. So it's going to be on my headstone: The Mother Chukar."

Greene, who is from New York originally, was not familiar with the bird, so he looked it up and then asked around to see what stakeholders thought.

"A chukar is a game bird, kind of indigenous to our region out here," he said. "I didn't even know what a chukar was, so I started calling people, season seat holders. I did a little test marketing, and everyone I ran the idea by liked it."

As Balginy said, the word chukar is pronounced roughly the same as the word chucker, which gives it a basebally double entendre, and that is included in the team's visual identity.

"If you look at our hat logo, for example, the chukar, the bird is clutching a baseball and he has it in the throwing position, so the chukar did have that dual meeting," Greene said.

While the chukar is not the most intimidating bird in real life, the logo, created by Dan Simon of Studio Simon, has a bit of menace about it.

"There's nothing fierce about them," Greene said. "I guess our logo makes it look a lot more fierce than it is."

The Chukar nickname and brand have remained unchanged since the 2004 season. So long as he's in charge, Greene says, that will remain the case. So for the foreseeable future, Idaho Falls will play host to the fiercest fat little partridge in the Pioneer League.

Inland Empire 66ers

Inland Empire 66ers
2003–Present

Current Team Data

Parent
Los Angeles Angels

Class
High-A

League
California

The Inland Empire 66ers, an affiliate of the LA Angels and three-time champions of the Single-A California League, are located in San Bernardino, California, a town noted for its place along the iconic highway Route 66. Since their inception in 2003 (they were previously the San Bernardino Stampede), the 66ers have played on their relationship with Route 66 in the most literal way possible—with a logo that looked like a highway sign.

In a minor league baseball landscape littered with Chihuahuas and RubberDucks and Flying Squirrels, among much else, the road sign did not exactly stand out, and the team felt it was time for a change.

"We really felt one-dimensional with what we could do," said 66ers' general manager Joe Hudson. The team reached out to the San Diego-based firm Brandiose, which has developed new identities for lots of teams in recent years. "One of the things that we brought to Brandiose was that feeling that we wanted to be able to have fun with this thing."

After a process that lasted about a year and a half, the team unveiled a new identity for the 2014 season. The result was a lively new primary logo—a cartoon mechanic swinging a giant wrench like a baseball bat—and perhaps a new professional record for sheer number of secondary logos. (I've counted seven so far, but I keep finding new ones in different places.)

While some teams have it easy, developing a look for a team named after a highway has its challenges. "It's easy if your team name is the Grizzlies," Hudson said. "What are you? You're a bear! You know, the Knights. You're the Knights!"

But the 66ers' challenges in developing an identity were also opportunities. Hudson said, "We could have gone different routes with this thing." [Editor's note: So to speak!] "The previous brand was, We're Route 66 so we're a road sign. We had to put a road sign on it. But that's not necessarily the only thing.... We wanted to have our logo have a little bit of everything about Route 66. So you have the mechanic as one of the logos. You've got an alternate logo with a wrench, you've got a hood ornament as one of them, and you've got an engine."

The new logo offers opportunities for the team to be creative with promotions, marketing, and scoreboard animations. "We can have more fun with it," Hudson said. "That's what a lot of minor league baseball is about. We're a young front office, and we like to really have fun with what we're doing here. The new look has definitely given us a lot more flexibility to do it."

While the 66ers' new look is a lot more fun and a lot more flexible than the old look, I did have one concern. I asked Hudson about the mechanic's mechanics. That is, how do baseball people feel about the form of his swing? Hudson felt that he was not qualified to comment, so

I turned to former collegiate baseball player Scott Mealey, who batted clean-up behind future Major League All Star Sean Casey at the University of Richmond in the 1990s.

Scott said that the mechanic's hip rotation and forearm rotation are good, but that's about it for the positives. The biggest concern is his head. "Looking in the direction of the shortstop is not a key to success," Scott said. "See Adam Jones's head on any outside slider for reference."

Additionally, the mechanic's front foot should be flat on the ground, and he's off balance. ("Inside pitch would tie him up.") Finally, Scott said, "Teeth gritting and overall tension in the face muscles are not conducive to a loose, fast swing."

Scott also expressed a concern that the mechanic's bushy eyebrows would interfere with his vision and that maybe he should work out his legs at the gym every once in a while instead of just doing upper body stuff all the time.

But hey, he's in Single-A ball, right? The mechanic has time to work on his mechanics.

While the mechanic might be the team's new identity, the face of the franchise remains their mascot Bernie, who was named 2011's craziest mascot and has been with the team since they were the San Bernardino Stampede in the 1990s. "He's a fan favorite and to a certain extent, he's truly the face of our organization," Hudson said. "So, he's not going anywhere. It doesn't mean that there isn't a chance of having this new character become a sidekick kind of situation. But Bernie's still the guy."

While there was some early resistance to the new look (as there always is), the team's decision to rebrand was a good one. The mechanic—even if he needs to work on his wrench-swinging form a little—and his bottomless toolkit of secondary logos will be a vital source of entertainment at the ballpark. The old street sign logo had a certain kitschy appeal (appropriate for Route 66), but the new look is unique, appropriate to the place, and most importantly—fun.

Kannapolis Intimidators

Kannapolis Intimidators
2001–Present

Current Team Data

Parent
Chicago White Sox

Class
Single-A

League
South Atlantic

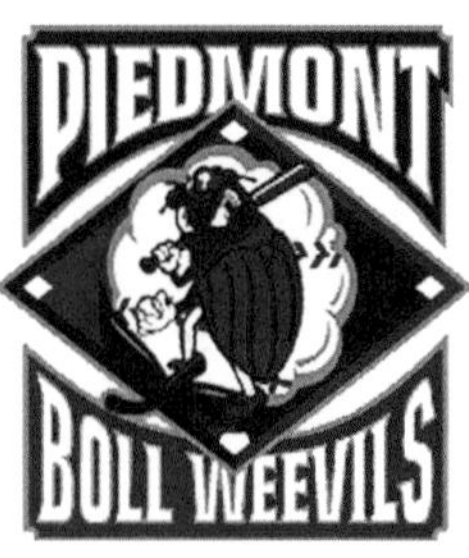

As with most baseball stadiums, Intimidators Stadium in Kannapolis, North Carolina, has a standings board that shows up-to-the-minute league results. The board at Intimidators Stadium, home of the South Atlantic League's Single-A Kannapolis Intimidators, however, is a bit different from what you might find at most ballparks.

"We've got a NASCAR Cup Series standings board in the ballpark that we update along with the South Atlantic League leader board," said Josh Feldman, the team's director of communications. "We embrace the motorsports racing roots here."

Those motorsports racing roots run deep in Kannapolis, and not just because it's in the heart of NASCAR country. It's the hometown of the late Dale Earnhardt Sr., NASCAR Hall of Famer and seven-time Cup Series winner, who is immortalized in a nine-foot bronze statue in Kannapolis's Dale Earnhardt Tribute Plaza.

Late in 2000, Earnhardt purchased a minority share of the Piedmont Boll Weevils. (Piedmont is the name of the region in which Kannapolis is located, and boll weevils are bugs that eat cotton plants—serious pests in a part of the world that relies on the textile industry.) The team was going through some changes, including switching affiliation from the Phillies to the White Sox, and a new name was in order.

With the hometown hero in the fold as part owner, naming the team in Earnhardt's honor was a popular choice—not always the case when it comes to sports teams changing identities.

"Everyone for the most part knew the team's name was going to change when the affiliation with the Phillies was ending," Feldman said, pointing out that the Boll Weevils logo was so tied to the Phillies that it had a Phillies P on the bug's hat. "People were open to a transition, especially with the name that we picked."

The team's new name was a reference to Earnhardt's nickname, The Intimidator, which he earned in the 1980s because of his reputation for driving aggressively in races. "That nickname has a lot of meaning for the folks in this community, and NASCAR fans nationwide," Feldman said.

While most sports teams adopt nicknames based on animals, weather phenomena, or even groups of people, it's not typical to see a team named for a specific individual.

"There's a very small number of minor league teams that are named for people," Feldman said. "When you get a chance to have a team that's named for someone who means a lot to the community, who is a sports hero, I think that's a pretty meaningful thing."

Earnhardt was only a few months into his new role as part owner of the team named in his honor when he was killed in a crash in the final lap of the Daytona 500 on February 18, 2001. The entire sports world felt the loss, but in his hometown and for the tiny team he had just become a part of, it was particularly hard.

"He was going to be more involved," Feldman said. "Obviously, we never got that opportunity to fulfill that dream and to see him be a part of it."

Earnhardt's presence is still felt at the ballpark. There's a number 3 tribute car in front of the stadium, a popular spot for fans to take photos. And speaking of that number 3, you won't see it on the backs of any Intimidators players at the ballpark.

According to Benjamin Hill, who spends the summer months road tripping and writing about stadiums for Minor League Baseball's Ben's Biz Blog, "The Intimidators have retired three numbers, only one of which is in honor of a baseball player. #50 is retired throughout the South Atlantic League in honor of John Henry Moss, who served as league president for 50 years. #42 is retired throughout the entirety of professional baseball in honor of Jackie Robinson. And #3 is, of course, Dale Earnhardt."

The logo was created in 2001 by Sam Bass, whose claim to fame is that he was the first artist officially licensed by NASCAR. Among much else, he's created original paintings for nearly 80 consecutive program covers for races at the Charlotte Motor Speedway since 1985.

"I'm a race fan first, who just happens to be a NASCAR/motorsports artist," Bass said, quoted in *USA Today*. "NASCAR and the fans allow me to live out my dream of painting, drawing, and designing race cars and creating artwork for great drivers and sponsors."

Bringing Bass in to create the logo for the Intimidators just made sense. "We've had NASCAR tied back to early management of the organization," Feldman said, "so I think from that standpoint, it makes sense that they would use their guy."

Because it was created by an artist from the motorsports industry, the Intimidators logo has a different feel from minor league baseball's normal visual vernacular.

"I think it's different. I think it's simple," Feldman said. "A lot of different logos, there's so much extra meaning and you can't see half the symbolism. Once you know what you're looking for, you realize, oh this actually spells this or you see this symbolic meaning. We're not really going for that."

The Intimidators have used the same logo since 2001, though in 2011, the team introduced an alternate logo featuring a NASCAR-y letter I and Dale Earnhardt in what Feldman described as the "victory pose."

The Intimidators stand out from the minor league baseball crowd because the origin of their team name and the artist who created their logo come from outside the sport. It's the sort of schizophrenic multiple-sport crossover that only works in certain communities, and Kannapolis, North Carolina, is definitely one of them.

Kansas City T-Bones

Kansas City T-Bones
2003–Present

Current Team Data

Class
Independent

League
American Association

Just across the river from Kansas City, Missouri, home of the 2015 World Series champions, lies another Kansas City in another state with another baseball team. While the Royals, the better-known team in the better-known Kansas City, are steeped in tradition, carrying a regal name and a classic baseball identity since 1969, the other Kansas City, this one in the state of Kansas, plays host to a minor league team in the American Association of Independent Professional Baseball—one with a notable identity of its own.

One of the things people associate with Kansas City, Missouri, is meat—residents will argue that their tomato- and molasses-based sauce is the only way to consume barbecue. But the other KC, the one in Kansas, has its own claims to steak fame, including the nationally known Kansas City Steak Company, which was founded during the Depression and is still headquartered in Kansas City, Kansas. Another claim the Kansas-based KC can make is that it's home to the only meat-themed baseball team on either side of the river.

Before the 2003 season, when the independent Duluth Superior Dukes relocated to Kansas City, the team took to the local paper, the Kansas City Star, to ask fans to suggest new names.

"Obviously with Kansas City being the capital of barbecue and steaks and cows and that type of background, those were a lot of the names that were submitted," said the team's vice president and general manager Chris Browne. "A lot of Cowboys, Steaks, Kansas City Steers, Kansas City Stars, but definitely the barbecue and the steak flavor that Kansas City is known for—the KC Strips was one of the names."

The name T-Bones, which comes from one of the more prized cuts of steak, caught on immediately with the locals.

"They laughed at it, they enjoyed it, they thought it was cool, fitting for our history," Browne said. "At the end of the day, it was very catchy and apropos for the Midwest and Kansas City."

The team debuted with a slogan that they still use today, "Fun Well Done," and a promotion that gave fans four T-bone steaks with the purchase of season tickets. Their mascot, Sizzle, named for the sound he himself would make while being cooked, is the bull featured in the logo.

In terms of a baseball brand, the T-Bones differentiate themselves from their big league neighbors in three ways: the game on the field, the atmosphere at the park, and the style of their logos.

As for the game, independent baseball features young players trying to get noticed for an opportunity to play in a Major League team's farm system, as well as players who have had their opportunity—some of them even having played in the bigs—and who are trying to make their way back. (I saw a game in 2016 and the starting pitcher was onetime San Francisco Giant Mike Kickham.)

"The players on the field," Browne said, "those guys are keeping the dream alive, trying to get to the next level."

More importantly for the team, they're not trying to compete with the Royals for fans, but rather offer a different kind of experience.

"We all love the Royals here," said Browne, who once worked as a Royals clubhouse personnel guy, and who has been with the T-Bones since the team debuted. "We love the Royals, but as you know, minor league baseball, we have a different niche. It's laid-back, it's free parking, it's easy in and out, it's family fun, family price points, economical, and I think that's where our niche is."

One distinctly minor league feature of the ballpark is a sign beyond the left field wall that offers a fan the opportunity to win $100,000 if a home-team player hits a bull's eye—literally. The sign, which seems to be Kansas City's version of the Durham Bulls' famous "Hit Bull Win Steak" sign, features a target in a bull's eye. The sign has paid off once in the team's 14 years.

"I want to say it happened in our 12th year, a couple years ago, toward the end of the season," Browne said. "It was fun to present that fan a check for $100,000." (Given the paychecks that players are pulling at this level, I was kind of hoping the check would go to the player who hit the home run rather than a random fan.)

The logos, which were designed by the team's ad agency at the time and have remained essentially unchanged since, are fun and quirky. The suite includes a primary logo featuring Sizzle the bull holding a bat as well as a cap logo with the bone of a T-bone steak forming the letter T.

All of this adds up to a baseball brand that embraces the kitsch of minor league baseball. The whimsical source of the name, the cartoonish nature of the logo (and I'm pretty sure that "B" in "Bones" is set in Brush Script, a default font you have on your own computer), and the quirky fan experience at the ballpark create an identity that is completely (and intentionally) different from the World Series champs across the river.

Lakeland Flying Tigers

Lakeland Flying Tigers
2001–Present

Current Team Data

Parent
Detroit Tigers

Class
High A

League
Florida State

In March of 1941, the US was not yet officially involved in World War II—that would come in December after the attack on Pearl Harbor. Despite their official neutrality, though, the Americans were sending supplies to allies like Britain, Russia, and China.

With China on the cusp of succumbing to Japanese invasion, one particular arrangement had American pilots from the Navy, Air Corps, and Marine Corps formally resigning from the American military and signing on as volunteers with the Chinese airforce, which, in the words of pilot RT Smith, "was never a match for the Japanese and by 1940 had nearly ceased to exist."

Despite being outnumbered by the Japanese, the American pilots, officially called the First American Volunteer Group, were wildly successful in China. They would earn the nickname the Flying Tigers—complete with a logo created by the Walt Disney Company's Roy Williams. Though the Flying Tigers were disbanded seven months after their inception and replaced officially by the US military, their legend lives on.

One of the specific places where the legend of the Flying Tigers lives on is Lakeland, Florida, which was once home to a tiny municipal airport called Lodwick Field, where roughly 2,000 British and American World War II pilots trained. In 1953, Lodwick Field closed and was purchased by the Detroit Tigers, who built their Tiger Town spring training complex on the site.

The Tigers' spring training facility, Joker Marchant Stadium, is also home to Detroit's Single-A Florida State League affiliate, the Lakeland Flying Tigers.

The Flying Tigers baseball team, which is owned by its parent club, had simply gone by the name Tigers since the 1960s. But in 2007, the Detroit Tigers took note of the marketing and retail success of the Phillies' Clearwater Threshers, another Florida State League team owned by its parent club, and they placed a call to Brandiose, the firm that created the Threshers' brand.

"The Detroit Tigers organization called us up and said, hey we notice what the Phillies have done there and we'd love to bring the same process to Lakeland," said Brandiose's Jason Klein.

Given the historic nature of the site in Lakeland, there was not much debate about which direction this identity would go.

"We took a tour of this place," Klein said. "They still have the airplane hangars from World War II, they still have the mess hall, which is now the cafeteria for Spring Training. There is a very palpable sense that this is an old airfield from World War II."

Klein credits the Tigers' director of Florida operations Ron Myers, whom he describes as a huge history buff, with the idea for the name.

"It allowed us to find the center of this Venn diagram of the Detroit Tigers and the World War II training ground," Klein said. "And the idea of this being the training ground for the players. They're moving themselves up the big leagues."

COURTESY BRANDIOSE

The logo itself combines a reference to the Detroit Tigers' tiger with iconic pilot wings. But as with all things Brandiose, there were some deviations along the way.

"When we started off," Klein said, "[Brandiose partner] Casey [White] had this great idea of the imagery from the Wizard of Oz, the idea of these flying monkeys, and so some of the early sketch concepts had a very flying monkey, Wizard of Oz feel to it."

A version of the flying tiger monkey did end up in the logo set, but it's one of the lesser-used marks.

Another lesser-used mark that exists in the official logo set is a pin-up girl based on those seen on WWII jackets and decals featured on the shark-toothed airplanes that the Flying Tigers flew. Ultimately, however, Klein said, "the Tigers organization wanted to downplay it."

The design process led to an extensive suite of logos, all exploring the narrative of World War II aviation.

The final collection includes, among others, those based on a National Aircraft Insignia, Tiger Town USA, pilots' wings, a shield, and a tiger character in a distinctive pilot's jacket.

Another unique twist on the Flying Tigers' identity is that they're the first team, according to Klein, to feature an on-field manager's cap that's different from the one the players wear.

"The players have normal hats and the manager has scrambled palms, because he's the captain," Klein said.

I'll admit that I was not familiar with the history of the World War II Flying Tigers or the fact that Lakeland was a training ground for military pilots, so my first impression of this logo was that a minor league team had simply tweaked its parent club's identity. It wasn't until I started exploring the meaning behind the logo that I was able to appreciate it as it was meant to be.

I asked Klein if this was a good thing or a bad thing.

"One of the old sayings that used to go around was, if a logo has to be explained then it's a bad logo," Klein said. "We entirely disagree with that. We think that a good logo should be almost a question that lures you in to learn more about it.... The purpose of a good brand is that it gets people talking, it gets people discussing, it gets people learning about these great towns in America."

There are a lot of unique identities in minor league baseball, and nearly all of the time, there's a connection between the team's nickname and the town in which it plays. Some of those connections are stronger than others, while some just hang on by a thread. In the case of the Flying Tigers, the relationship between the town of Lakeland and the training of World War II pilots, along with the sheer happenstance of the team's parent club being called the Tigers, makes this one of the most meaningful team names in the minors.

Lexington Legends

Lexington Legends
2001–Present

Current Team Data

Parent
Kansas City Royals

Class
Single A

League
South Atlantic

Baseball goes way back in Lexington, Kentucky. But after playing host to a handful of teams dating back to the 1800s, the city went without baseball for most of the second half of the 20th century. After the Negro Leagues' Lexington Hustlers and the independent Lexington Colts disbanded in 1954, baseball was dormant in the city for decades. In 1984, the first rumblings about bringing the sport back to Lexington began. After 15 years of false starts, in 1999 a group of investors bought the rights to a Single-A franchise, which would debut in Lexington as a member of Single-A South Atlantic League in 2001.

If there was any question whether the city was glad to have a team in its midst after half a century without, the popularity of a name-the-team contest held in conjunction with the *Lexington Herald-Leader* was one of the first clues. The contest started in February of 2000.

"By mid-May, Lexington Professional Baseball Company had received over 5,400 entries consisting of 674 different names," says the team's website. "During the last month of the contest, over 14,000 fans voted for their favorite nickname—that's more than voted in the 2000 congressional primary in Lexington!"

The team's name and brand evoke a connection to Lexington's storied baseball past.

"What are the Legends?" asked Jason Klein of Brandiose, the firm responsible for the team's 2013 rebrand. "There are some loose connections to old-timey baseball."

The brand, pictured here in its original 2001 iteration, centers around the team's mascot, old-timey ballplayer Big L, whose back story, according to the team's website, is notably intertwined with horses.

Before the rebrand

"Big L was raised by two horse trainers who worked on many of the beautiful horse farms in the area," the team's website says. "He spent his childhood days playing the game of baseball in the fields of these sprawling farms.... Now, with his playing days over, Big L has decided to return to Lexington as the original Lexington Legend."

Given Big L's ties to horse farming and the popularity of horse racing in Kentucky (Lexington itself is home to race courses the Kentucky Horse Park, The Red Mile, and Keeneland) Brandiose's early discussions about the 2013 rebrand focused on that sport.

"We tried to incorporate horse racing a lot early on," Klein said. "There's some stuff like the white picket fence, which is a staple in Lexington for horse farms."

But ultimately, as with all things Lexington Legends, the rebrand ended up focusing on Big L himself. "They really wanted to focus on this mascot of theirs, Big L," Klein said. "We were like, this is a great character, let's figure out where we can take this character."

There are a few alternate logos that evoke granite, "which is also big there," Klein said, but the real identity is found in the team's storied mascot.

The logo that defined the rebrand and caught the national imagination was one that reduced Big L to his most prominent feature.

"It was sort of like when the hipster mustache movement was getting started," Klein said. "We were like, hey, why don't we put the mustache on a hat, and it will be a tribute to the mascot?"

JOSH SPANGLER

The mustache logo caught the attention of the national media, but the team was quick to explain they weren't just catching a passing bandwagon.

"Minor League Baseball is all about the 'wow' factor, and we wanted to go beyond the normal stuff you'd see at the ballpark," said Ty Cobb (no, not that Ty Cobb), the Legends director of creative services and graphic designer, quoted on MiLB.com. "And we wanted to be the team to do this first, to have a mustache on a hat. Our mascot, he actually has a mustache, so we're not just hopping on a fad."

The team treaded lightly at first, using the mustache logo sparingly.

"First it was the road and alternate cap," Klein said. "Quickly it became the official home cap when the popularity took off."

And that popularity did take off. The mustache found its way pretty much everywhere, including a Legends T-shirt that was best described by Ben Hill, author of Minor League Baseball's Ben's Biz Blog: "This is real: a piece of officially licensed Minor League Baseball apparel that explicitly references the time-honored act of mustache riding."

The guys at Brandiose probably didn't have that idea in mind when they created the mustache logo, but when they hand off a suite of logos to a team they work with, they're happy to see that team take the ball and run.

"Like any concept, you really want it to have legs," Klein said. "You want the staff to be able to creatively run with it. The mustache was something where the staff found themselves creatively coming up with ideas faster than anything else."

In just over 15 years, the Legends brand has made the jump from retro kitschy to hipster irony, but in the world of minor league baseball, that sort of jump can be just the thing that gets you noticed. You never know what's going to catch the public's imagination, but the simple mustache logo has become the centerpiece of this relatively young brand.

Lincoln Saltdogs

Lincoln Saltdogs
2001–Present

Current Team Data

Class
Independent

League
American Association

The city of Lincoln, Nebraska, has a lot going for it. With a quarter-million residents, it's the state capital (its skyline is highlighted by the nation's second-tallest capitol), it's home to the University of Nebraska, it hosts an expanding tech industry, and it's named for a president who guided the United States through one of its most turbulent eras.

So you can forgive fans of the Lincoln Saltdogs, one of twelve teams in the American Association of Independent Professional Baseball, if they have a certain question about their hometown team.

"When people come take tours," said Charlie Meyer, the team's president and general manager, "that's one of the most frequently asked questions—what is a Saltdog?"

If you Google the question (depending on your "safe search" settings), you might stumble across *salty dog*, which is either a slang term for lifelong Marines or a cocktail made with grapefruit juice and vodka or gin. The baseball team has nothing to do with either of those. The actual answer goes back to the mid-1800s, when the area was called Lancaster County and had a population of 500 people.

"When we were putting the team together back in 2000 and trying to identify what the name of the team was going to be, we were really looking to the history," Meyer said.

In coming up with a name, the team considered going by Capitals, playing off the fact that Lincoln is the state capital. However, at the time of their founding, the team was part of the Northern League (which disbanded and kind of reformed as the Northeast League, which is now the CanAm League) and the Northern League already had the Québec Capitales, so it was back to the drawing board. (The Saltdogs would leave that league to become one of the founding members of the American Association after the 2005 season.)

"What we were trying to do was tie it to the history of Lincoln," Meyer said. "A lot of people didn't realize it was founded on a salt flat back in the mid-1800s."

Basically, from 1853 to 1887, the area that is now Lincoln was settled by individuals and companies who couldn't help but notice that the ground was covered in salt. Two local bodies of water—Salt Creek, which fans have to cross in order to reach the Saltdogs' stadium, Haymarket Park, and a basin that now goes by Capital Beach Lake—are naturally salinated through deposits left by the vast inland sea that once covered the area.

The salt mining industry would never really pan out it Lincoln, but the town took root and continued to grow. More than a century after any serious attempts at salt mining in the area, the local baseball team brought that history back to the forefront.

So that explains the salt part of the name. But the question remains, what is a Saltdog? It turns out that the team turned to that time-tested minor league baseball team-naming formula to round out their moniker:

City + Geological Feature + Any Animal = Your Team Name!

"It was a matter of whether we were going to be called Saltcats or the Saltdogs," Meyer said. "And our owner has dogs."

Given that the history of Lincoln as a salt resource has been obscured by time, and the fictional animal Saltdog is an invention of the team, I asked Meyer if the name often required explaining.

"Yeah, absolutely," he said.

But it's not without precedent! Meyer invoked the names of some other teams in minor league baseball whose names require a little explaining.

"It's kind of like, what's a River Cat?" he asked. "I think that's the uniqueness. It's kind of like a Mudcat. Spinners. All those types of things." (For the record, the origins of all three of those teams are detailed in this book.)

Of course, as with all brands, consistency and persistence rule the day. The Saltdogs have had the same name and identity for 16 years. While the team added a front-facing logo to celebrate their 15th anniversary, the primary logo, created by Dick Sakahara, who was with the Lincoln-based agency Swanson Russell at the time, still remains.

SETH GALLAGHER

From the get-go, the team had to pick a direction—do we go adorable or intimidating. While the team's mascot, Homer, is decidedly adorable—he makes regular appearances in the community and he's the namesake for Homer's Heroes, a baseball program for disabled children in the area—the logo has a bit of an edge to it for a reason.

"The ferociousness of the logo is because we've got guys playing baseball," Meyer said.

The Saltdogs' branding is complicated somewhat by the fact that they share Haymarket Park with the University of Nebraska. It's a great park (named best playing field in the Northern League and the American Association for every year that the Saltdogs have existed), and its location half a mile from the University of Nebraska's campus is ideal, but the teams share the branding that fans see when they attend a game.

"There are Husker things around the concourse as well as Saltdogs, so it's more a community ballpark and we share the facility," Meyer said. "Their season ends here in May, we start up in May. We run through early September, so it's been a great partnership for 15 years."

The Saltdogs' name was basically created out of thin air—or at least salty ground—but a decade and a half of consistent branding have made it a household name throughout Nebraska. Fans will continue to ask what a Saltdog is, and those in the know will tell them, it's not a sailor or a drink, all that matters is that it's a baseball player.

New Hampshire Fisher Cats

New Hampshire Fisher Cats
2004–Present

Current Team Data

Parent
Toronto Blue Jays

Class
Double-A

League
Eastern

The original logo

The 2008 update

Here are some important facts about the small carnivorous animal known as the fisher cat: 1. It is not a cat. 2. It does not eat fish.

Fisher cats are members of the weasel family, and their name derives from a linguistic quirk of European settlers in North America, who thought it looked like a European polecat. The name *fisher cat* comes from *fiche* or *fichet*—French terms for a polecat pelt—and the middle Dutch word for nasty, *visse*.

"There are tons of them all over New Hampshire," said Rick Brenner, president and general manager of minor league baseball's New Hampshire Fisher Cats. "They're a pretty mean, aggressive animal, to be honest with you."

Much of the fisher cats' range is in the forested lands of Canada, so it seems appropriate the New Hampshire Fisher Cats, who play in the Double-A Eastern League, are an affiliate of Major League Baseball's only Canadian team, the Toronto Blue Jays. (Until we get the Expos back. Am I right, Montreal?!)

As a sports franchise that plays in New England but is an affiliate of a divisional rival of the beloved Red Sox, the Fisher Cats don't expect their fans' team loyalty to extend so far beyond the city limits of Manchester, New Hampshire.

"It's a great, rabid sports market to be in," Brenner said. "People love their teams, they love their sports, so it's a great atmosphere to be in and be a part of. We work hard to make sure the Fisher Cats are our community's minor league team, and who they choose to be their Major League team is certainly something that's their choice."

The Eastern League's other New England team is the Portland Sea Dogs, a Red Sox affiliate, so you can bet that when the Fisher Cats and Sea Dogs get together, their fans fight like two different kinds of animals who do not typically get along that well. (Again, I can't emphasize this strongly enough: Fisher cats are not actually cats. And as I point out in my article about Portland, sea dogs are not actually dogs.)

The Fisher Cats' inaugural logo, designed by Studio Simon, featured a menacing version of the animal gripping a bat and a ball, with New Hampshire's evergreen forests in the background.

A change in team leadership took the team in a new direction in 2008, this one designed by Rickabaugh Graphics. "We were just kind of looking for something a little friendlier, a little bit more able to relate to the kids and the families that come in the park," Brenner said. "Our goal was really to freshen up the look and take it a little bit down the friendlier road than the aggressive one. We were looking to change the color scheme up, brighten it up a little bit."

In 2011, the team underwent another identity shift, this time from a conceptual color standpoint. "We felt that green was important to be a part of New Hampshire," Brenner said. "Then we got to a point where we thought, you know, so much of New England is patriotic, and the red, white, and blue would be a great fit for our marks. We took a look at it and decided to go that direction."

Alternate logos include the animal's tail wrapped around the letters NH and a clawed paw gripping a baseball.

Speaking of patriotic, the Fisher Cats would not have actually been the Fisher Cats if things had gone to the original team management's plans. When the team was first announced in 2003, they were introduced as the New Hampshire Primaries, named for the state's role in hosting the first ballots cast in the early stages of the USA's never-ending presidential election process. Local fans hated the name—probably because they were in the midst of an election cycle at the time, and it's a soul-crushing, horrible process—and the team turned to a fan vote to decide on another name.

This Primaries identity was vetoed by fans

That said, the Fisher Cats have not abandoned the Primaries name altogether, occasionally using it as an alternate identity. The team primarily (get it?) uses a patriotic Uncle Sam instead of the original concept for the primary logo (GET IT?!), which featured a Republican elephant and Democratic donkey eying each other suspiciously, seemingly about to bash each other with baseball bats.

"It's an undeniable part of the team's history, and it's an undeniable part of the state of New Hampshire, so it just made sense to continue to use it and have it be part of some of the things we do here from time to time," Brenner said. "I think it's always important to hold on to your history and celebrate it and bring it out and keep it alive and celebrate the roots of your franchise."

Instead of elephants and donkeys, though, baseball fans opted for a different nasty animal to represent their team. They could have been named for politicians and instead they went with Fisher Cats. What this means in the end, of course, is that they simply traded one kind of weasel for another.

The team uses this Primaries logo for promotional nights

Omaha Storm Chasers

Omaha Storm Chasers
2011–present

Current Team Data

Parent
Kansas City Royals

Class
Triple-A

League
Pacific Coast

There are a lot of sports teams named after severe weather or natural disasters—Avalanche, Hurricanes, Quakes, Storm, Thunder, etc. But very few teams are named for the people who actually head out into the world in intentional pursuit of extreme weather events.

The term *storm chasing* is most commonly associated with people who track tornadoes in the American Midwest, though it can apply to anyone who pursues extreme weather, either recreationally or for science. It is also commonly associated (in my mind, anyway) with the 1996 movie *Twister* featuring Helen Hunt, Bill Paxton, and a bunch of flying cows. As we know from the movie, people who chase storms have to be brave and a little bit reckless and ruggedly attractive, in a mussed-hair, ruffled-clothing sort of way.

"Being a storm chaser, I wouldn't say is the most safe thing in the world," said Martie Cordaro, president and general manager of the Triple-A Omaha Storm Chasers. "It takes a special, unique individual that's trained to be a storm chaser."

Omaha's minor league baseball team had been called the Royals after its parent club for nearly its entire existence, beginning in 1969. (There was an ill-fated three-year stint from 1999 to 2001 when they were the Omaha Golden Spikes, a reference to the transcontinental railroad that had more to do with Utah than Nebraska.) But with the big league Royals mired in longterm mediocrity and the name Royals not applying to the local Omaha community, the team asked itself some soul-searching questions.

"Are we Omaha Royals because we always have been, because we were affiliated with Kansas City, or is there really a connection there?" Cordaro asked. "The Royals had lost for a number of years, plus the Royals were in Kansas City. The Royals were not in Omaha."

When the rebrand process began in 2010, a name-the-team contest turned up a consistent theme.

"We got over 1,500 unique name suggestions, 5,000 total names," Cordaro said, "and there were a lot of weather-related ones in there, from hail, wind, rain, storms, flooding, you name it. Anything that had to do with weather, it was in there."

The thing that makes the Storm Chasers' name-the-team contest unique among all the others I've written about in this series is that the fans genuinely selected the team name. The organization chose 24 appropriate entries based on their own market research, conducted in concert with the design firm Brandiose (known as Plan B at the time), then a series of fan votes narrowed down the options to nine, three, and the final selection. Unlike most minor league baseball name-the-team contests, which are basically farces intended to generate publicity, in this instance, the name that got the most votes was what the team would be called.

With fan voting actually selecting the team name, it seems that Omaha might have circumvented the normal cycle of annoyed traditionalists horrified at the new identity who then almost immediately turn around and start loving it. But it was not to be.

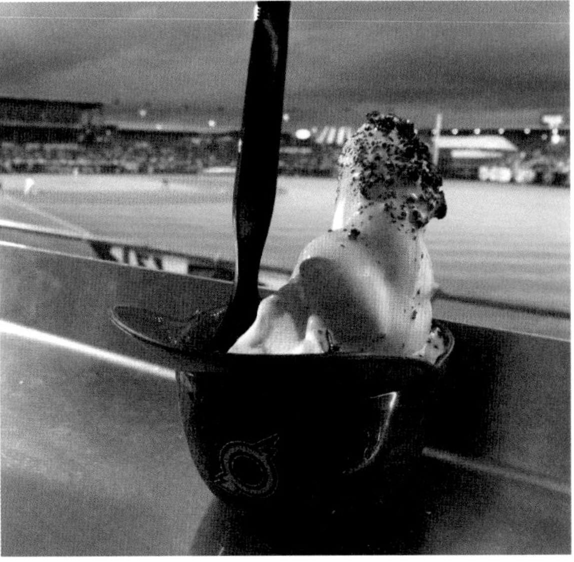

"Any time you have a change, you're going to have frustrated people. We dealt with those as any team does when they make changes," Cordaro said. "We didn't have a lot of, 'I can't believe you're not the Royals anymore.' We did have some of, 'I can't believe you're the Storm Chasers.'"

Of course, the new look has afforded the club opportunities that being named after their Major League affiliate did not. "We actually have a brand," Cordaro said. "We can tie in with meteorology and weather programs. There's a lot of things we're able to do now that we weren't able to do prior to the rebranding."

The most popular element of the new logo set is a tornado named Vortex with a baseball bat for a nose. He exists as a three-dimensional, inflatable character (above) and is featured on the home cap, seen at right on catcher Francisco Pena.

Other design elements include what Cordaro called the O-bolt, featured on the team's road caps (and their helmet sundaes), and alternate logos with the letters SC—presumably for Storm Chasers, though there are competing theories.

"It does stand for Storm Chasers," Cordaro said. "I will tell you, the county we're based in is Sarpy County. People do feel that it is for Sarpy County. It was not intended to be that way, but yes, it is both for Storm Chasers and for Sarpy County." (Cordaro also pointed out that his wife, Sarah Cordaro, has her own theory about what the SC stands for.)

The Storm Chasers' rebrand coincided with a resurgence of Kansas City's farm system, which has translated to success on the field for Omaha. The Storm Chasers made the playoffs the first four years that they existed and they won not only the Pacific Coast League title, but the one-game Triple-A championship game against the International League champion in 2013 and 2014.

Not only that, but Omaha hosted the Triple-A All-Star Game in 2015 in Werner Park, the Storm Chasers' new home as of 2011.

So with consecutive championship seasons, the fifth anniversary of their ballpark, and hosting the All Star Game, there has been a fair amount going on in Omaha. You could even say—or better yet, let Martie Cordaro say it for you, "It kind of was the perfect storm. Pun intended."

The most interesting thing about the Storm Chasers' name is that it connects the team to extreme weather without actually being specifically named for extreme weather. A sports nickname that conjures the people who pursue tornadoes rather than the tornadoes themselves is a twist (as it were) on the traditional approach. The Storm Chasers have had early success with their new look, which, combined with success on the field, has made them one of the more recognizable brands in the minors.

Quad Cities River Bandits

Quad Cities River Bandits
2008–present

Current Team Data

Parent
Houston Astros

Class
Single-A

League
Midwest

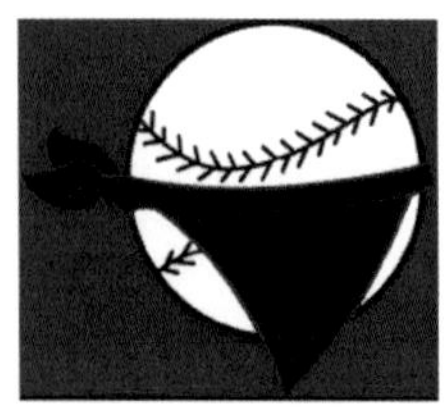

The Quad Cities River Bandits, the Midwest League's Single-A Houston Astros affiliate, have done things a little differently. They are embodied perfectly by their logo and mascot, Rascal the raccoon—scrappy, undersized, and kind of adorable, but they'll hold their own in a fight. In a market a fraction of the size of most higher-level minor league teams, the River Bandits finished fourth among all 160 teams in Minor League Baseball's 2014 logo popularity contest, the Clash of the Caps—and they were the top finisher among the 100 Single-A and rookie league teams in the contest.

"You can't compete with a club that's in a much, much, much larger market, like Nashville, where they have NFL football, or Charlotte, where they have NBA basketball and NFL football, or San Antonio," said Dave Heller, one of the team's owners. "We're not that big. We have a quarter million people in our media market. To be able to win that kind of voting means people all over the country are seeing our cap and liking it and in many instances buying it."

The River Bandits play in Davenport, Iowa, one of a cluster of cities on the Mississippi River known as the Quad Cities. Like many minor league teams, they adopted the names of their various Major League affiliates for many years, but ultimately rebranded with a unique identity.

From 1992 to 2003, the team was known as the Quad City River Bandits, a reference to the nefarious bandits who killed the town's namesake, George Davenport, in 1845. The first iteration of the River Bandits featured a popular logo of a baseball with a bandana.

After horrific floods in 2001 and 2003, then-owner Kevin Krause chose to distance the team name somewhat from the river, and rebranded as the awkward and ill-fated Swing of the Quad Cities in 2004.

"That name was based on a triple entendre," Heller said. "It referenced the swing of the bat, and Davenport sits on what some people like to call the swing of the river, where the river turns and actually runs east-west at one point, and then the swing of the old jazz era. Davenport and the Quad Cities are right on the Mississippi, where there's a long blues history."

When Heller and his partner Bob Herrfeldt purchased the team at the end of the 2007 season, they chose to put the name of the team back in the hands of the community, and the community made its voice heard in a name-the-team contest.

"With six finalists of names suggested, the River Bandits name took something like 82

ELISTA ISTRE

Bandits are everywhere at Modern Woodmen Park.

percent of the vote," Heller said. "In a six-way race, that's a pretty significant landslide, so we rechristened the team the River Bandits."

But there were changes. First, the original River Bandits in the 1990s were the Quad City (singular) River Bandits, whereas their current name is the Quad Cities (plural) River Bandits. Heller explains:

> If the question is, "Where are you from?" you would never answer, "I'm from Quad City." Nobody would say that. You would say, "I'm from the Quad Cities." My thought was, we're going to put this name on a visiting jersey and we're going to wear it with pride, it ought to say what the answer would be if anybody asks, "Where are you from?"

Another important change was the team's logo, designed by Francis Santaquiliani of FS Designs, who has designed other sports logos, but none in affiliated minor league baseball, according to Heller. The logo features a raccoon, Rascal.

"We wanted something that could be both friendly and fierce at the same time," Heller said. "And we thought a raccoon with basically a mask around its eyes already, was the ideal way to depict a bandit that could be both friendly and fierce."

Before the 2014 season, the River Bandits redesigned their primary logo to be more appropriate to their location, specifically relating to Davenport's well-known architectural centerpiece, the Centennial Bridge. The bridge is a prominent feature of the skyline as seen from the team's home, Modern Woodmen Ballpark, which was voted minor league baseball's best park in a *USA Today* poll in 2013.

"The reason we did that is we wanted to really localize the logo," Heller said. "We wanted people to have it be instantly identifiable as the Quad Cities. Our ballpark sits right below the Centennial Bridge and the new the bridge in the logo is really a more geographically accurate representation of the Centennial Bridge."

Not only that, but the team unveiled a series of alternate logos, each with a specific purpose.

"What we've tried to do with our logos," Heller said, "is really very intentionally use each one as a means of telling the story of what this team means to the community and what you get when you come to Modern Woodmen Park."

It begins with water. "We are right on the Mississippi River, the biggest river in the nation," Heller said. "And so we wanted something that would reflect the river. That's why we have the ball landing in the river. If you're a strong left-handed hitter, you could easily pull the ball over the fence and plop it down in the river."

A second alternate logo "is Rascal in the gondola, because we added a Ferris wheel to the ballpark this year," Heller said. "We're the only minor league park in the country with our own Ferris wheel inside the ballpark."

But most importantly, "the third piece is the paw holding the baseball," Heller said. "There's all kinds of different ways, with the rides and the views, the boats going by, and the bridge, to enjoy yourself at the ballpark. But at the end of the day, we're still about baseball, and so the paw holding the baseball very prominently reminds people, first and foremost, we're a baseball team."

And finally, speaking of baseball, "We thought, for a BP cap, we'd have Rascal taking BP," Heller said. "So we put a bat in his paws."

The River Bandits' approach is not unusual—minor league teams everywhere are using cartoon characters to appeal to children. (It worked on my 10-year-old son, who has never been to Davenport, but owns a River Bandits T-shirt.) Indeed, the Bandits fared well in this year's Clash of the Cap contest because fans liked their logo on a superficial level—it's fun and eye catching. But on a deeper level, the River Bandits' design decisions are meaningful in a specific way to their hometown, and intentionally create a narrative related to their own ballpark experience. This is not typical of every Single-A minor league baseball team, and it's what make this identity worth a second look.

Reno Aces

When I reached out to the Reno Aces, Triple-A affiliate of the Arizona Diamondbacks, to talk to them about their logo and team name, I did not expect to end up talking about Ewoks. But when I asked Aces marketing director Brett McGinness about how the team's sophisticated, traditional look bucks the trend of new minor league logos that cater exclusively to children, he used Ewoks as a metaphor. It boils down to this: Ewoks are basically *Star Wars's* way of talking down to children, and Ewoks are annoying. And don't get us started on Jar Jar Binks.

"*Star Wars* was fantastic, and adults love *Star Wars*. We didn't need Ewoks in *Return of the Jedi*," McGinness said. When it comes to baseball, he continued, "I don't think you need an Ewok-ish logo or mascot. Give kids a little bit of credit."

In the interest of fairness, I am compelled to point out that while the Aces did not name themselves after a *Star Wars* character, they did have a *Star Wars* night this season, because they're a minor league baseball team and that's the law.

Reno Aces
2009–present

Current Team Data

Parent
Arizona Diamondbacks

Class
Triple-A

League
Pacific Coast

All of that said, there's a reason the Aces, who debuted in 2009, felt like they did not need a glorified teddy bear as the face of their franchise:

"Two-thirds of the fans that attend our games do not have children under 18 in the home," McGinness said. "Even among the people who do have children in the home, I think it was 40 percent said that there weren't any children under 18 with them at their most recently attended game."

The Aces' nickname is a double entendre. It references both star pitchers in baseball and a playing card, appropriate for Reno, a tourist destination noted for its legal gambling. Though McGinness points out that kids also play card games, such as Crazy Eights and Go Fish.

"I don't think card games in and of themselves necessarily represent gambling," he said. "At least around here, nobody thinks, 'Oh that's not very family friendly.'"

While the team name and logo are more sophisticated than some of the other new ones out there, there's still something for the kids when they're done with their Crazy Eights and Go Fish tournaments. The team's mascot, Archie, is named for the Reno

Your trusty author in the Aces clubhouse in 2013.

Arch, which proclaims Reno the "Biggest Little City in the World." Not much is known about Archie, but McGinness offers this: "He's just a big red fuzzball." (He's definitely not an Ewok.)

The Aces' cap logo features a stylized letter A, as you might see on a playing card, with one particularly meaningful design element: "I think it's lost on a lot of people," McGinness said, "but in the A, there's a tiny red diamond in our logo, and that's a nod to the Diamondbacks."

The team's alternate logo features a spade instead of a diamond (unless you count the baseball diamond, of course) so they'll still be able to use it if they ever switch Major League affiliates, as teams do every season.

Despite playing in the smallest market in Triple-A baseball, according to McGinness, the Aces have the highest attendance per capita of any Triple-A team, in large part because their downtown stadium, which hosted the 2013 Triple-A All Star Game, attracts visitors.

"When people look out their windows," McGinness said, "and they're looking for something to do aside from the gaming, the eating, the drinking, all the stuff that goes along with vacationing here, you know, here we are."

The close relationship of the team's identity to gambling, the primary reason that tourists visit Reno, helps fuel the popularity of merchandise. The Aces have been among the top 25 sellers in minor league logo merchandise on a regular basis.

"It's not necessarily Diamondbacks fans saying, 'Oh I gotta have our Triple-A affiliate,'" McGinness said. "It's a lot of people saying, 'Oh, that's a fantastic logo.' It might be folks who like the name, folks who are amateur poker players, things like that."

The Aces moved to Reno after the 2008 season. Their previous iteration, the Tucson Sidewinders, was a much more obvious nod to the parent club than the current subtle reference to diamonds. After moving to Reno, many local fans wanted the team to acquire the rights to the nickname of the city's longtime independent Golden Baseball League team, the Silver Sox (a reference to Nevada's nickname, the Silver State). But at the time, that team's future was still in question and the name was not available. (The Silver Sox eventually folded.)

The Aces nickname was selected from a name-the-team contest that drew more than 1,600 entries with more than 1,100 unique name ideas. (I'd be really curious to see a complete list of 1,100 potential baseball team names.) Ultimately, the team went with a clever, appropriate nickname, and traditional visual identity with mass appeal. Of course, you have to wonder what might have been if the team had taken a different approach.

"We didn't have to roll out and be the Reno—I can't even imagine—Mountain Goats or God knows what," McGinness said. "We didn't need to be the Reno Ewoks."

Round Rock Express

Round Rock Express
2005–present

Current Team Data

Parent
Texas Rangers

Class
Triple-A

League
Pacific Coast

More than a century and a quarter before the world was introduced to the Round Rock Express baseball team, Triple-A affiliate of the Texas Rangers, the International and Great Northern Railroad brought trains to Round Rock, Texas. The railroad industry changed the face of the city forever.

According to the city's website, "Round Rock can claim that the most significant event in its history was the coming of the railroad in 1876. This event precipitated the relocation of the town's central business district and changed Round Rock forever."

So it stands to reason that the town's baseball team would feature a train in its logo. In fact, the train is such a prominent part of the Express's identity, it sometimes causes confusion.

"People who are new in town," said Jill Cacic, the team's Vice President of Public Relations and Communications, "they may see the Round Rock Express and think we're a newspaper or a train company or a transportation company or something like that."

To help spread the word that they're a baseball team and not some other company, the team rewards fans for wearing Express gear when they're out and about on the town. "We have an initiative locally where if you're caught wearing Express gear in public ... it's good for two free tickets to a future game," Cacic said.

By now, though, there shouldn't be too much confusion over who the Express are. They've been around since 2005, moving to Texas from Canada after playing as the Edmonton Trappers from 1981 to 2004. (It was a bad time for baseball in Canada, as the Trappers were an Expos affiliate, but that changed after 2004, when both teams left for cities to the south.) The Trappers were purchased in 2003 by the RSR Sports group, which bought the team with the intention of moving it to Round Rock. RSR Sports is named for its principals, Hall of Fame pitcher Nolan Ryan, business person Don Sanders, and Nolan's son Reid Ryan.

PEGGY SIMME

Spike the mascot with fans

The fact that the team is partially owned by one of the biggest names in baseball history, and that his nickname from his playing days sounds an awful lot like something to do with trains is a lucky coincidence—and one the team would have been crazy to ignore when naming the team.

"The name comes from Nolan Ryan, who is one of our principal owners and he was the Ryan Express when he was playing," Cacic said. "There's also a train that runs right by the stadium, so it was a natural fit."

Being that the Express play in Texas, where Nolan Ryan played roughly half of his 27-year career with the Astros and the Rangers, you can forgive Round Rock Express spokespeople for making bold claims about their owner.

"We have the luxury of having, you know, the greatest pitcher in all of baseball to be one of our owners," Cacic continued, "so it's something that's easy to pull from."

Indeed, Nolan Ryan holds Major League records with 5,714 career strikeouts and seven career no-hitters, plus his 383 strikeouts in 1973 is the most in a single season in the live ball era. But in terms of best pitcher ever, the likes of Bob Gibson, Pedro Martinez, Randy Johnson, Greg Maddux, Sandy Koufax, and Dazzy Vance might raise their eyebrows at that claim. (Unresolvable baseball debate alert! Who's the best pitcher in baseball history? While you're at it, should Pete Rose be in the Hall of Fame and is the designated hitter good for the sport?)

The current logo, designed by Dan Simon of Studio Simon and adopted in 2011, prominently features a cow catcher and an eye-catching detail that combines baseball and trains.

"If you look at the primary logo, there's a baseball," Cacic said. "I always think of it as the light on the front of the train."

The cow catcher and headlamp are particular of note for trains in Round Rock because of a unique feature of an early train to frequent the city. One of the first lines to run out of Round Rock was to nearby Georgetown, where there was nowhere for the train to turn around, so the train had to make the return trip backwards. According to *The Railroads of Roundrock,* "To facilitate this process, the 'J.J. Dimmitt' was outfitted with cow-catchers and headlamps on both ends."

With a name that draws from baseball royalty and a logo that explores their hometown's ties to the railroad industry, the Round Rock Express have a strong logo and two converging backstories that make it one of the more fun identities in the minors.

Sacramento River Cats

In the course of writing this series, I have been surprised on many occasions to learn of connections between the names of sports teams and their home towns. So when I called up the Sacramento River Cats to learn the story behind their nickname, I was expecting to find that Sacramento, California, was perhaps the feral cat capital of the world, or maybe it has the highest percentage of cat ownership on the west coast, or possibly it's the secret breeding ground for a species of super house cat with extra purring power.

I asked Robert Barsanti, the team's coordinator of media relations, how come you guys are called the River Cats?

The reason for the *River* part of the team's name is obvious. The Sacramento River is the largest in California, flowing 445 miles from the Klamath Mountains to the San Francisco Bay. It has enormous natural importance, playing host to wildlife like chinook salmon, serving as the watershed for a huge swath of northern California, and feeding lakes and other scenes in a beautiful part of the country. And it's culturally significant, with ties to Native American heritage dating back thousands of years, Spanish exploration in the 1700s, and the California Gold Rush, to name just a few examples. Among the many notable landmarks along the river's course, it flows right past Raley Field, home to the Triple-A Sacramento River Cats.

As for the second part of that name, why is the team called the River *Cats?*

"I don't think the Cats has any real tie to anything," Barsanti said.

No connection between Sacramento and the largest population of orange tabbies in the western states? No record for fattest house cat in North America? No huge kitty litter manufacturing plant on the outskirts of the city?

"When the team moved to Sacramento from Vancouver—we made that move in the '99–2000 offseason—we actually held an open vote for our team name. We asked the city and the surrounding areas to submit names that they thought would be great for the team, and took some of the more popular ones and considered them," Barsanti said. "It was one of the more popular ones that was submitted, and you know, our team here liked it."

So while the Cats part of the name was pulled out of thin air back before the 2000 season, some of the more interesting parts of the team's brand are much more recent. Until recently, the River Cats had been an affiliate of the Oakland A's for the entire duration of their tenure in Sacramento. Minor league baseball teams change parent clubs all the time, but when the River Cats signed on with the San Francisco Giants before the 2015 season, it

Sacramento River Cats
2000–present

Current Team Data

Parent
San Francisco Giants

Class
Triple-A

League
Pacific Coast

The River Cats' first logo

Sacramento's Tower Bridge is visible from Raley Field.

generated more publicity and public reaction than any other move that offseason (with the possible exception of the Los Angeles Dodgers, who ended their affiliation with the Albuquerque Isotopes to purchase the Oklahoma City Redhawks and change the name of that team to the OKC Dodgers).

"The biggest thing is, while there was a strong reaction, I think it was stronger on the positive side," Barsanti said. "There are a lot of Giants fans in the Sacramento region, even before our affiliation switch. Obviously, when you win three World Series in the span of five years, you get a lot of fans everywhere."

That last point—that the River Cats have their own established brand independent of their parent club—is a driving force behind alternate uniforms the team wore in 2016. The new identity, created by the team's in-house designer Mike Villarreal, connects the team to San Francisco with Giants colors and an image of the Golden Gate Bridge, but it plays up the city's nickname, Sactown.

"The River Cats really are Sacramento's team," Barsanti said. "People aren't just A's fans, or just Giants fans. They're River Cats fans."

Of course, some people who are not fans of the Sacramento River Cats are their intrastate rivals, the Fresno Grizzlies, the team the San Francisco Giants left to become parent club to the River Cats.

As a part of a strong Oakland A's farm system, the River Cats had substantial success over the last decade and a half. Meanwhile, the Giants have had success at the Major League level, but they've done so at the expense of their farm system. When the River Cats switched parent clubs from the A's to San Francisco, the caliber of Triple-A player wearing that Sacramento uniform dropped. The Fresno Grizzlies, on the other hand, signed on with the Houston Astros, who had one of the strongest farm systems in the Majors.

The River Cats and the Grizzlies have spatted on Twitter and in the real world since the affiliation change, to the point where the Grizzlies put up anti–River Cats "Wackramento" billboards in Sacramento. The Grizzlies won the division for the first time since 1998 in 2015, but perhaps more importantly, defeated the River Cats 3-1 on that season's "Grumpy Cat Night," a promotion in which they compared Sacramento's logo to the grumpy cat of internet meme fame.

SACRAMENTO RIVERCATS

"After so many years of the River Cats being the top team in our division, I think that Fresno saw it as an opportunity to take a jump at us and have something to attack us with," Barsanti said. "I think they were using it as an opportunity to kind of strike back for all the years of them not being as good of a team."

Of course, one of the things about minor league baseball is that no one really cares that much who wins on the field—it's a system designed to move those who excel on to the next level. But the River Cats have won on one of the profession's most contested off-field battlegrounds—branding. The team is consistently on the annual list of top-25 minor league baseball teams in terms of merchandise sales.

The River Cats are one of those increasingly rare minor league teams where, to paraphrase Dennis Green, they are who we thought they were. There's no contorted message or twisting and turning to give the name significance beyond "Hey, we thought it was cool." This obviously has worked for the River Cats, and with a solid history of building their brand, there's no reason for it to change any time soon.

Salt Lake Bees

Salt Lake Bees
2006–present

Current Team Data

Parent
Los Angeles Angels

Class
Triple-A

League
Pacific Coast

The origin of the Triple-A Salt Lake Bees' nickname traces back a couple thousand years—to the Biblical "land of milk and honey." Utah's Mormon settlers called the state "Deseret," a word from the Book of Mormon that means honey bee in the Jaredite language. It's the reason the state uses beehive imagery everywhere, from highway signs to a sculpture in front of the capitol.

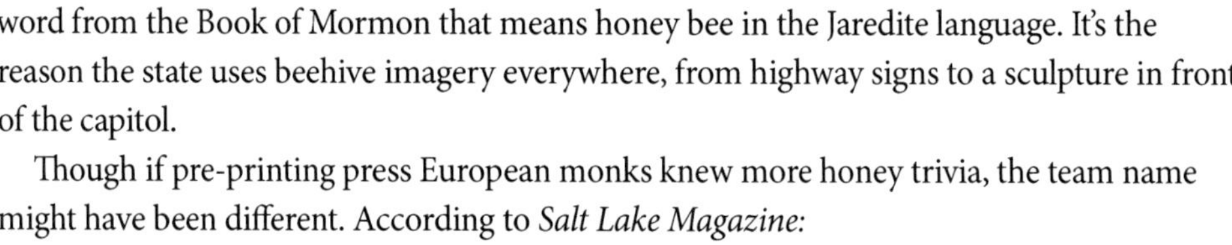

Though if pre-printing press European monks knew more honey trivia, the team name might have been different. According to *Salt Lake Magazine:*

> "The beehive has been used as a symbol for thousands of years," according to historian Mark Staker, an expert on early Mormon anthropology at the LDS Church's Family History Center. "The Bible refers to the Promised Land as 'the land of milk and honey.'"
>
> Of course, there were no honeybees in the ancient Middle East.
>
> "The European monks whose scriptoria kept the Bible in print before Gutenberg came along had no way of knowing that Biblical honey was most likely date honey and had nothing to do with bees. So they incorporated bees and the cooperative life of the hive into early Christian symbolism," explains Staker.

However it came to be, it's safe to say that it's probably for the best that baseball teams in Salt Lake City over the years have been named for bees rather than dried fruit.

The current baseball franchise in Salt Lake City debuted in 1994 as the Salt Lake Buzz after moving from Portland, Oregon. (I'm going to have to research this, but I'm pretty sure nearly every franchise in minor league baseball was once the Portland Beavers.) The team's nickname and teal logo (because it was the '90s and that was the law) were popular, but the team was forced to change for reasons beyond their control.

"Everybody enjoyed it. It was a good logo, and it went over pretty well here," said Steve Klauke, the team's director of broadcasting, who has called more than 3,000 games in more than 20 years as the voice of the Bees. "Unfortunately, Georgia Tech had trademarked Buzz for their team mascot and eventually filed suit against our old owners. I guess our old owners lost, so we had to change the name."

"It doesn't make any sense to me." Klauke continued. "The mascot of an ACC team against a Triple-A team 2,000 miles away, but so it goes."

Ironically, the reason the team was not called the Salt Lake Bees when it moved from

Portland in 1994 in the first place was a legal hurdle. The team's owner, minor league baseball legend Joe Buzas, didn't want to deal with the hassle of negotiating with another Bees team, the Midwest League's Single-A Burlington Bees.

"Burlington already had it," Klauke said, "and that was something Joe wasn't interested in dealing with. He wanted to have his own identity."

After the demise of the Salt Lake Buzz, the team had a name-the-team contest, which resulted in another bee-themed nickname. The Salt Lake Stingers debuted in 2001, the same year the team switched parent clubs from the Twins to the Angels. From 2001 to 2005, the team went with a logo that was, frankly, terrible (not to put too fine a point on it).

"I was not a big fan of the name or the logo," Klauke said. "Let's put it that way."

The Stingers identity was also not popular with one very important person: "In 2005, the owner of the Utah Jazz, Larry Miller, purchased the ballclub, and he was not a big fan of that name," Klauke said.

So new owner Larry Miller set about changing the name to the one he remembered from his childhood, the Salt Lake Bees. It's a nickname that other teams in the city had used off and on since 1915.

"For years and years, from the mid-teens all the way up through probably the mid- to late-'60s, any professional baseball team, whether it be Pacific Coast League or Pioneer League, was called the Bees," Klauke said, "and [Miller] always thought the nickname should go back to that, because that's the name that many people of his generation grew up with here."

The centerpiece of the negotiation to bring the Bees name back to Utah was Salt Lake City's special connection to the town of Nauvoo, Illinois, less than 30 miles from the other Bees' home in Burlington, Iowa.

"Nauvoo, Illinois, is kind of a town that our local population, the LDS population, goes back to, because that's where their trek west back to Utah began," Klauke said. "So every year, in our game program, the Burlington Bees get a full-page ad and the ad basically says, 'Hey when you come to visit Nauvoo, stop by and see a Burlington Bees game.'"

The Bees wear their primary cap logo, the right-handed batting bee, during home games, but their road caps feature a classic interlocking SL for Salt Lake—not an SLC for Salt Lake City. According to Klauke, the Bees don't use the word "City" in their name because the county of Salt Lake contributed to their stadium, so the moniker Salt Lake represents both the city and the county.

After some legal wrangling and some false starts, the Bees have one of the most consistent identities in Triple-A baseball. According to Klauke, the team has the second-longest continuous stretch of nickname, location, and affiliation in the Pacific Coast League, behind only the Colorado Springs Sky Sox. Strong colors, a clean look, and a nickname with a strong connection to place make the Bees' identity a good one—dare I say, the Bees' knees.

Tennessee Smokies

Tennessee Smokies
2000–present

Current Team Data

Parent
Chicago Cubs

Class
Double-A

League
Southern

The Smokies logo prior to the current look

Ask most people what the most-visited national park in the United States is and their minds will almost certainly go first to one of the iconic sites out west. But the answer to that question is not the Grand Canyon or Yosemite or Yellowstone, but Great Smoky Mountain National Park, which sits on the border between Tennessee and North Carolina. In fact, Great Smoky Mountain National Park drew 11 million visitors in 2017, more than the next two parks on the list, Grand Canyon and Yosemite, combined.

The Great Smoky Mountains—the Smokies, for short—get their name from the mist that often shrouds the mountain range. The mist, which from afar looks like plumes of smoke, is caused by the dense vegetation in the area's almost 200,000 acres of old-growth forest.

The Great Smoky Mountains have another claim to fame that those other parks out west don't have—they have a minor league baseball team named for them. The Tennessee Smokies, Double-A affiliate of the Chicago Cubs, play in Kodak, Tennessee, near Knoxville, a city whose minor league baseball credentials date back to 1897.

Over the years, teams with names like the Knoxville Sox (1972–1979), Knoxville Appalachians (1909–1911), Knoxville Pioneers (1921–1924), and my favorite, the Knoxville Baseball Club (1904) have graced the city's fields. Among those teams, two iterations of the Knoxville Smokies (1925–1967 and 1993–1999) bore the nickname of the current club, which has been playing as the Tennessee Smokies since 2000.

Aside from the mountain range, another association many people bring to the word "Smoky" (or "Smokey," in this case) is the moniker of one Smokey Bear, the anti-forest fire mascot of the U.S. Forest Service and later the National Park Service. (Author's pet peeve side note: There is no "THE" in Smokey Bear's name!) (Also, while I'm at it with the pet peeves, there is no "S" on the end of "Cracker Jack" in Take Me Out to the Ballgame!)

Before the 2015 season, when the team worked with Dan Simon of Studio Simon to update its logos, there were several givens to what the new visual identity would include: The colors would be determined by the team's parent club, the wordmark would remain roughly the same, and there would be a bear.

"We knew there was going to be a bear in the logo," Simon said. "It was a team called the Tennessee Smokies. It already had a bear.... We knew that it was going to be a bear-centric identity."

A Cubs affiliate since 2007, the Smokies wanted to reinforce their connection to their parent club with the new brand. The existence of a bear in the logo was a start, but a bear in a blue and red logo cemented the deal.

The direction Simon received from the club was this: "We really want to play up our connection to the Cubs," Simon was told. "That's something we haven't had with our previous identity."

It's not just the colors and the animal that tie the Smokies' identity to that of their parent club, but the form of the design itself.

"If you at the Chicago Cubs logo, you will notice that their logo has a blue circle on the outside, then it's got white, and then it's got red," Simon said. "If you look at the Smokies' primary logo, it's got a blue circle on the outside, a white in-line inside of that, and then red in that. So that circular shape that encompasses the primary logo is directly based on what the Cubs do."

One of Simon's favorite alternates in the suite of logos is one that was fraught with peril early on—the fear that trotting out a tired trope would look too familiar to sports fans.

"They wanted a bear claw logo," Simon said. "One of the things I said to them was, there are so many bear claw logos out there."

Simon fretted over how to create a logo that would not look derivative of others out there in the sports world already. Aware that there are countless logos, not just of bear claws, but any number of animals clutching baseballs, Simon turned to fellow designer and friend Joe Bosack to discuss the issue.

Bosack's suggestion, according to Simon, was this: "Instead of clutching the baseball like a paw would, why don't you have him clutch it like a baseball pitcher would? So we've got him doing a four-seam fastball grip there, what it did was put a different spin on an otherwise familiar theme." [Author's note: SO TO SPEAK!]

The Smokies have generations of tradition behind their brand. With a nickname that derives from a misty mountain range and a set of logos that ties to both America's most famous bear and the team's parent club, the Tennessee Smokies' new suite of logos builds on that tradition rather than replacing it.

Vancouver Canadians

Vancouver Canadians
2000–present

Current Team Data
Parent
Toronto Blue Jays
Class
Short Season-A
League
Northwest League

Vancouver, Canada, is a fascinating, beautiful city. More than half of its population claims something other than English as a first language. Vancouver's population density is Canada's highest and North America's fourth highest, but it also has the 1.5-square-mile Stanley Park. The city sits in an astonishing geographic location on the Burrard Peninsula, and is home to impressive architecture, remarkable ethnic diversity, and perhaps most importantly, one of the best all-you-can-eat sushi places I've ever been to.

So in 2014, when Brandiose partners Jason Klein and Casey White set about updating the brand of the Vancouver Canadians, the city's baseball team, they looked forward to delving into some of what makes Vancouver unique.

"We're always looking for something that has to do with the city," Klein said. "We said, what sort of local things do we want to incorporate? And they were like, we want it to be a celebration of Canada."

That's a lot to put on the shoulders of a short-season Single-A baseball team, and Klein admits that the Brandiose partners struggled to get their head around the idea of representing an entire country in a minor league baseball team's identity. So they put the question another way.

"Canada is so proud of the maple leaf, and so proud of, just, Canada, and everything Canada, Canada, Canada," Klein said. "We were like, what about Vancouver? And they were like, no, no, no, it's all about Canada."

While it's a lot to take on, it makes sense that the Canadians would want to represent all of Canada in their brand. The team is (of course) an affiliate of its in-country neighbors the Toronto Blue Jays (a short 40-hour, 4,400-kilometer drive to the east), and it is the only one of 160 affiliated minor league teams to play in Canada.

So with their marching orders in hand, Brandiose set about updating the team's current brand and adding a mark that would walk the line between a serious brand and minor league frivolity.

"The owners and the management are very about classic, traditional, major league approach," Klein said. "They're not really into the minor league, tongue-in-cheek stuff. They wanted to keep it real buttoned up."

To that end…

"Back in the '80s and '90s there was a Disney show called the Wuzzles. They're like mash-up animals," Klein said. "[Brandiose partner] Casey [White] had this idea of creating kind

2000

2005

2008

of like a Wuzzle character that was half moose, half orca, half beaver. Because we were trying to figure out how to bring a minor league, tongue-in-cheekness to the whole thing. It was dead on arrival. They were like, no way, this is not going to work."

For real this time, Brandiose set about creating a brand that honored the team's wish to avoid the outrageous minor league identity while also being fun.

The first step was to update the primary logo, which debuted in 2000 and was updated in 2005, 2008, and most recently in 2014. (Prior to the current short-season Single-A Vancouver Canadians, a Triple-A team of the same name played from 1978 to 1999 before relocating to California to become the Sacramento River Cats.)

The real strength of the new brand, as Klein sees it, is the custom typeface.

"It's a very northwestern typeface that we created for them," Klein said. "It looks like it could have been made out of wood. It's got a craftsman feel about it."

Of course, the most notable departure from anything the team had done previously is an alternate logo depicting a burly Mountie—a member of the Royal Canadian Mounted Police—running with not one but three baseball bats over his shoulder. The idea to use an image of the Mountie came from the team, in part as an homage to a Pacific Coast League team called the Vancouver Mounties that played in the 1950s and '60s, and in part because it's basically the most Canadian Canada thing ever.

In keeping with the team's wishes to have a Major League feeling while expressing minor league fun, the Brandiose partners used another team they have done some work for as a model.

"We really treated it like it was a Cincinnati Reds type brand," Klein said. "That was part how we approached it to ownership and management. Hey, we're going to look at the Reds as an example. They have like an old-timey character. We'll do an old-timey character."

Even with a cartoon Mountie in their suite of logos, the Canadians' brand is downright sophisticated, especially compared to some of the other teams that play in the Northwest League—like the Hillsboro Hops, Everett Aquasox, and Tri-City Dust Devils. A strong use of color, a commitment to the meaning behind the brand, and just a sleeve patch's worth of minor league fun make the Vancouver Canadians' identity work.

Vermont Lake Monsters

Vermont Lake Monsters
2006–present

Current Team Data

Parent
Oakland A's

Class
Short Season-A

League
New York–Penn

The last professional baseball team to carry the nickname Expos was not from Montreal, but rather Burlington, Vermont. When the Montreal Expos moved to Washington DC after the 2004 season, the team's short-season Single-A affiliate did not have time to change names before the 2005 campaign started.

"When Major League Baseball owned the team at that point, they kind of wanted to forget the Expos and move on to the Nationals," Vermont's general manager Nate Cloutier said. "With our name piggy-backing on theirs, they had asked us to consider renaming the team, and at that point, we just didn't have enough time to do so. It was a couple months before the season, and anyone in the industry knows that it takes months and months and months to not only rebrand but also get inventory in terms of merchandising and uniforms and stuff like that."

In the process of deciding on a new nickname during that 2005 season, a name-the-team contest generated overwhelming support for naming the team after their own mascot, Champ, the legendary and mythical* lake monster of nearby Lake Champlain. (*Note: MAYBE.) The legend of Champ dates back to a sighting by French explorer Samuel de Champlain in 1609. The mascot Champ (who shares my birthday, in case you're curious) dates back to the inception of the Vermont Expos in the mid-1990s. But despite overwhelming support for naming the team after its mascot, there was a problem.

"Champs was the number one vote," Cloutier said, "but having not made the playoffs since 1995, we didn't figure it was an appropriate name."

While the Vermont Champs were never meant to be, the team realized that their future identity had been right under their noses all along. "Every time we would think of something unique like Snow Devils or something like that," Cloutier said, "everyone would ask us, 'What's going to happen to Champ?' At that point the bell went off and it was like, 'Wow, we're sitting on something special and we're thinking of changing direction away from our biggest asset?' That just didn't make any sense."

The team adopted the nickname Lake Monsters in 2006, changing the logo from the Vermont Expos' gray cartoon lake monster, which appears to be part golden retriever, to a more sophisticated green monster. But while the Lake Monsters logo was a good one, something didn't sit right about it. There was a disconnect between the logo, which was a pointy, kelly green monster, and the beloved mascot, a roundish, lime green goof ball. So the team unveiled a new logo before the 2014 season.

"Champ is a lime green monster," Cloutier said. "He is our identity and that is why we have the new look that we have today.... You see him in the community and you recognize the big lime green figure. Why would our team colors not resemble that as well?"

The Lake Monsters' new logo didn't feel new at all to fans of the team. It was the familiar face of the franchise that they had known for years—probably better than they knew any of the team's players. "Being a short-season team, our players aren't around enough to even promote," Cloutier said. "If they're good enough, then they're typically not here very long."

SCOTT CASTIGLIA

Basing a baseball team's nickname on an urban legend, which is something the Las Vegas 51s have also had success with, inevitably leads to questions. Specifically, is it real?

"I've never personally seen anything," Cloutier said. "But it's something that the community holds onto, and tourists love.... I know one thing: You can see Champ 38 times each summer at Centennial Field."

I may be predisposed to liking the Lake Monsters because I miss the Expos (Vermont is an A's affiliate now), but I like the logo and the nickname. I can't think of another instance in which a team has named itself after its own mascot, but I think that some Major League teams should follow suit—like the Philadelphia Phanatics, the San Diego Chickens, or the New York Mr. Mets. I've long advocated for a return of the Montreal Expos, but if they ever do come back, I hope the team in Vermont remains the Lake Monsters—and that some day they win a New York-Penn League title and can call themselves the Champs.

Winston-Salem Dash

Winston-Salem Dash
2009–present

Current Team Data

Parent
Chicago White Sox

Class
High-A

League
Carolina

Winston-Salem Warthogs, 1995–2008

I've discovered a lot of unique team name origins in the course of writing this series, but just when I had given up my dream of finding a team that combined two of my passions, baseball and punctuation, I stumble across the Winston-Salem Dash.

The town of Salem in what would become North Carolina was settled and established by members of the Moravian Church in the mid-1700s. About a century later, the town of nearby Winston was established. The two existed separately for decades—including for more than 30 years after a failed referendum to unite the cities in 1879—until the US Post Office, always the forward-thinking fashion-maker, established a post office in 1899 that referred to the towns as the unified name of Winston-Salem. In 1913, another public referendum in the two cities established what the Post Office already knew, that Winston-Salem should be united as one.

Another entity that referred to the two cities as one was the minor league baseball Winston-Salem Twins, who first appeared on the scene in 1905—a full eight years before the official merger of the cities. The Twins' name came from Winston-Salem's nickname among locals, the Twin City. (It's worth noting that another of Winston-Salem's nicknames is the Camel City because of its importance to the tobacco industry. Seems like there's a potential minor league nickname there.) When the current team was choosing a new name in 2009, there was one important reason not to reprise that original Twins moniker.

"A White Sox affiliate probably couldn't be named the Twins," said Brian Boesch, the team's Associate Director of Media Relations and Broadcasting.

Between 1945 and 2008, baseball teams in Winston-Salem would go by the names Cardinals (1945–1953), Red Birds (1957–1960), Red Sox (1961–1983), Spirits (1984–1994), and Warthogs (1995–2008). When the team moved to its shiny new home at BB&T Ballpark, named for the financial services giant headquartered in town, they decided it was time for a new name.

"The Warthogs are still well regarded and well remembered in this town and they will be for a long time," Boesch said. "It was the main motivation there, going downtown, going into a new ballpark. Let's have a new, fresh, modern look.... We wanted it to kind of signal a whole new period of time in our organization."

That new name for the team in the new ballpark would come from that tiny but symbolic bit of punctuation between Winston and Salem.

"The Dash represents the dash in Winston-Salem," Boesch said. "Beyond that, it

represents the connection within the community. Winston-Salem has always been a community that has had a kind of a unique connection, one that a hundred-plus years ago didn't exist. So that's where it comes from."

Of course, the word *dash* has other connotations pertinent to baseball, and the logo plays off the most obvious one, that of running fast. "We'll sometimes do some marketing toward some different definitions of dash," Boesch said. "This year, our slogan was 'Time to Dash.'"

If you can't quite shake the image of your grade school English teacher sadly shaking her head in admonition, it's because there's a word for that punctuation mark between Winston and Salem, and it's not dash.

"I know, technically, the word for it is hyphen," Boesch said. "We've gotten that before."

Grammar nerds will tell you that dashes are not the conjoiners of words that hyphens are, but rather serve to separate thoughts within a sentence (among other uses). Those grammar nerds will then be happy to go on and on about the differences between hyphens, en-dashes, and em-dashes and their various lengths and purposes. But guess what? Those grammar nerds will be sitting at home crying in their *Chicago Manual of Style* while everyone else is out living their lives.

Yeah, it's technically not a dash between Winston and Salem, but the Winston-Salem Hyphens would be a terrible name for a baseball team. "The dash represents not just the punctuation in the city name, but also the unique, special connection within this whole city, this whole community," Boesch said.

The Dash's primary logo, designed by Terry Smith, features a forward-moving baseball character, and has a certain sideways shape to it. "When you see the horizontal logo, it kind of looks like a dash," Boesch said. "It lends to that secondary meaning of, it's not a racing thing, but dash, you're going quickly."

The team's alternate logos feature a dashing, unnamed baseball character and the team's initials set in purple. The color choice is not unique to the city, but was chosen for being a little bit different. "There's no sort of Winston-Salem connection to purple," Boesch said. "It was just sort of something clean and modern.... Purple definitely jumps off the page, that's for sure."

What the Winston-Salem Dash lack in grammatical correctness, they make up for in having a nickname that's kind of adorable. The dash (hyphen) is the symbol of a union of two cities that goes back more than years, and it's endearing that the local baseball team chose to celebrate this enduring relationship with the only nickname I know of based on punctuation.

The Wacky Era

HEIDI KAY

MODERN-DAY MINORS

Every time a team rebrands or a new team is introduced, it seems that they have to get just a bit more outrageous to out-do the latest wacky nickname. The Wacky Era traces its roots back to the likes of the Lansing Lugnuts and Carolina Mudcats in the 1990s (one team in this chapter dates back to the 1950s, placed here because of a new logo), but the era took off in earnest in the 2000s, with the teams like the Montgomery Biscuits, Albuquerque Isotopes, and Lehigh Valley IronPigs. The trend has led us to today, when teams named Baby Cakes and RubberDucks and Yard Goats are the norm rather than the exception.

Dunkin' Donuts Park in Hartford, Connecticut, home to the Double-A Hartford Yard Goats

Akron RubberDucks

Akron RubberDucks
2014–present

Current Team Data

Parent
Cleveland Indians

Class
Double-A

League
Eastern

It's okay if you heard the name of minor league baseball's Akron RubberDucks, Double-A affiliate of the Cleveland Indians, and you thought, "Okay, now they're just flipping open the dictionary and naming teams after the first word they point to." But the RubberDucks' name has a specific and meaningful origin story that you'd never have guessed without knowing some of the city's history.

Let's start with the first half of the name, rubber: "Akron was the rubber capital of the world for years," said the team's general manager, Jim Pfander. "My grandfather actually worked down the street from the ballpark, two blocks away, where BF Goodrich was, when Akron was the tire capital of the world, and the rubber capital of the world. Tying in the rubber industry makes a lot of sense."

And while Akron's rubber heyday climaxed in the 1950s, the industry is still a major factor in the city's culture and economy. "Not only is the rubber industry part of our past, it's also part of our future," Pfander said. "Goodyear moved their headquarters back to Akron about a year and a half ago, and built a brand-new headquarters. Firestone has a service and tech center that they just built about two years ago."

So okay, there's a connection to rubber in Akron. What about the second part, ducks?

The team's stadium—Canal Park—is built on the Ohio and Erie Canal. "What usually comes with canals are ducks," Pfander said. "We have a number of ducks that float and swim and fly around the ballpark, especially behind the ballpark in the canals."

And how do you tie a neat little bow around the rubber industry and real ducks and the history of Akron?

"When the rubber industry was rocking here years ago," Pfander said, "one of the first rubber ducks made in the United States was made here in Akron as well. So there's a lot of different tie-ins."

Of course, the danger in naming your team after a bath toy is that maybe you've taken the trend of hyper-marketable, kid-friendly logos one step too far. "A lot of people think of rubber ducks, they think of the yellow squeaky bath toy in Bert and Ernie," Pfander said. "But when you see this logo, it's a 180. You're like wow, that's a tough-looking duck."

The RubberDucks' first season with their new nickname was 2014, but the franchise has been playing in Ohio since 1989, first in nearby Canton as the Canton-Akron Indians, then moving to Akron in 1997, where they adopted the cryptic nickname Aeros. (The team initially announced that it was going to be called the Akron Blast in honor of Judy Resnik, who died in the Space Shuttle *Challenger* disaster. That decision was widely considered to be in poor taste, especially given that the mascot's name is Kaboom, and the team quickly changed plans.)

After setting Eastern League attendance records in their first three years in Akron, attendance declined over the course of the next decade, dropping from more than half a million in 1999 to just over 250,000 in 2012, as fans felt ownership was not maintaining the stadium. In 2011 and 2012, new management and ownership took over the team, invested in renovating the stadium, and looked at making a change in branding. What they learned in their market research was that there was not a strong attachment to the name Aeros, in part because no one knew what it meant.

"We'd meet with groups of 15 people at a time and we'd sit them in a room and say, 'What does the name Aeros mean to you?' Pfander said. "As you'd go around the room, you'd get 15 different answers. No one could identify what an Aero was. Some people said it was Ohio's contribution to air flight with the Wright brothers, some people said it was aeronautics with the Goodyear Blimp. Akron's contributions to astronauts was another one."

And while fans took to the name RubberDucks quickly, they didn't do so immediately. Pfander's friend Scott Hunsicker, general manager of the Reading Fightin Phils, had just gone through his own rebranding effort, and warned that it would be tough going for a few months. "I tell you what," Pfander said, "I was ready for three months of it and we only got three days."

But those three days were eventful. "I got a call that was, 'Is this an April Fool's joke?' People thought we were out of our minds," Pfander said. "But once people saw the name together with the logo, immediately, the radio stations were saying, 'Hey, look at it. This is a pretty good-looking logo.'"

That acceptance was reflected in merchandise sales. "We almost sold more merchandise by opening day than we did the previous year," Pfander said. "We had merchandise sold in all 50 states within a week of us announcing the rebrand."

The RubberDucks' primary logo, designed by the prolific firm Brandiose, features tire tracks and a duck gritting its teeth. (Pfander admits, "I've never looked inside a duck's mouth, but I would think that a duck doesn't have any teeth.") The next most popular logo, a duck face with tire tread arms, is featured on the team's batting practice caps. Next up is the letter A made from tire treads, featured on the team's Sunday cap, and finally, the team's road cap logo, a duck foot A.

The team colors started with black and gold, but there was a place-specific problem. "If you keep it black and gold those are Steelers colors, and here in northeast Ohio that's a bad word," Pfander said, "so we can't be identified with the Steelers or even the Pirates for that matter. Black and orange, well that's the Cincinnati Bengals, and you know again, we want to separate ourselves from Cincinnati."

So the RubberDucks needed an accent color, which would be inspired by a family moment. "I have a pond real close to my house and I was taking my daughters down there for a walk," Pfander said. "We actually got a chance to get up close to a duck and in the duck's feathers, they have a blue feather."

Conversations about what sort of blue the team should use landed on what Pfander calls electric blue, and a unique uniform design. "We're the only team in baseball to have an electric blue jersey," Pfander said.

Of course, ducks and baseball are forever intertwined, so the team has renamed certain parts of the park ("You know, fowl territory, F-O-W-L") and certain expressions are used frequently ("You have ducks on a pond when the bases are loaded," Pfander said, "you've got a duck snort when a ball just gets over the shortstop's head and lands in the outfield").

And sometimes, ducks are incorporated into the entertainment in ways not specific to baseball, such as one promotion in 2014 when the team gave away woopie cushions. "'Oops, I Stepped on a Duck Night' was pretty entertaining," Pfander said.

Perhaps more than any other, the RubberDucks are one of the poster teams for team nicknames geared for children. Not only does their logo have a cartoonish quality about it, but they're actually named for a toy. But the connection of their name to the history of their home city adds a level of meaning to an otherwise whimsical name that many casual observers might not expect.

Albuquerque Isotopes

Albuquerque Isotopes
2003–Present

Current Team Data

Parent
Colorado Rockies

Class
Triple-A

League
Pacific Coast

In a March 2001 episode of *The Simpsons,* Homer Simpson staged a nine-day hunger strike to thwart plans by Springfield Isotopes owner Howard K. Duff VIII (of Duff Beer fame) to move the local baseball team to Albuquerque, New Mexico. The ordeal ended with Homer victorious, standing on the outfield grass being showered with food by grateful fans for exposing the threat. It seemed it was safe to believe that a dystopian future that included the Albuquerque Isotopes was never meant to be.

But just two years later, Homer's worst nightmare came to fruition in real life when the Florida Marlins' new Triple-A affiliate, the Albuquerque Isotopes, debuted in New Mexico. (They're a Rockies affiliate now.) Even worse for Homer, it seems that the move from Springfield to Albuquerque has paid off, because according to *Forbes* magazine, the real-life Isotopes are the fourth-most valuable franchise in minor league baseball. In a game that I attended in 2015, the team set a single-game attendance record with 16,348 fans—more than a few Major League teams get on certain nights.

Before the Isotopes, Albuquerque was home to a number of different teams dating back to 1915, many of them called the Dukes, including a Triple-A Pacific Coast League team that played there from 1972 to 2000. That team left Albuquerque to become one of roughly a million different minor league teams that have been the Portland Beavers.

The franchise that brought baseball back to Albuquerque in 2003 had been the Calgary Cannons since 1985 and before that, the Salt Lake Gulls from 1971 to 1984. When the franchise held a name-the-team contest after moving to Albuquerque, the final vote included five options, including the Dukes. *The Simpsons* episode ("Hungry Hungry Homer," season 12, episode 15) was still fresh in the imaginations of fans and Isotopes won convincingly, receiving more than half the tally. So the baseball team approached the TV show about using the name.

There is no formal relationship between the baseball team and the TV show, but the team's logo type looks very *Simpsons*-y, the stadium plays host to statues of characters from the TV show, and Ken Levine, who wrote the *Simpsons* episode in question, threw out the first pitch at a game in 2014 and was interviewed by the team about the name.

"We don't sell any *Simpsons*-type things in our pro shop or anything like that, so it's not gone that far," said Laura Verillo, the Isotopes' director of public relations through the end of 2014. "But there is an agreement to an extent that we can use the Albuquerque Isotopes name that was in that episode."

While the Simpsons connection is the overwhelming reason behind the nickname, there's more to the Isotopes than that. "The area that we are in is a big scientific area," Verillo said. "We have the Sandia Labs over here, so that's part of it—the science background on it." (Sandia National Laboratories, according to Wikipedia, are "two major United States Department of Energy research and development national laboratories.")

Not only that, but one particularly famous high school science teacher and chemist, one Walter White, once lived in Albuquerque and supported the team, evidently, wearing the team's cap on an episode of *Breaking Bad*.

This connection to science poses a unique challenge to the team's employees. "We get the question, What is an isotope to begin with?" Verillo said. "Our staff has to know some chemistry, and I don't think you really have that with any other Major or minor league teams."

The Isotopes have achieved what minor league baseball teams everywhere strive for. Their merchandise sells across the USA and internationally, and not just because big league fans want to support their highest-level minor league franchise. Sometimes it's simply scientists who like the actual image of something scientific on a hat.

"It's not just for baseball fans," Verillo said. "I think people are attracted to the uniqueness of our logo. It's not your typical animal mascot."

The Isotopes logo is definitely not typical. It's the only one I know of that is based on a 16-year-old episode of a kids' TV show and that features baseball-shaped neutrons circling the nucleus of an atom in a pattern that forms a capital A. In a way, the team lucked into a great situation (every city should have a wildly popular cultural reference to name their new team after), and it's very much to their credit that they took advantage of the opportunity that was presented to them.

Biloxi Shuckers

Biloxi Shuckers
2015–Present

Current Team Data

Parent
Milwaukee Brewers

Class
Double-A

League
Southern

Nearly two months into their inaugural season, the Biloxi Shuckers, whose previous life was as the Huntsville Stars in the Double-A Southern League, still had not played a home game. Because of construction and funding issues, the Shuckers opened the season on an epic 55-game road trip.

The Shuckers' makeshift home-away-from-home games took place in locations like Jacksonville, Florida; their former home in Huntsville, Alabama; and Pearl, Mississippi. (It's very much of note, to me, at least, that a team with an oyster as a logo was playing in a place called Pearl—the oysters in Pearl rather than the other way around.) When the Shuckers took their actual home field for the first time midway through the 2015 season, they did so wearing a popular new logo from Brandiose that pays homage to the prevailing local industry.

"There's a big oyster industry around here," said Christina Coca, the team's director of social media and publications. "The shucker is the actual person who prepares and shucks the oyster, basically opening it into that half shell look that's so iconic that everybody knows."

Something was picking at the back of my mind as Coca explained this reasoning. "However you eat them, whether you eat them charbroiled or Rockefeller," she continued, "it's a tribute to the whole seafood industry around here."

Then it clicked: The team is named for the people who prepare oysters to be eaten, and the logo is an actual oyster. Isn't there a disconnect there?

"It's minor league baseball," Coca explained. "Everybody enjoys the fun names, the fun logos. I don't think there's a disconnect. I think everybody looks at it and kind of laughs about it because it's cool, it's unique."

Speaking of laughing, you have to have a certain sense of humor to name your team something that rhymes so clearly with a famous curse word. "With a name like that, you kind of have to embrace it," Coca said. "We have a little call at the end of our promotion for our radio broadcast is 'Biloxi Baseball: Get Your Shuck On.' You see license plates that say 'Shuck it' on it. It's funny." Coca also pointed out that the hash tag #shuckit has become a popular rallying cry for the team on Twitter.

Another indication that the team isn't afraid to accidentally-on-purpose invoke an expletive through branding is its road cap logo, which uses interlocking letters—a classic baseball tradition, to be sure, but not when those letters are the infamous "BS."

"Maybe they take it as 'BS,'" Coca said, "but it's a symbol now that everybody will start recognizing—the BS on the hat, that's the Biloxi Shuckers."

As one of the individuals responsible for the team's in-house graphic design, Coca embraces the opportunity to work with unique design elements, including the type ("We have our own font," she said. "I think that's amazing") and the colors, which she identifies as Gulf blue, sand, coral, and black. "We're the first professional team that's used that color combination," she said.

The team's most popular mark, according to Coca, is their alternate cap logo, which features the oyster wearing a white Gilligan hat and holding a baseball bat—not swinging it baseball-style like many Brandiose character logos, but cocking it back like a mobster who doesn't like that you think he's funny like a clown.

"It kind of looks badass," Coca said.

The hat is typical of the fishing hats you see on the docks in Biloxi, Coca said, and if oysters had feet, this one would be wearing what locals call "Biloxi Reeboks," distinctive white rubber boots that local fishermen wear.

Part of what makes the oyster badass is his glowering stare, which the team used to tease their new identity before their first season. "He does have those iconic angry eyes," Coca said. "When we did our logo unveiling and our name unveiling, all we put up there as a hint was just those two eyes."

Early sketches of the logo from Brandiose show that the team considered logo options such as a seagull, a fishing boat, a citrus wedge with those angry eyes, and the as-of-yet-unnamed oyster in various baseball scenarios. (Note that the oyster in the logo does not have a name, but the team's mascot is called "Shuck Norris.")

While much of the Shuckers' identity is whimsical and fun, part of their identity has a decidedly serious backstory. The name Beacons, a reference to the town's iconic lighthouse less than a tenth of a mile from the new stadium, was one of the finalists in the name-the-team contest. With that in mind, the team developed a logo that would feature not only the lighthouse, but some of the state's recent history.

"It has the waves at the bottom," Coca said. "Those are majestic, huge storm waves… basically a dedication to those who were here and survived the storm, not just Katrina but Camille."

The Shuckers found early success in their first season. They were a finalist, along with the Richmond Flying Squirrels, in *Baseball America's* Logo Mania bracket. The Shuckers achieve that balance of connecting their identity to the local community while appealing to a national audience with a wacky, character-based logo.

Binghamton Rumble Ponies

A lot of small towns proclaim themselves the Something Capital of the World. There are multiple cities that claim the title of Blueberry Capital of the World, Music Capital of the World, or Financial Capital of the World, to name a few—but only one city lays claim to the title Carousel Capital of the World, and that is Binghamton, New York.

Binghamton, with its roughly 50,000 residents, has gone by the nickname the Valley of Opportunity for its history of economic success in such areas as transportation, cigar production, and computers, among others. But it's the city's collection of antique carousels dating back to the late 1800s scattered around the city that gave rise to the local Double-A baseball franchise's nickname, the Binghamton Rumble Ponies.

Carousels have long been part of the city's cultural landscape.

"They were free for people to go and ride in the summer," said Eddie Saunders, the Rumble Ponies' director of marketing. "You had adults taking their kids, and then when those kids grew up they were taking their own kids."

The winning entry in a name-the-team contest was submitted by a woman who asked to be identified only by her first name, Nicole, in the official press release. Her connection to the area's carousels is personal.

"She wrote to us about how she remembered her dad taking her to the carousels in the summer, and now she's passed those memories on to her children, taking them, and hopefully one day they'll do the same," Saunders said.

The team went by the name Binghamton Mets from 1992 to 2016. Because naming minor league teams after their parent clubs is inherently boring, the team announced plans to adopt a new name after the 2016 season. Of the six proposed names, four of them had to do with carousels—Stud Muffins, Rocking Horses, Timber Jockeys, and, of course, Rumble Ponies. The other two proposed names were Bullheads (for catfish found in the Susquehanna River) and Gobblers (because of turkey hunting).

The B-Mets (it makes me yawn just to type it) have long been on the short list of minor league franchises that might relocate due to a lack of fan support. The decision to rebrand had a lot to do with a new ownership group, Evans Street Baseball, led by primary owner John Hughes, wanting to reengage the fan base.

"Basically when John came in, the big thing that he wanted to do was to give this team back to the community," Sanders said. "That was his mission from day one. This is not my team, this is not our team, this is really the community's team."

Binghamton Rumble Ponies
2017–Present

Current Team Data

Parent
New York Mets

Class
Double-A

League
Eastern

Binghamton Mets

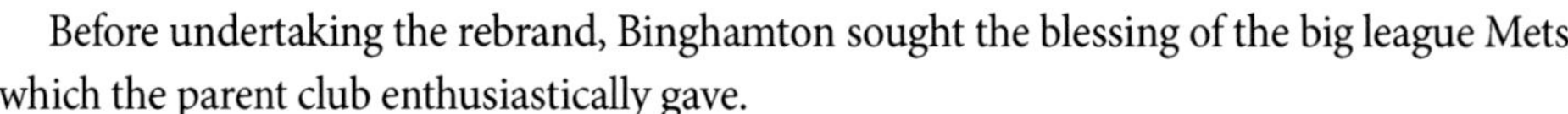

Before undertaking the rebrand, Binghamton sought the blessing of the big league Mets, which the parent club enthusiastically gave.

"The way John thought about it, that Mets name deserves to be in Queens with the big league team," Saunders said. "That's their identity. We want one that allows them to have that while at the same time we have one that's unique to us here."

Obviously, the team is aware that their new name is a bit non-traditional, especially in a community that's fielded a team named for their parent club for the last quarter-century. In coming up with the new name and logo, the team set about creating a conversation piece, even if it caused a bit of a stir.

"If somebody has to have a conversation about why there's a carousel horse connected with Binghamton, that is a five-minute advertisement about the Rumble Ponies," said Jason Klein, a partner in Brandiose, the firm responsible for the new look. "We want the design to be a question. We want the design to spark a conversation."

Brandiose told the team to brace itself for a negative reception to a wacky new name.

"You're going to have people who are naysayers," Saunders said. "We deal with it on an everyday basis, people asking, why did you guys change the name?"

The reason to change the name, of course, is the nature of who attends minor league baseball games.

"If you're a Major League Baseball team, you're in the baseball business. If you're a minor league baseball team, you're in the entertainment business," Klein said. "For the 80 percent of the population at a game that's there just to have fun, that doesn't even remember the score, they're excited."

As is typically the case, fans have started coming around, not just locally, but around the country. "We're seeing people from New York, we're seeing people from California, Florida, all over the country, that are buying Binghamton Rumble Ponies stuff," Saunders said. "You might have been a Seattle Mariners fan out in Seattle but you've seen our alternative boxing pony logo and you think that's great. I can say that right now, when we started this, we released our name on a Thursday, and by Friday morning, basically, 75 percent of our alternative hats were all sold out."

Of course, the mention of carousels conjures a certain mental image, which Brandiose set out to subvert in the team's visual identity.

"That's one of the strategies that we've found successful, understanding that there's a current mindset about a certain subject matter, and going in and flipping the script," Klein said. "We looked at Binghamton, and carousels are a little old-timey and grandfatherly. They can be a little old fashioned. So we said, how are we going to take this story of the carousel capital of the world and flip the script?"

The answer to this dilemma came with a simple re-envisioning of the carousel horse. "What would happen if the carousel music starts playing Back in Black by AC/DC?" Klein asked. "What if we had a bad-ass battle horse with flame-maned hair and rivets—somebody that looked like he was going into battle?"

The Rumble Ponies are another in an increasingly long line of minor league teams adopting hyper-local, non-traditional nicknames. Fifteen or twenty years ago, it may have been hard to imagine a city's connection to historic carousels leading to a baseball team with a bad-ass battle horse for a logo, but that's the landscape of the industry now, and it shows no signs of changing any time soon.

Columbia Fireflies

Columbia Fireflies
2016–Present

Current Team Data

Parent
New York Mets

Class
Single-A

League
South Atlantic

From mid-May to mid-June, Congaree National Park in South Carolina is home to a rare natural display that can only be seen in a few places around the world. The mating rituals of *Photinus carolinus*—also known as synchronous fireflies—create a hot, steamy, Christmas-in-Springtime wonderland of lightning bugs blinking in unison. The fireflies can be seen in several places in North America—most famously in Great Smoky Mountains National Park in Tennessee—as well as southeast Asia. (On a personal note, I saw them once along a river in Malaysia, and it was amazing.)

In 2015, when the Savannah Sand Gnats announced that they were leaving Georgia to play in Columbia, South Carolina, less than 20 miles from Congaree National Park, the team abandoned a nickname based on a hateful, biting nuisance in favor of a bug people flock to see.

As the identity for a baseball team, naming a team for the synchronized blinking of lightning bugs has a conceptual meaning in addition to the literal connection to the nearby natural phenomenon.

"It's kind of a symbol for the city and all the history that's happened here in the city, how everybody comes together and works in unity and synchronizes together," said Abby Naas, the team's Vice President of Marketing and Public Relations. "We had a lot of floods in 2015, and everyone just kind of worked together to rebuild."

"It's a great metaphor," Naas continued, "but it's also just a fun, local, unique tie to our community."

The name itself, which was submitted to a name-the-team contest by six different individuals, flies in the face of the regional nickname for glowing insects, which Naas said most people in the area call lightning bugs.

"We went with Fireflies not because it's the scientific name for them, but because [fire] is one thing Columbia is known for," Naas said. "The slogan for the city up until just a few weeks ago was 'Famously hot,' so it was a flame icon. Because of that we wanted to tie in the fire, the heat."

A notable aspect of the Fireflies logo, on-field caps, and most of their merchandise is that they glow in the dark, which puts them in league with the Asheville Tourists and the defunct Casper Ghosts. While you can't see the caps glowing in the dark under the stadium lights, Naas said it's always fun to see them out in public, especially in places like concerts where the glow-in-the-dark aspect is prominent. The whole glow-in-the-dark thing took on a special meaning when the team planned a special event for the much-anticipated solar eclipse in August 2017.

"At first we treaded lightly on that and said let's just make the kids' shirts glow in the dark," Naas said. "And then they ended up turning some of the adult shirts glow in the dark, and then the adults wanted them. We didn't know adults would want that. But it's such a unique thing. Why not?"

Of course, the Fireflies, a Mets affiliate, were in the news for more than just their glow-in-the-dark identity in 2017. Former Denver Bronco, New York Jet, practice squad Philadelphia Eagle, and practice squad New England Patriot Tim Tebow started his baseball career with a .223 average, three home runs, and 20 RBIs in 56 games in the Single-A South Atlantic League. In order to deal with the rarity of their situation, the Fireflies reached out to staff members of the Birmingham Barons who were around in 1994 when Michael Jordan was making a run at a baseball career. In the end, having Tebow on the roster has been a positive for the brand.

"It's helped us get our name out there," Naas said. "I've got a *Sports Illustrated* sitting on my desk with our logo in it."

The Fireflies' nickname and identity, which was created by the Atlanta-based firm Sky Design, whose first minor league baseball logo was with the Fireflies' sister club, the Fort Wayne TinCaps, have worked well for the team. Even before any Heisman-winning football players joined the roster, the brand was getting noticed. The Fireflies were one of only four Single-A teams to make Minor League Baseball's list of the top 25 teams in terms of merchandise sales in 2016, along with the Dayton Dragons, Lake Elsinore Storm, and South Bend Cubs.

Early on in their existence, the Fireflies stand out as a unique new brand in a sea of outrageous new identities in minor league baseball.

Daytona Tortugas

Daytona Tortugas
2015–Present

Current Team Data

Parent
Cincinnati Reds

Class
High A

League
Florida State

For 22 seasons, the Florida State League was home to the Daytona Cubs. But after the 2014 season, when Chicago switched its High-A affiliate from Daytona to the Myrtle Beach Pelicans, the team in Daytona signed on with the Cincinnati Reds and started the process of developing a new identity.

"We were with the Cubs for 22 years, and so for 22 years, being the Daytona Cubs, it worked," said Jim Jaworski, the team's assistant general manager. "To be the Cubs for 22 years, and especially, to have that Cubs brand, which is obviously a fantastic brand, you know, it was a pretty tough transition."

Not only is the Cubs brand a solid one for a minor league baseball team that wants to ride the coattails of its parent club, but Daytona had just refreshed its logo three seasons prior. Forced into coming up with a new identity, the team approached Dan Simon of Studio Simon, who had created the Daytona Cubs identity that the team used from 2012–2014.

"They weren't coming to me because they didn't like their old identity," Simon said, "they were coming to me because they had to come up with a new identity, which is really a shame, because they really loved the new Cubs identity that we did for them. I really loved it. It's a shame that it had to die an early death."

In searching for a new name, the team explored a lot of options.

"Being in Daytona Beach, there was a lot of different ideas that came to the floor," Jaworski said. "Do we want to associate ourselves with being by the beach, do we want to associate ourselves with NASCAR, with Bike Week, with different things that are going on here in the area?"

In the end, the team went with what is becoming something of a tradition in their league.

"We have the Manatees, we have the Threshers, we have the Hammerheads, so there's definitely a theme down here in the Florida State League," Jaworski said. "Because of the turtle population that's here in Volusia County, because of nesting season that ties in with our season, it seemed to be a pretty natural fit."

Once the team decided on the sea turtle as the main visual identity, there was still the business of deciding which sea turtle to adopt. Of the five species of sea turtles in the area—loggerhead, leatherback, green turtle, hawks bill, and Kemp's ridley—only two seemed like they might make good names for a minor league baseball team.

COURTESY DAN SIMON

General manager Josh Lawther approached Dan Simon with the options of Loggerheads and Leatherbacks.

"As soon as they came to me with those names, I said, those are great names, but I've got one that's even better for you," Simon said.

Simon's friend Kurt Hunzeker, who is currently vice president for marketing strategy for Minor League Baseball, had once during a casual conversation suggested Tortugas, the Spanish word for turtles, as a great name for a team. Simon suggested the name to Lawther, and the rest is history.

One of Simon's early concepts was to combine the sea turtle idea with another idea that had come up in conversations.

"They were considering motor sports," Simon said, "what with Daytona being a motor sports Mecca with Dayton International Speedway, the Daytona 500, and a long history of motor sports in Daytona."

After getting a quick sketch on paper, though, everyone involved decided that was not the path to take.

"I had drawn the turtle with the helmet, liked it, but then I realized, now I've got to bring baseball into it as well," Simon said. "You're going to have a turtle with a racing helmet and a baseball bat. It's too much."

Another idea was to celebrate Ponce de León, the first Spanish explorer to set foot in present-day Florida. In fact, Ponce de León Inlet is located just 12 miles from the Daytona Tortugas' home field, Jackie Robinson Ballpark. It's worth noting here that one of Ponce de León's most celebrated achievements was the 1513 discovery of the Gulf of Mexico's Dry Tortuga islands, so named for a preponderance of sea turtles and their lack of fresh water.

The Tortugas came about out of necessity following a somewhat unexpected affiliation change, but the result has been one of the sport's most popular identities. The Tortugas have been celebrated as one of minor league baseball's top new brands.

"We won Minor League Baseball's Clash of the Caps last year, we won *Ballpark Digest's* best rebrand last year," Jaworski said, "so it's starting to get noticed."

The logo's success is likely the result of a number of factors. There's a certain cool factor to the name itself, which Simon said he first heard in reference to the Haitian island of Tortuga in Pirates of the Caribbean. ("I remember watching that movie and thinking, what a cool word," he said.) Also, pretty much everyone likes sea turtles—have you ever heard of someone having a turtle phobia? Finally, the logo itself, has a soothing, tropical feeling about it.

"It was a fresh color palette—fresh both in its uniqueness as well as in the feel of those colors. They feel fresh," Simon said. "It wasn't like, what can we do that hasn't been done before? It was based on, what's going to feel like a sea turtle? And those colors just felt right."

Whether it's the name, the turtle, or the colors, the Tortugas have tapped into something that's captured the imagination of baseball fans. The exact reason is something of a mystery, perhaps best summed up by Crush, the sea turtle in *Finding Nemo:* "Well, you never really know, but when they know, you know, y'know?"

El Paso Chihuahuas

El Paso Chihuahuas
2014–present

Current Team Data

Parent
San Diego Padres

Class
Triple-A

League
Pacific Coast

Admit it, the first time you heard the nickname for the El Paso Chihuahuas, Triple-A affiliate of the San Diego Padres—you thought of Paris Hilton. Or possibly Taco Bell.

This is one of the reasons the announcement of the new nickname in El Paso before the 2014 season was met on social media with comments like, "Really?? Chihuahuas??" and "Worst. Name. Ever. Yo quiero name change," and "Oh well. As long as the beers are cheap."

Tim Hagerty, the team's manager of broadcasting and media relations, admitted, "Your average sports fan in El Paso may have been a little bit shocked."

Even he wasn't sure at first: "I have to admit I was a little bit startled," he said.

But that negative tide turned quickly, sometimes even with individual fans. "We're tracking the Facebook comments," Hagerty said, "and there's this one gentleman that, the day the team name was announced, wrote a paragraph and there were a couple swear words in it. He was furious. And that same exact guy, same exact profile picture and everything, 10 days later he wrote us a message saying, 'Hey, are the fitted caps in yet?'"

The nickname is based on the team's proximity to the Chihuahuan Desert, as well as the fact that chihuahuas, according to general manager Brad Taylor, "represent fun and are fiercely loyal." The branding firm Brandiose, who designed the logo, toured El Paso, interviewed people, and found the locals to be feisty, with something of a chip on their shoulder.

"For that reason," Hagerty said, "they made the dog a little bit damaged. There's a rip in the top of the ear, and the same with the baseball, it's a torn-up baseball.... A chihuahua might be the smallest dog on the block, but he's not intimidated by anybody."

Hagerty can speak with some authority about minor league baseball nicknames. He is the author of a 2012 book about minor league team names, *Root for the Home Team,* and has been with this franchise since they were the Portland Beavers and more recently the Tucson Padres. He understood the initial reaction to the nickname, but the thing that turned fans around was the design of the logo itself.

"It really shows you how impressive these graphic artists are because when I heard the name Chihuahuas, I didn't even know what to picture," he said. "I had no idea what that was going to look like. But then, when they showed me these logos, I liked it 50 times better.... Even in those couple days where reaction was mixed after the team name announcement, I did not hear or see a single thing that criticized the logos."

The team's alternate logos feature the chihuahua swinging a gnarled bone like a baseball bat (though from a baseball perspective, his form leaves a little to be desired), a torn baseball and crossbones, and one that feels a little incongruous next to the others, a clean, stylized EP for El Paso.

Of course, the identity lends itself to small-dog-related promotions and frivolity at the ballpark. For instance, fans park in the "barking lot," they call the upper deck the "woof top," and fans can buy nachos in a souvenir plastic dog bowl. (I have one that my cat uses. Feels a little like sacrilege.)

Before the team's first season started, Tim Hagerty would not rule out the possibility that Paris Hilton would be the team's mascot. The mascot turned out to be Chico the Chihuahua, half adorable and half terrifying, so kind of like Paris Hilton after all.

The nickname and logos do what every minor league team is trying to do now—appeal to children. ("They're fascinated by it," Hagerty said.) That said, Chico's bloodshot eyes, torn ears, evil grin, and ill-fitting studded collar hint at a backstory not every three-year-old fan is going to want to fully embrace.

Early negativity in response to an unusual nickname in minor league baseball is predictable. What's been atypical about the Chihuahuas is how quickly fans have come around. Their cap featuring a Chico head logo was voted best in the minors, narrowly edging out the Richmond Flying Squirrels in an online "Clash of the Cap" contest conducted by Minor League Baseball in the team's inaugural season.

Even before the team set foot on the field in their brand-new downtown ballpark, the Chihuahuas had sold logo gear from their website to people in more than 40 U.S. states and six countries. Within six months after the team announcement, that number had grown to include all 50 states and nine countries.

ELISTA ISTRE

Chico, half adorable, half terrifying, greets fans at Southwest University Park.

"We're finding that people smile when they talk about it," Hagerty said. "When people have memories at our ballpark, they wouldn't picture anything else."

El Paso has a reputation as being a rough and tumble border town, so it's an understatement to say that the team subverted expectations by choosing a somewhat delicate, if not annoying, animal to represent it. And with that decision, the Chihuahuas have become the poster child for the era of the wacky minor league baseball nicknames. After initial misgivings, the team found success in embracing the outrageous and focusing on family-friendly fun. And serving food to people in dog bowls.

Eugene Emeralds

Eugene Emeralds
1955–present

Current Team Data

Parent
Chicago Cubs

Class
Short Season A

League
Northwest

Of all the documented sightings of Bigfoot, known in the scientific community as Sasquatch, roughly a third of them have occurred in the mountain forests of the Pacific Northwest. There's an obvious reason for this: That is where Bigfoot lives.

Since 1955, the Eugene Emeralds, currently a short-season Single-A affiliate of the Chicago Cubs, played in the heart of Sasquatch country without even realizing it. Their logos were pleasant, almost soothing, like one you might use for a bed and breakfast promoting the serenity of the Pacific Northwest.

"This whole area is called the Emerald Valley," said Allan Benavides, the team's general manager. "It's known as that because of how beautiful and how green it is—gorgeous trees and rolling hills and big mountains, just green for miles."

If you're feeling really calm right now, like you want to strap on a backpack and delve into a misty forest to discover your inner self, that's not the effect the team was looking for. So they changed their logo.

"We had seen all these fun logos come out throughout the country, all these great teams coming up with these really fun logos that they could manipulate, have some fun with them. Ours was technically just a cursive E," Benavides said. "It was a very nice logo in a traditional font, but we wanted something that was a little more modern—something that we thought was a little more minor league."

The rebranding process started with an attempt to overcome the most deadly reaction a person can have to a minor league baseball logo. "The one thing I hated about our old brand was apathy, the 'I don't really care about it. It's there, you know?'" Benavides said. "That's the worst emotion to have about a brand, isn't it? You don't care? Doesn't that have to be the worst reaction to your logo or your brand?"

The first challenge the team faced in its rebrand? "It's just a color. We're basically named after a color," Benavides said. "How do you brand around a color?" Not only that, but their nickname is often shortened to "Ems," so they were basically an episode of Sesame Street, sponsored by the color green and the letter M.

They started thinking about why they had the name they had—because of the Emerald Valley. And what lives in the Emerald Valley? Lots of stuff—deer, beavers, gnomes—but none of it was really inspirational when it came to a team name.

"All of a sudden it hit us," Benavides said. "We're like, it's Sasquatch! Sasquatch lives here, obviously, right? He's in the hills. He's in the mountains. He's in the trees."

The Emeralds early logos were super pleasant.

The team worked with Brandiose to develop a new look, to take their identity in a new direction while maintaining a name with six decades of tradition under its belt. For the unveiling in November 2012, the team packed about 300 fans into a local brewery to watch a video featuring their mascot Sluggo venturing into the woods to retrieve a home run ball.

"He goes in there and this big hand comes out and rips the ball away from him, and it shows kind of like these claws ripping through the old logo and the new one pops up," Benavides said. "I remember being like 'Oh God, here it comes.' And it was huge cheers. Huge."

And then the team breathed sigh of a relief. "Obviously we were so nervous at the unveiling because had gone to such an extreme," Benavides said.

The new logo set features Oregon resident Sasquatch carrying, chewing on, or swinging a bright green tree, as well as a green E footprint. (That fluorescent green has proven to be problematic for a minor league team with a limited printing budget, because getting it right on printed materials often requires additional steps beyond a traditional four-color printing process. "We love it, which is why we still have it," Benavides said, "but for a small team like us, it's like, 'God dangit, we have to spend how much more to print this?'")

Of course, with this logo being designed by Brandiose, one of the alternate logos features a character swinging a thing. While this is something of a signature look for Brandiose logos, the Emeralds had their reasons. "We did it because we were a Padres affiliate," Benavides said. "We were trying to mimic the swinging friar."

With such a drastic change in direction, not everyone has loved it. But that's okay with the team. "I'm sure there are people who hate our logo, which is fine," Benavides said. "I want you to either to either hate it or love it. Because if you hate it, if you think we're the biggest idiots for doing this, you're going to tell somebody. You're going to tell a lot of people. And they might say, 'You know what, it's not that bad. I kind of like it.' And it's going to create a conversation."

One concern over the new identity was that the team would get rid of its beloved mascot, Sluggo. (They would not.) Another concern was that the logo inadvertently promoted another Oregon institution. "People tell us all the time, 'You know you guys have Nike swooshes throughout the whole thing," Benavides said. "We're like, 'No, those aren't Nike swooshes.' We get that a lot."

Yet another issue involved the delicate sensibilities of the children the team was appealing to. "When we unveiled it, some of the criticism that we got early on was like, 'Oh my God that's scary. Kids aren't going to want to wear that,'" Benavides said. "I'm like, 'Really? You see what's on TV nowadays? Get out of here!'"

In fact, one of the effects of the new logo set is that the team has been picked up by Minor League Baseball's Little League uniform program. "It's fun to get people from all over the country, 'Hey my kids play on the Tallahassee Emeralds,'" Benavides said. "You get a call or an email, 'Hey my kid played for the Emeralds in Little League.' We never had that before, ever."

The Emeralds reflect their new Cubs affiliation with more traditional uniforms than what they've worn previously. The redesigned pinstripe uniforms are Emeralds black rather than Cubs blue and feature the Cubs logo on the sleeve.

While the team's uniforms are taking on a more traditional look, the story of the Emeralds' identity is decidedly the opposite. Their switch from a milquetoast (though pleasant) reflection of the local scenery to a logo that embraces the spirit of minor league baseball has worked for the team. In short, it's more fun, it's bright green, and it reminds the world just where Bigfoot lives.

Florida Fire Frogs

Florida Fire Frogs
2017–present

Current Team Data

Parent
Atlanta Braves

Class
High A

League
Florida State

The Florida Fire Frogs have ambition. First, they're one of only a handful of minor league baseball teams named for an entire state. A few others spring to mind, like the New Hampshire Fisher Cats, Arkansas Travelers, and Connecticut Tigers—and hey, the Carolina Mud Cats are named for two states—but they're the exception rather than the rule.

When the team, formerly the beloved (by me, anyway) Brevard County Manatees, relocated this past offseason from Florida's Atlantic Coast to Kissimmee, just south of Orlando, they needed a new way to identify their location. But there were some road blocks that those of us not from there might not be familiar with.

"In Florida, they have stigmas," said Jason Klein, a partner in the firm Brandiose, which created the new look. "People from this county don't go to that county. People from that county don't go to this county. We wanted to be inclusive. We didn't want there to be any barriers for people to attend a Fire Frogs game."

The team's president, Joe Harrington, put it a bit differently: "This is a big area, and our name signifies that we have the expectation of being big," Harrington said, quoted on MiLB.com. "We want to be the community's team, to bring more people to the table."

When it came time to choose a new name and settle on a brand, the team looked even farther afield. The frog featured in the logo is a coquí, which is the common name for a handful of species of frogs native to somewhere not Florida.

For details, we turn to noted minor league baseball chronicler Ben Hill: "That the coquí frog is of Puerto Rican origin is no coincidence," Hill said on MiLB.com, "as the greater Kissimmee area is home to a large percentage of people who are of Puerto Rico heritage."

"There's a very large Puerto Rican community that they're embracing," Klein said. "One of the symbols of Puerto Rico is the coquí frog. Part of it was, what if we incorporate a coquí frog? That allows us to connect to a degree with the Puerto Rican community. It also allows to reach the swamp area that the region is so known for."

The Fire Frogs name was selected in a name-the-team contest, beating out other finalists Dragonflies, Mud Kickers, Rodeo Clowns, Sorcerers, and Toucans. One of the reasons the team went the way it did was to be unique.

"If you look at minor league baseball teams and names and things like that, it is one of those ones that you don't really see a lot of frogs as mascots," said Fire Frogs President Joe Harrington, quoted in the *Orlando Sentinel*. "We will do well here. Since I have been living a short time in Florida, I have seen a ton of them.'"

While the primary logo is a coquí, the suite of logos features variations on the frog theme. Klein credits the idea of a family of frogs (because going to a minor league baseball game is a family outing) to team owner David Freeman.

"He said, 'Man, here's a great idea,'" Klein said. "'Why don't we have a family? We can have a kid frog, a mother frog, we can have the crazy uncle frog.' We thought David had a great idea."

That crazy uncle turned out to be a kind of fantastical take on the notion of a bull frog.

"[Brandiose partner] Casey [White] had done this joke sketch of bull frog—a frog with bull horns, because they're known for the Kissimmee Rodeo," Klein said. "Somehow it stuck. They were like, we really like this idea with the bull frog. It was mythical, so we kind of had this uncle who was this bull frog character—a frog with horns."

Some of this Fire Frogs' identity comes from the "Form Follows Function" files. For instance, the team's colors of fire red, navel orange, and golden sun were somewhat predetermined.

"Like everything in minor league baseball, you have to think economically. How are we going to make this fit in this ballpark?" Klein said. "A lot of the colors that we chose came from the colors that already existed in the ballpark. So the ballpark looks like it was colored to match the team identity, when the opposite is true."

The roundel logo, while something of a trend anyway, also had its origins in the team's home in Osceola County Stadium, spring training home to Houston Astros from 1984 to 2016 (not to mention the awesomely named Kissimmee Cobras from 1995 to 2000).

"There were these giant metal round Astros logos throughout the entire park," Klein said. "We knew that it was going to be really expensive to take those logos off and put Fire Frogs logos up in their place. So one of the tricks that we did was we made sure that the primary logo was a roundel so that they could just take one circle logo and cover it up with another circular logo."

The Florida Fire Frogs are not the wackiest or most outrageous nickname in the minors. Heck, they might not be in the top five wackiest nicknames to debut in 2017. But they've got a lot going for them. Before the Gwinnett Braves rebranded as the Stripers for 2018, they were the only Braves farm team not nicknamed the Braves. They have a brand that's meaningful to the area and their target audience, plus it walks the line between being minor league fun and also a fierce animal. With the alliteration in the name, a good color scheme, and fun logo, this one works for me—though I still miss the Manatees.

Fond du Lac Dock Spiders

Fond du Lac Dock Spiders
2017–present

Current Team Data

Class
Collegiate

League
Northwoods

The town of Fond du Lac, Wisconsin, sits at the southern tip of Lake Winnebago—its name, translated from French, means "bottom of the lake." (Lake Winnebago, I was sad to realize as I started writing this article, is not to be confused with New Hampshire's Lake Winnipesaukee, where the movie *What About Bob* took place).

The idyllic setting plays host to boating, swimming, fishing, and all of the other recreational activities you would associate with the largest lake located entirely within the state of Wisconsin. It is also home to a creature that locals know well, but might not be entirely familiar to people on other parts of the continent—the dock spider.

I was not familiar with the term *dock spider*, so I had to look it up. An article on the website *Cottage Life* offers this as one of its 10 reasons that we should celebrate dock spiders instead of being squeamish about them: "They don't spin webs to catch their prey. Instead, they stalk their victims, using two large fangs to inject them with venom, paralyzing them."

So that's good.

When Brandiose partners Jason Klein and Casey White visited Fond du Lac to work with the town's new team in the collegiate summer level Northwoods League, they did not expect to be thinking about spiders.

"We went to Wisconsin, first time in Wisconsin, got to tour a dairy farm, which was incredible, ate cheese curds. We went all in," Klein said. "Early on, we had anticipated a dairy name, because there wasn't really any dairy brands out there in minor league sports. We thought we could really do a lot with dairy."

There was one evocative dairy-themed name that had potential, but made people nervous, even in today's wackadoodle world of minor league baseball branding.

"The name that we really liked, and everyone was on the fence, was the Udder Tuggers," Klein said. "Everybody who heard it thought, I love that name. It sounds like there's something wrong with it, but no one could really land on what was offensive about it, because everything you think is offensive about it is not."

While no one could quite put their finger on why Udder Tuggers made people squeamish, the name did not make the final cut. Brandiose had been brought in to be part of the naming process, but the final choice was something they had never heard of before visiting Wisconsin.

"We didn't grow up with dock spiders in San Diego, where we live," Klein said. "We started doing research. The staff told us about the lake.... They talked about these relentless, evil spiders."

Dock spiders as a species (actually, it's a common name for a handful of species) have something of a public relations problem. (As a Richmond Spider myself, I can attest that not everyone loves arachnids as sports mascots.) But the team had fully bought in and was ready to run with the idea.

"One of the things that is important to us is that the staff has to love the idea," Klein said. "The staff has to be able to go, Oh, we could name the kids' club this, and we could name the team store this. The staff said at some point, we're more emotionally invested in Dock Spiders."

For the uninitiated, like me, I asked Klein just what a dock spider is.

"They're these big, fuzzy spiders," he said. "It's pretty straight forward. They live under docks. They're kind of nasty, and they're kind of furry."

The Dock Spiders name won the name-the-team contest, beating out other finalists Barn Owls, Lake Flies, Pipsqueaks, and Shantymen, and since its debut in the 2017 season, has garnered a fair amount of attention, even competing against affiliated minor league clubs like the Binghamton Rumble Ponies, Florida Fire Frogs, and New Orleans Baby Cakes. The battle to get brands noticed has trickled all the way down to collegiate summer level ball, and the Dock Spiders are the natural outcome of that process.

Hartford Yard Goats

Hartford Yard Goats
2016–present

Current Team Data

Parent
Colorado Rockies

Class
Double-A

League
Eastern

The Hartford Yard Goats, Double-A affiliate of the Colorado Rockies, are named for the most unglamorous, squat, workhorses of railroad locomotives. In the rail industry, yard goats, or switchers, hardly ever leave the rail yard. Instead, they toil in obscurity, spending their days moving trains around to get them ready for long-distance locomotives, who swoop in like big shots and head out on the open rails to be cheered on by children and rail enthusiasts everywhere. It's like a dystopian episode of *Thomas & Friends* written by Kurt Vonnegut.

What's worse is that in their previous life, the Yard Goats were superstars, living a life of glamor and excess. Before moving to Hartford in 2016, the team was based in New Britain, Connecticut, where they had played for two decades as the Rock Cats, with a logo designed by internationally famous cartoonist Guy Gilchrist.

And when it rains, it pours. Not only did the Yard Goats go from a life of luxury and superstardom to one of thankless toil, but they ended up homeless for a year. After moving to Hartford, the team famously played all of its games in 2016 on the road after construction delays and lawsuits delayed the opening of Dunkin' Donuts Park (which is the most New England name for anything ever). They've finally started playing games in Hartford, and the team is settling nicely into its new identity.

The Yard Goats nickname was entered in a name-the-team contest by New Jersey schoolteacher and 1998 University of Connecticut graduate Anthony Castora. His was the only entry out of more than 6,000 with the suggested name.

So what do Yard Goats have to do with Hartford, Connecticut, and why would you name a minor league baseball team after them? The team explains the latter like this: "A minor league baseball player is like that Yard Goat, working hard in his minor league city to keep his Major League affiliate on track."

The railroad connection is another story. Hartford's history is tied to an important rail system, the New York, New Haven, and Hartford Railroad, which operated from 1872 to 1968. The first line in the system was from Hartford to New Haven. While Hartford's claim to fame now is as the "Insurance Capital of the World," its growth as a city in the 1800s is the result of manufacturing, which was facilitated by its access to railroads.

Hartford's railroad history is the inspiration for one of the cleverest and most elegant design elements in minor league baseball branding. The distinctive typeface used in the New York, New Haven, and Hartford Railroad's logo is the basis for the Yard Goats' wordmark.

The team's colors pay homage to a different aspect of the city's past. Royal blue and kelly green were the colors of the city's beloved Hartford Whalers, who left town two decades to the day before the Yard Goats' first home game.

"That was a no-brainer, to use the Whalers colors," said Jeff Dooley, the team's Director of Broadcasting and Media Relations.

The Yard Goats embrace another tradition related to their city's bygone hockey team: "Sometimes they'll play Brass Bonanza, the song they played with the Whalers," Dooley said. "They'll play that at some games for home runs just to bring back that feeling."

For players in the Colorado Rockies system, it's a fun trip, branding-wise anyway, through the minors. In addition to the Yard Goats, the Rockies farm teams include the Triple-A Albuquerque Isotopes, High-A Lancaster Jethawks, Single-A Asheville Tourists, and Short-Season Boise Hawks. If we could get the Rookie League Grand Junction Rockies to reprise their moniker from their days in Casper, Wyoming—the Ghosts—the Rockies farm system would be a clean sweep in unique nicknames.

The Yard Goats, whose logos were created by Brandiose, are evidence of how quickly minor league baseball teams can go from outrageous newcomer to an established brand. When the nickname and logo were announced, beating out other name-the-team contest finalists Hedgehogs, Praying Mantis, River Hogs, and Whirlybirds, the reaction from fans was similar to what we saw in 2017 with teams like the Binghamton Rumble Ponies, Jacksonville Jumbo Shrimp, and New Orleans Baby Cakes. While the Yard Goats nickname was initially criticized, because it's a wacky minor league baseball logo and that's the law, the team was fully part of the community by just its second year in existence—and its first year with actual home games.

"We were in the Saint Patrick's Day parade in downtown Hartford and there were goats marching with us," Dooley said. "People wanted selfies with the goat."

It's not automatic that wacky nicknames will be accepted by fans and the local community. The Yard Goats have used successful marketing (including a very funny Twitter account) and what is ultimately a solid brand, and now feel—to borrow a term from the Yard Goats' neighbors, ESPN—something like an instant classic.

Hillsboro Hops

Hillsboro Hops
2013–present

Current Team Data

Parent
Arizona Diamondbacks

Class
Short Season A

League
Northwest

Minor league baseball is an industry whose main goal is to appeal to families, if not specifically children. So the Hillsboro Hops, short-season Single-A affiliate of the Diamondbacks, went out on a limb when they based their entire identity on one of the four main ingredients of beer. In fact, when the team unveiled its new team name after relocating from Yakima, Washington, before the 2013 season, there was concern about the direction they were taking.

"Right away there were some people that just jumped right to the beer side and had this picture in their head that we would have drunks all over the stadium and Thirsty Thursday was going to be every night and all this stuff," said K.L. Wombacher, the team's executive vice president and general manager.

But Wombacher is quick to point out that the name Hops isn't just popular with any old beer drinkers, it's popular specifically with beer snobs. Hops are commonly associated with craft brewing, which accounts for an increasingly large percentage of the beer industry.

"Craft beer drinkers are more like wine drinkers," he said. "They get offended if someone is drinking a Bud Light next to them."

And besides, the team name is about more than just beer. With 4,000 acres of hops fields, Oregon ranks second among states that produce the crop. While Hillsboro has become something of a tech town, located in the so-called Silicon Forest, the town's roots are in agriculture.

"There were a ton of hop fields here back in the day," Wombacher said. "So the agriculture theme kept coming back to us when we were looking at the name."

The Hops had a couple other goals in selecting a name. After 23 seasons with a generic name, they wanted something unique. "We were the Yakima Bears before," Wombacher said, laughing. "There are only about 300 of those logos."

With all of these factors met, there was one final criteria: It needed to sound good. "It came off the tongue well," Wombacher said. "It's the Hops. It's real simple to say. 'Have you been to the Hops game?' 'Have you seen the Hops play?' 'Go Hops!' 'Hops Nation.' All that kind of stuff."

So the name is borne of the town's agriculture roots, it's captured the imagination of the growing craft brew culture, it's unique, and it sounds good. In addition to that, it relates to the game the Hops play. "It also ties into baseball with the terminology," Wombacher said. "Short hops, crow hops, bad hop."

To say that the logo has been a success would be an understatement. When they debuted, they sold out of their first batch of T-shirts in 23 hours, and in their first year sent orders to all 50 states and a handful of foreign nations. Then they accomplished something that you don't see often with short-season Single-A teams playing in tiny markets.

"When we cracked the top 25 in merchandise last year, we threw a huge party," Wombacher said. "Playing only 38 games and going up against Triple-A and Double-A teams that play 70 home games—I mean, 80 or 90 percent of your merchandise sales comes from the games, so we never thought we'd be able to beat out Triple-A and Double-A teams."

Wombacher credits much of the logo's success to designer Dan Simon of Studio Simon, who immediately saw potential in the name. "He started looking at pictures of a hop and was like, 'Yeah we can make this guy into a superstar,'" Wombacher said.

Another reason for the success is good timing. "I think we just launched it at the perfect time," Wombacher said, referring to the increasing popularity of the craft brewing industry. "Craft beer, hopheads, it's just such a different culture.... We've been able to have minor success with it on a national basis with craft beer drinkers."

The team's color palette of blues and greens is intended to convey a soothing feeling of the Pacific Northwest, but if Dan Simon hadn't intervened, things might not have been that way. Since they already had green, which connected them to the University of Oregon, the Hops toyed with the idea of using orange to bring in Oregon State fans.

Wombacher is glad Simon insisted on a cool palette. "The colors are a big part of our logo's success—more of a sustained success than initial success," he said. "I think the flashy colors probably get attention up front ... but I would be surprised if they had staying power over a 10-, 20-year period."

Another design element that Wombacher credits to Simon is the tiny, subtle references to an iconic mountain and surrounding forests. "You can drive to Mount Hood, you can drive to the forest, but you're not in them," he said. "I thought that was a brilliant way to add a little regional scenery to the logo without it overpowering things."

Speaking of the local surroundings, the Hops play about 13 miles from the city of Portland, which has been home to roughly a million minor league baseball franchises, all named the Portland Beavers. I was morally obligated to ask if the Hops considered becoming the million-first Portland Beavers.

"We did a couple of contests for name suggestions and it certainly came up numerous times," Wombacher said. "But for us our biggest goal—and it was kind of a reason to go to Hillsboro rather than Portland—was to develop our own identity, to start a new generation of baseball."

The Hops tapped into the cultural phenomenon of craft beer at just the right time, and somehow found a way to walk a fine line between being family friendly and appealing to beer snobs. The success of their logo in a crowded minor league baseball marketplace is particularly remarkable, given that they play against teams in much bigger markets playing at higher levels. It just goes to show, everything goes better with beer.

Jacksonville Jumbo Shrimp

Jacksonville Jumbo Shrimp
2017–present

Current Team Data

Parent
Miami Marlins

Class
Double-A

League
Southern

Whenever the term *oxymoron* comes up, "Jumbo Shrimp" seems to be the first example people can think of. *Jumbo* means big, *shrimp* means little. In a way, the oxymoronic nature of the term makes it a perfect fit for the name of a minor league baseball team that plays in the biggest little city in Florida.

"Jacksonville is the largest land-mass city in the country. At the end of the day it really has a small town, tight-knit feel," said Noel Blaha, the team's assistant general manager. "Jumbo Shrimp is a bit of a play on that large city, but small town feel."

The Jacksonville Jumbo Shrimp are the latest iteration of a team that's been around for a long time. Prior to rebranding before the 2017 season, the baseball team in Jacksonville had been called the Jacksonville Suns since 1962, with the exception of a stint from 1985 to 1990, when they went by the name of their then-parent club, the Expos.

The Jumbo Shrimp are unusual in minor league rebrands in that the team didn't go through the pretense of a fan vote before renaming the team. The higher-ups simply decided that it was time and came up with a name. As with nearly every rebrand, the name was not received with open arms.

"The reaction was incredible. Everyone had an opinion," Blaha said. "Right off the bat social media hit us with angry folks, including a petition that 10,000 quickly signed to revert the name back to the Suns."

The team anticipated a certain amount of backlash and early on sold a T-shirt with the team logo and the slogan, "Haters Gonna Hate," which they promoted on Instagram with the caption, "If you're BOLD enough to go against the mainstream and proudly rep the Jumbo Shrimp then this is the shirt for you."

If the Jumbo Shrimp thought they might fly under the radar with the timing of the announcement of the new name in late October 2016, they may have misjudged how much local communities care about their ballclubs.

"Here we were announcing the Jacksonville Jumbo Shrimp the same day as Game 7 of one of the most storybook World Series in recent memory [Indians-Cubs] and less than a week from one of the most volatile presidential elections ever," Blaha said. "The headline the next day in the *Florida Times-Union*, with a massive above-the-fold, full-color photo, was, 'Suns Become Jumbo Shrimp.' There were tiny blurbs stating 'Cubs Win First World Series Since 1908,' 'President Obama in Town Today,' and 'Donald Trump Visits Today.'"

The origin of the team name has to do with Jacksonville's role in the fishing industry.

"Modern shrimping methods were refined in nearby Fernandina Beach around 100 years ago and to this day the best-tasting shrimp in the world gets hauled in at Mayport on the St. Johns River here in Jacksonville," Blaha said. "The day we announced the new name, we received phone calls from local shrimpers and seafood retailers that were thrilled with the name and the recognition it would bring to their industry here locally."

While the team maintains that their seafood-based identity has nothing to do with their parent club, the Miami Marlins, it's hard not to notice a pattern in the nicknames of nearby minor league teams.

"We joke that along I-10, it's the Southern League Seafood Division," said Jason Klein of Brandiose, the firm responsible for the logo. "You've got Shuckers, the Blue Wahoos, and now you've got the Jumbo Shrimp. We call it the seafood buffet."

The team colors derive from the preponderance of water in the area, along with the team's namesake. "We knew it was going to be some kind of a shrimp color," Klein explained. "One of the challenges is that a shrimp is pink, and do we want to go full pink?"

Ultimately the colors were influenced by a strong military presence in Jacksonville. "We just went full patriotic," Klein said.

Speaking of patriotic, Blaha noted this in regards to the custom typeface, "Our wordmark features a font loosely based on the GI Joe font."

In designing the logo, Brandiose was faced immediately with the challenge of the oxymoron in the name.

"One of our biggest challenges was, how do you make a shrimp look jumbo?" Klein asked. "To do that, you need to juxtapose it to something. You can't just show a shrimp or they'll never know it's jumbo. So you have him giant coming out of the cauldron, and you have him giant wrapped around the state of Florida."

Some of the Jumbo Shrimp logos have some hidden visual elements, and some not so hidden:

"People generally really like the road logo where our shrimp is holding the State of Florida with his fist firmly grasping Duval," Blaha said, referring to the county in which Jacksonville is found.

There's another visual element that Blaha feels should be more obvious. "What I'm still taken aback by is the amount of people that don't immediately realize our primary logo features the shrimp in the shape of a J," he said.

And finally, the batting practice cap logo requires a second look to take it all in. "That logo is great because not only does it feature corn and sausage getting dumped out of a pot with our shrimp," Blaha said, "but the idea of shrimp boil—good eats dumped out around a table of family and friends—is a perfect tie in to minor league baseball."

The oxymoron in the term Jumbo Shrimp is something of a metaphor for branding in minor league baseball overall. How do you take something big, like sports marketing, and make it appropriate to countless small towns, each of which has its own unique identity? The Jumbo Shrimp reflect the current, wildly successful trend in minor league baseball to answer that question in the extreme: A silly or unusual name (which everyone hated at first) derived from a hyper-local aspect of a community (which everyone loved), then was formalized with a highly polished brand (which is selling like crazy).

Joliet Slammers

Joliet Slammers
2011–present

Current Team Data

Class
Independent

League
Frontier

When Jake Blues makes his dramatic exit from prison at the beginning of the 1980 classic *The Blues Brothers,* he emerges from beneath a guard tower atop the east gate of the Joliet Correctional Center, a real prison that opened in 1858. Jake finds his brother Ellwood waiting for him in a 1974 Dodge Monaco—a police car that he had purchased at an auction in nearby Mount Prospect, Illinois. Reunited, the brothers set off to get their band back together in pursuit of their ultimate quest—*their mission from God*—to raise $5,000 to save the Saint Helen of the Blessed Shroud orphanage from closure.

This memorable opening scene—along with the fact that John Belushi's character is called "Joliet Jake"—put the town of Joliet, Illinois, on the cultural map as the home of the most iconic prison this side of Alcatraz. The prison has been featured in songs from Memphis Minnie's 1932 "Joliet Bound" to Bob Dylan's "Percy's Song," released in 1985. Countless fictional characters are former inmates of the prison, and since its closing in 2002, the building itself has been used as the setting for TV shows like *Prison Break* and *Breakout Kings* and movies like *Derailed* and *Let's Go to Prison*. (Hey, they can't all be *The Blues Brothers*...)

So when a new independent Frontier League baseball team debuted in Joliet in 2011, the club decided to fully embrace their hometown's identity.

"Joliet is a prison town," said John Dittrich, who was the Slammers' general manager when the team debuted (he was calling from his "retirement job" at the Cleveland Indians' spring training camp). "It was at one point home to a federal penitentiary, as well as a state penitentiary, as well as the county seat, so it had the county jail. Of course, it's a city, so it has a city jail. It has a youth detention facility. It's well known as a prison town."

The Joliet Slammers replaced the town's previous team, the Northern League's Joliet Jackhammers, who struggled with low attendance and were sold amid substantial financial debt. The Slammers' logo, designed by Dan Simon of Studio Simon, focuses on the imposing impression left by the prison.

"The primary logo is full of details that link back to the prison, with wire-topped walls and a guard tower included," said the team's current general manager Heather Mills.

A little-used alternate logo featuring an officer's shield (which Simon submitted for consideration as a primary logo) reinforces the law-enforcement aspect of the Slammers' identity.

The decision to name the new team for a well-known penitentiary, as with many team names, was not immediately embraced. "Some people didn't like it at first," Dittrich said, "but a lot of the more creative logos are not popular at first, and then they hit a home run. This one, I think, hit off pretty well after it was unveiled."

Of course, while the name Slammers is most notable for being a euphemism for prisons, there is a connection to the game on the field.

"We thought Slammers was a pretty good name because it not only signified the main industry in town—at one point, it was the main industry—but also it was a baseball term," Dittrich said. "Grand slammer, a good hitter, whatever it might be, is a slammer."

The Slammers identity is unusual in sports in that it focuses on law enforcement rather than lawlessness. It's far more common to see teams named for criminals—Bandits, Outlaws, Gunslingers, etc.—than for say, police officers, and the team made it a point to focus on that aspect of the identity.

It's for this reason that the logo featuring a prisoner, which Simon submitted and says is one of his favorite creations ever, was not adopted as the team's primary logo. He explains, "They opted not to go with this direction because … they wanted the primary logo to focus on the law side of the Joliet prison story, not the lawless side."

That being said, "there was no escaping the fact that there are inmates in the prison," Simon said, "and in minor league baseball, a lot of times, teams don't want to do a person in the logo. They want to have some kind of a character."

So while the primary identity focuses on the prison instead of a prisoner, it seemed inevitable that an inmate would be part of the team's identity in some way, and the bird made its way into the identity system.

"The secondary logo includes the mischievous mascot J.L. Bird," Mills explains. "Say it quickly now and it makes more sense."

There are a handful of things that a baseball team in Joliet could have seized on for an identity—Al Capone used to hang out in the Rialto Square Theatre, it sits on Route 66, and the first Dairy Queen opened there, to name a few ideas—so it's notable that the Slammers seized on the town's notoriety as a prison town. Insomuch as a logo based on a prison can be, it's a fun identity, and it's been part of a turnaround for baseball in Joliet. The team was awarded the Frontier League's Commissioner's Award of Excellence after the 2015 season, and look to be on firm footing going forward.

And while I haven't been to a game there, I look forward to some day visiting Joliet (the town, not any of its prisons), stepping up to a concession stand at a ballgame, and ordering dry white toast, four fried chickens, and a Coke.

Las Vegas 51s

Las Vegas 51s
2001–present

Current Team Data

Parent
New York Mets

Class
Triple-A

League
Pacific Coast

Here's how much I like the nickname and logo of the Triple-A Las Vegas 51s: I bought myself a 51s hat and shirt, even though I am a Phillies fan and the 51s, at the time of this writing, are a Mets affiliate. I love their primary logo, the stand-alone alien head with the baseball seam forehead, and what I just recently learned is called their "orbitron" logo.

The 51s' nickname and the alien-themed identity derive from nearby Area 51 (okay, it's 83 miles away), where the US government secretly stores spaceships and actual, living extra-terrestrials who have crash landed in the desert. *(Legal notice: *Allegedly.)* The 51s, however, are suffering one of the worst fates known to minor league baseball: The novelty is wearing off.

"Compared to some of the other nicknames now, really, to be honest with you, 51s is really not that wacky of a nickname," said 51s media relations director Jim Gemma. "It's really not that far out."

The 51s franchise dates back to 1919, when they were founded as the second iteration (of many) of the Portland Beavers. They moved to Spokane in 1972, where they played under the moniker Indians through the 1982 season before moving to Las Vegas. For 18 years beginning in 1983, the Triple-A baseball team in Las Vegas was a San Diego Padres affiliate called the Stars. When the team's affiliation changed to the Dodgers in 2001, they seized the opportunity to rebrand with a not-uncommon goal in mind: "The kids really do love the alien stuff," Gemma said.

Seamhead alien

Orbitron

To that end, the 51s introduced a mascot named Cosmo, whom Gemma says has been very popular. According to the 51s website, Cosmo is from a planet called Koufaxia and crashlanded on Earth, where he spent time in Area 51. (My theory is that Cosmo is actually Jar Jar Binks in an intergallactic Witness Protection Program. Cosmo—just coincidentally—debuted two years after Star Wars Episode 1 hit the theaters.)

Of course, people fear change, and the reaction to the new identity was not universally positive. "It's kind of weathered the storm," Gemma said. "People hated it, and a lot of people liked the Stars."

But time heals all wounds, and now after more than a decade in Las Vegas, the 51s are a fixture.

"Like it or not, if you say 51s to somebody … they know it's Triple-A baseball, Pacific Coast League, they play at Cashman Field," Gemma said. (As if it's totally normal for a minor league baseball team to base its identity on the sort of government conspiracies they make Will Smith movies out of.)

Given that they are named after a controversial, alleged, top-secret government facility, the team's uniforms are fairly traditional. In fact, the only place the 51s' wackiest visual element, the baseball-alien head, appears on the uniform is on the primary logo cap. And this is just fine with Gemma, who has players wear alternate LV logo caps when he takes player photographs.

"Our alternate hat is the LV hat, which we wear occasionally," Gemma said. "I think the LV hat looks better, but the alien head sells, and that's our primary hat."

The only change to the 51s' uniforms in recent years came when they switched affiliations to the Mets in 2013, after being a Toronto Blue Jays affiliate from 2009 to 2012. "We kind of had the standard blue and red and we decided to change the number on the front to orange," Gemma said.

Gemma is happy with the team's traditional look when it comes to the uniforms and the placement of the various logos. "To me, the cleaner the better," he said. "Our 51s orbitron logo I think looks great. The alien head on the hat, it's simple, but it's good."

The orbitron logo appears on the shirt sleeves. (I point this out primarily because I like the word *orbitron*.)

The 51s play in a stadium that is more than 30 years old, Cashman Field. It has held up fairly well over the years, though it does not have much of the glitz and glamor you'd expect in Sin City. One devastating detriment to Cashman Field: They do not sell ice cream helmet sundaes with the 51s logo—no soft serve helmets, no Dippin' Dots helmets, no shave ice helmets, and no cheese curd or nacho helmets. Here they have one of the most popular and distinctive logos in minor league ball, and fans are sent home with no helmet sundaes to add to their collection.

Since becoming the 51s in 2001, they have had multiple ownership groups. The current ownership group, Summerlin Las Vegas Baseball Club LLC, is exploring the possibility of a new stadium in the Vegas suburbs in the next several years, which may signal more change: "They're trying to get a new ballpark," Gemma said, "and when the new ballpark goes up, maybe they will change the name."

And what would become of the popular Cosmo if the team name did change?

"We'd probably just keep him," Gemma said. "That would be my vote. Just tell everybody the spaceship left without him."

If they do change the name, they have a high standard to meet. After all, the current one made a Phillies fan buy Mets stuff.

Lehigh Valley IronPigs

Lehigh Valley IronPigs
2008–present

Current Team Data

Parent
Philadelphia Phillies

Class
Triple-A

League
International

One of the reasons many minor league baseball teams adopt wacky nicknames is that they want to emphasize the fun, family-friendly atmosphere of a game at their ballpark. As I've spoken with representatives from different teams for this series, it's become clear to me that a lot of minor league baseball fans care more about the game experience—promotions and between-inning activities and whatnot—than they do the game itself. Regardless of how well the actual baseball team plays, a fun, unique logo creates a brand that people become attached to.

This is why one of the early challenges the Lehigh Valley IronPigs had to overcome was unusual.

"People here care more about baseball than your average minor league baseball fan," said IronPigs Media Relations/Broadcasting Director Matt Provence, who has worked in minor league baseball for almost two decades. "They didn't see the need to have this hokie, fun, state-of-the-art entertainment. They saw the need for baseball."

The Triple-A Lehigh Valley IronPigs' nickname derives from a simple inversion of the phrase "pig iron," which is forged in the steel mills of eastern Pennsylvania. The steel-themed logo perfectly represents the area's gritty roots. (Awesome, true fact! The nickname was submitted to a name-the-team contest by a man named Ronald Steele.) However, Provence said, the team's hometown of Allentown, Pennsylvania, is increasingly populated by transplants from New York and Philadelphia who might not be familiar with the area's history, let alone mining terminology.

"It wasn't like it was a slam dunk that everybody understood the play of words on pig iron," he said.

Not only that, but some people just didn't like the name. "Especially older people," Provence said. "They thought it was gross. You know, *pigs* in your name. Ugh, how awful."

Fans have come to embrace the team and its porcine nickname, though. In fact, when I mentioned to Matt that my six-year-old daughter chose a pig snout from the team's gift shop during a game last season, he exclaimed, "The number one seller in the store is the pig snout!"

The IronPigs are among the best-attended teams in the minors, ranking first, second, or third for several years running, and they have consistently been on Minor League Baseball's list of top 25 teams in terms of merchandise sales. The year the IronPigs debuted in 2008, their big-league parent club, the nearby Philadelphia Phillies, won the World Series and the second of five consecutive National League East titles. Provence ties some of the IronPigs' early success in merchandise and attendance to the Phillies' run of success on the field (which, to be fair, has come to a crashing halt the last couple seasons). Baseball fans in the IronPigs' hometown of Allentown, Pennsylvania, are likely to root for the Phillies, and are likely to want to see the team's highest-level prospects.

"We've been blessed to be in this area because the sports fan in the northeast is a different bird, it's a real diehard, it's a real loyal fan, it's a fan that cares," Provence said. "When you're always one or two in attendance, you're usually going to sell more merchandise.... Everything was a perfect storm for baseball in this region, the Phillies fans, the brand-new ballpark, getting a Triple-A classification from the get-go."

The IronPigs have been known to push the envelope when it comes to edgy promotions. An in-urinal video game received international attention, and the team once famously gave fans "Number One" foam fingers sponsored by a local urologist. "You want everything wholesome and clean, maybe a little bit toward the extreme without going overboard," Provence said.

The IronPigs unveiled a series of alternate logos in 2013, including a molten-lava pig face (to tie in with eastern Pennsylvania's steel mills), a three-quarters angle pig face (just because), a Liberty Bell, (to tie in with Philadelphia), and one that is simply a strip of bacon (because everything is better with bacon)—complete with a scratch-n-sniff bacon T-shirt. (The designers at Brandiose received a request from IronPigs' staff: "We'd like to see more bacon.") The new logos complement the existing "Pork Racer" mascots, Hambone, a hot dog named Diggity, and Chris P. Bacon.

The new logos and the IronPigs' focus on all things porky drew the attention of the Washington DC-based Physicians Committee for Responsible Medicine (PCRM), which objected because bacon is horrible for you. They launched a campaign to encourage the IronPigs to "stop glorifying bacon," including putting up a billboard outside the stadium saying, "Keep Kids Safe: Ban Bacon from Ballparks." In response, the IronPigs wrote a response thanking the PCRM for their letter and all of its baseball metaphors ("Ban the bacon and hit a home run for health"), then launched a #saveourbacon social media campaign and rode a huge wave of free publicity generated by the story.

As a Triple-A team, the IronPigs' roster often includes Major Leaguers on rehab assignments or who have been sent down to work out some kinks. Provence said that the big leaguers get a kick out of the wacky gear. When he asked members of the Phillies to shoot a commercial promoting IronPigs gear, they had fun with it. "Ryan Howard making noises of what he thought an IronPig would sound like was great footage," he said.

That said, in 2012, when then-IronPigs manager Ryne Sandberg had to sport a Christmas-themed uniform, he may have felt his career had bottomed out. Provence said, "Ryne Sandberg wearing a Santa Claus IronPigs shirt for Christmas in July was like, 'Really? This is where it's gone? From my Hall of Fame plaque to wearing Santa Claus?'" (Sandberg took over as the Phillies manager for a short while and was spared having to wear promotional gear like a tuxedo-themed uniform, which landed the IronPigs on the SportsCenter "Not Top 10.")

In the end, the IronPigs walked a fine line with their identity. They have the flexibility that all minor league teams need to appeal to families, especially kids, while also satisfying the serious Phillies fan who wants to see if his team's prospects have what it takes to make it in the Bigs. They needed a logo that could be fun but edgy, that is appropriate to the region as well as appealing to a national audience, and that could somehow smell like bacon, and it seems that they've succeeded on all counts.

Modesto Nuts

Modesto Nuts
2005–present

Current Team Data

Parent
Seattle Mariners

Class
High A

League
California

Modesto, California, is known for producing nuts, such as almonds, walnuts, pistachios, and George Lucas. And since they couldn't make a logo out of George Lucas, who was born and raised in Modesto and set his film *American Graffiti* there, the local baseball team decided to pay homage the industry that dominates the surrounding Central Valley with its logo.

"It's really an ode to the agricultural community in the Central Valley and Stanislaus County," said the team's general manager Tyler Richardson, who is himself a product of Modesto. "Agriculture—specifically almonds and walnuts—make up a huge part of who we are."

The Single-A Nuts debuted in 2005 after the then-Modesto Athletics switched affiliations to the Colorado Rockies. As is the trend in minor league baseball, the team rebranded with a nickname and logo appropriate to their own region rather than simply adopting the name of their Major League affiliate.

"One of the main benefits now is no matter who our affiliate is, our team name will always be the same," Richardson said. "We've always marketed ourselves as Modesto's team, Stanislaus County's team, and so to have a name that reflects who we are, which is agriculture, it just deepens those relationships even further."

The Nuts featured in the logo are Wally the Walnut and Al the Almond—whom I have always thought of as the Bert and Ernie of the baseball logo world. The team recently added another mascot, a female pistachio named Shelley. In an announcement on the team's website, Richardson said, "We feel a strong, independent female character will resonate with all of our fans." The options for Shelley's name, selected from suggestions that fans submitted online, were Penny, Patty, Shelley, Bella, and Polly. (The official stance of this author is that fans were to correct to go with Shelley, branching out from the alliteration of Wally the Walnut and Al the Almond.)

The mascots wear red caps with a white capital M, an homage to the erstwhile Modesto Reds, the local team from 1966 to 1974. This means that the caps that Nuts players wear as part of their uniforms feature a mascot wearing a cap. It makes you wonder, if Wally were wearing a cap with the current Nuts logo—a picture of himself wearing a cap—would we be caught in an *Inception*-style infinite loop of cap logos?

The Nuts' identity features another design element that might be lost on the casual observer, but is significant to people who know the area. The team's primary logo features the word Modesto in an arch—a nod to an actual arch in Modesto, which has welcomed motorists to the city with its motto, "Water, Wealth, Contentment, Health," since 1912.

"Everyone who knows Modesto knows about the arch," Richardson said, "and so we wanted to put 'Modesto' in the arch to signify our arch."

These place-specific details in the Nuts logo don't restrict its marketability. "Although the name is local, it has national appeal," Richardson said. "We get requests and comments and merchandise orders from all over the country."

The Nuts logo is highly regarded among minor league baseball fans for being lighthearted and well-designed—though botanists might complain that almonds, walnuts, and pistachios are technically drupes rather than nuts. That said, if anyone does complain about the technical definition of a nut versus a drupe, they don't do it at Nuts games. When I asked about it, Richardson told me, "You're the first person that's ever mentioned that." (For the record, a drupe is a fruit with a pit inside it, like cherries or plums. In the case of almonds, walnuts, and pistachios, we actually throw away the fruit and eat the pit.)

The Nuts seem to be a fixture on lists of people's favorite wacky sports logos. A strong color scheme, a unique mascot, and an identity that is meaningful at multiple levels—from the place-specific, agricultural roots of the name right down to details of the actual design—make the Nuts one of the most distinct logos in minor league baseball.

Montgomery Biscuits

Montgomery Biscuits
2004–present

Current Team Data

Parent
Tampa Bay Rays

Class
Double-A

League
Southern

In the interest of full disclosure, I should point out that at time of this writing, I have been on a grain-free, sugar-free diet for the better part of a month—and I use the word *better* loosely. This means no ice cream helmet sundaes, no beer, and for absolute sure no delicious Southern-style biscuits.

So my judgment may be colored a little when I look at the logo for the Montgomery Biscuits, Double-A affiliate of the Tampa Bay Rays, and think, that is the most delicious logo in the history of baseball, and I would knock over my own grandmother for a real biscuit with melty butter on it right now. I can tell just from looking at it that the Montgomery Biscuit is made from real flour rather than ground almonds.

I spoke with Sherrie Myers, co-founder of Professional Sports Marketing, based in Evanston, Illinois, which established and owns the Montgomery Biscuits. Because I have something of a one-track mind at the moment, I asked Ms. Myers about the presence of actual biscuits at a Montgomery Biscuits game.

"We're the first team in the country to sell biscuits in the stadium," she said, "and we still do. We have sold something like … 300,000 biscuits."

And it's not just a regular old biscuit with butter, which would be plenty. In Alabama, biscuits are a delivery mechanism for all sorts of goodness:

"It's outrageous," Myers said. "They put ham on the biscuit and they put chicken on the biscuit and they have honey on the biscuit, and you know, they think that's just like a normal thing to eat. And the rest of us, the rest of the country, we're like, *biscuits?!*"

And there's more. The team launches actual biscuits into the crowd during games. "Some people have a hot dog cannon," Ms. Myers said. "We have a biscuit cannon. And we shoot biscuits into the crowd."

This may go without saying, but in my current state, I would elbow you in the gut and step on your head to catch one of those biscuits. I might even try to take on the Biscuits' mascot, Big Mo, whom Ms. Myers describes as a "biscuit-eating, aardvarky sort of creature" who is *not scary*. ("If you're under two," Ms. Myers concedes, "you might still cry at the mascot just because this creature is big and you're still in that stage. But there are very few kids over two who don't like our mascots.")

The origin story of the Biscuits' identity is simple enough: A fan submitted the name as part of a name-the-team contest in 2003 after the Orlando Rays announced that they would be moving to Montgomery, Alabama. Professional Sports Marketing has been involved with the creation of nine teams (including the Lansing Lugnuts, their first, and the only other team they still own), and the name-the-team contest is a staple in their team-launching playbook.

"You want the community to be part of the architecture of the new approach to minor league baseball in that community," Ms. Myers said.

The name Biscuits was a surprise when it was submitted to the contest, but the team quickly saw its potential, and more importantly, they liked the connection to the place. Ms. Myers asked, "Biscuits—how much more Southern can you get?" By 2004, the Biscuits were in business, and today the team's unique logo has earned it a spot among the most popular minor league merchandise (through a team store called the "Biscuit Basket") and the name has lent itself to numerous puns and promotions.

As seems to be the case with most unique logos, though, it was not well received at first. "When we announced the Biscuits in 2003 you could hear a pin drop," Ms. Myers said, "and we were on a stage in this huge summer concert area." Fans wanted something serious, menacing, and revered, Ms. Myers said, but instead they got campy and delicious.

But all that serious, menacing stuff is best left to the big leagues, and the focus for minor league teams is different. "It's not about wins or losses," Ms. Myers said. "It's totally about the brand and the experience.... It's very different from the Majors, and so you need to market it as family, affordable fun."

When it comes to maintaining a high-profile brand in an increasingly competitive (and wacky) minor league landscape, the Biscuits have had success pinning their hopes on a proven formula: community involvement; a unique, place-appropriate nickname; a family-friendly experience; and weaponized baked-goods fired directly at hungry fans, some of whom have not eaten grains or sugar in weeks.

New Britain Bees

New Britain Bees
2016–present

Current Team Data

Class
Independent

League
Atlantic League of Professional Baseball

The official seal of the city of New Britain, Connecticut, features a beehive and the Latin inscription, *"Industria implet alveare et melle fruitur,"* which translates to "Industry fills the hive and enjoys the honey."

The city embraces the simile "busy as a bee"—an expression whose origins go back more than 600 years to Chaucer's *Canterbury Tales*—because industry has so thoroughly filled the proverbial hive in New Britain. The city earned the nickname "Hardware City" because of its rich manufacturing history, and more specifically because it's home to the headquarters for Stanley Black & Decker.

"The first professional ballpark, which is next door to New Britain Stadium, is Beehive Field," said Chris Knoblock, Director of Media Relations and Broadcasting for the New Britain Bees, "and New Britain's town mascot is a bee as well."

So when it came time to name the city's baseball team, a new franchise in the independent Atlantic League of Professional Baseball, before the 2016 season, it's not a surprise that a certain buzzing insect played a role. Bees beat out Stingers, Hornets, Hammer, and Hard Hitters in a name-the-team fan vote.

The logo, created by Skye Design Studios in North Carolina, who recently created the logo for the Atlantic League's 2018 All Star Game in Long Island, features a beehive, dripping honey, and the bee character, who is so adorable he almost makes you forget that he'll inject you with throat-closing venom in a heartbeat if you even look at him funny. (Caveat: It's possible I had kind of an incident as a child that involved me stumbling into a beehive and spending the next three days swelled up like the Michelin Man.)

The unaffiliated Bees assumed the mantle of the city's baseball team after the New Britain Rock Cats (née the New Britain Red Sox) left town to become the Hartford Yard Goats after more than three decades in the city.

"The response has been fantastic—fans have really embraced the Bees identity," Knoblock said. "Mostly people are thrilled to have baseball remain in New Britain—this being the 35th year of professional baseball between the New Britain Red Sox, Rock Cats, and Bees."

One thing the Bees share with their Double-A forebears is uniforms featuring their hometown's "Hardware City" nickname. The Rock Cats actually used Hardware City as their geographic locator for a season before switching to New Britain, and now the Bees wear gold alternate Hardware City uniforms on 11 "Hardware City Sunday Family Fun Days" throughout the season.

Fans of minor league baseball know that there are already a couple "Bees" teams out there. The Triple-A Salt Lake Bees and the Single-A Burlington Bees, both (purely by coincidence) affiliates of the Los Angeles Angels, are called the Bees because of strong populations of followers of the Church of Latter Day Saints in their respective locations, and Biblical references to the "Land of Milk and Honey."

According to Knoblock, the name of New Britain's team has nothing to do with either of the other baseball Bees, but they have had a little fun with it.

"The public voted on the team name and the public decided 'Bees' was the moniker that fit their team," he said. "We did a funny little interaction with Salt Lake on National Look Alike Day on Twitter, but that's been the extent of our interaction."

While many minor league teams seem like they're jumping up and down trying to be noticed, the New Britain Bees have achieved a brand that is both understated and minor league cute. It's a simple, clean look with nice colors, featuring a cartoon character that is fun without being childish or outlandish.

I'm still terrified of that stinger, though.

New Orleans Baby Cakes

New Orleans Baby Cakes
2017–present

Current Team Data

Parent
Miami Marlins

Class
Triple-A

League
Pacific Coast

It's possible that the New Orleans Baby Cakes are the first team in sports whose logo is a cartoon representation of a plastic toy that many people think represents baby Jesus. Let me explain.

Until this season, the Baby Cakes franchise, Triple-A affiliate of the Miami Marlins, had been known as the New Orleans Zephyrs (ostensibly named for a famous roller coaster in New Orleans), who brought the name Zephyrs from Denver (where there was a famous passenger train by that name). The Zephyrs had an understated, classy logo, and therefore were getting drowned out of relevance in a sea of outrageous minor league baseball identities.

So the team sought a new brand, one that would speak to the local community and get noticed by fans everywhere. The result is one of the most talked-about wacky new nicknames in a sport that basically is defined by its wacky nicknames. According to the team, though, the name is not just about shock value.

"We never once said, let's come up with something crazy that will make people go nuts," said Augusto "Cookie" Rojas, the team's general manager. "It wasn't our intent to be bizarre or exotic or way out there. It was basically our intent to craft something that was unique like New Orleans." (Speaking of unique to New Orleans, notice how the Baby Cakes' crest includes the logo of the early-1900s baseball team the New Orleans Pelicans, which saw the likes of Shoeless Joe Jackson, Dazzy Vance, and Earl Weaver in uniform.)

The name Baby Cakes comes from a traditional delicacy called a king cake, which is essentially a sugary bread with purple, green, and yellow icing. The three colors represent royalty (purple), faith (green), and gold (yellow), as well as the Biblical three kings who brought gifts to baby Jesus on the 12th day of Christmas. King cakes, which have come to be associated with Mardi Gras, traditionally have baked into them a small plastic baby, which to many represents baby Jesus.

In the original tradition of the king cake, which dates back hundreds of years to old Europe, it was a bean, pecan, or ring baked into the cake. The person who ended up with the slice of cake with the trinket in it was to be treated like a king for the next year.

The current tradition with the plastic baby began in New Orleans in the 1940s, where it was originally a porcelain baby. Nowadays, the person who gets the plastic baby Jesus is responsible for providing the cake at the following year's celebration. Because king cakes were first associated with the 12th day of Christmas, also called the Epiphany or the feast of the three kings, many believe that the baby in the cake represents baby Jesus, though this is not universally accepted.

The colors found on the cake, and in all things Mardi Gras, really, are featured (kind of) in the Baby Cakes' identity.

"Our colors are navy blue and gold—that dark, dark, dark navy blue, almost black looking. And then we sprinkled in our own Mardi Gras colors," Rojas said. "It's not the exact Mardi Gras colors; it's our take on it."

When you think of a minor league baseball team named for Mardi Gras, the possibilities seem endless, and all of them feel like they might end up a bit risquée. But the Baby Cakes take a different perspective on the holiday.

"Mardi Gras is more than what the rest of the world perceives it as," Rojas said. "It's not Bourbon Street. It's about families getting together and celebrating that time of the year."

He continued, "When we came up with the name Baby Cakes, it's really taking the whole king cake concept, flipping it on its ear, and focusing on the baby itself, and the cake.... Minor league baseball brings families and people together to have a good time, just like a king cake does."

Of course, the name and the Brandiose-designed logos generated a reaction when they were announced before the 2017 season, much of it predictably negative, because that's always how it goes with these outlandish rebrands.

"No one likes change. No one enthusiastically embraces change," Rojas said. "When it came out, the response was crazy, there was anger, there was passion, and it stirred something in people."

When fans were voting on a new nickname last season, Rojas went incognito and walked around the stadium listening to conversations. He would hear fans would say how they hoped the team wouldn't go with that crazy Baby Cakes nickname, but when Rojas interjected to see which names they preferred, more often than not, they couldn't even remember the other options.

This leads Rojas to proclaim the mantra of minor league baseball teams everywhere: "I'd rather be loved or hated, but never ignored."

In a sport where teams like the El Paso Chihuahuas, Albuquerque Isotopes, and Richmond Flying Squirrels seem rooted in tradition because they've been around for more than a few years, it's fair to wonder how far down this wacky path minor league baseball will go. Will there be a backlash against the wacky nicknames and a return to more conservative identities?

Rojas thinks the wacky nicknames are here to stay, because that's what the game is about, and he's glad to see the Baby Cakes contribute to it.

"I do see that we are part of that trajectory of really coming up with something that allows minor league baseball to keep its identity as fun and not taking itself overly serious," he said.

To be sure, the Baby Cakes are named for a significant cultural tradition in a unique location—the fact that the logo is based on a plastic toy that may or may not represent baby Jesus makes this backstory one of the most interesting in a landscape where it's harder every day to be noticed.

Normal Cornbelters

Normal Cornbelters
2009–present

Current Team Data

Class
Independent

League
Frontier

The plains of the midwestern United States are defined in many ways by their most prominent crop. Last year, four states produced more than a billion bushels of corn each: Iowa, Illinois, Nebraska, and Minnesota.

"They refer to it as the Corn Belt," said Steve Malliet, founder, president, and general manager of the Normal Cornbelters, an independent baseball team that plays in Normal, Illinois. "We're right in the middle of it right here, Corn Production, USA."

When they debuted in 2010, the Cornbelters seized on the importance of the corn industry, in part because it really is super important ("We happen to be in the richest corn-producing area in the entire world right here—at least it is in the United States," Malliet said), and also because the second option seemed even more boring.

"By far the agriculture business here is our number one," Malliet said. "The economy here is wrapped around that—that and insurance."

So the team set about creating a team identity based on the corn industry that would accomplish some specific goals.

First, Malliet said, "We wanted to do something a little bit different, that wasn't the same as everybody else."

This was accomplished with a logo created by Chris Henwood of JanSport that is part ear of corn and part Bill the Cat from *Bloom County*. "People have noticed the googly eyes, and it's different," Malliet said.

Second, they didn't want to hurt any feelings.

"What we didn't want to do was offend anybody in this process," Malliet said. "We tried to be careful. We worked with the Illinois Corn Growers Association to make sure that we didn't do that, that we weren't poking fun at anybody or the industry because we have a lot of respect for it."

Finally, they wanted it to sell. Independent baseball teams don't have access to some of the resources that affiliated teams benefit from, so a strong brand is essential if you want people to take notice.

"Minor league baseball does a great job of pushing the logos and marketing them," Malliet said. "You're pretty much on your own when you're marketing your logo here."

That said, the Cornbelters were almost not the Cornbelters. They toyed with the idea of going by the name Nuts ("Normal Nuts" has merit as both a team name and a medical diagnosis), but decided against it because the Single-A Rockies affiliate Modesto Nuts was already using it. (And the other option, Nutz with a Z to avoid a conflict, was terrible.)

Then came the name-the-team contest that ended in controversy and had to be scratched when a certain late-night television host's fans got hold of it. One of the options in the online name-the-team contest was the Normal Coal Bears, ostensibly a reference to the city's ties to coal mining. The team's fans would be called Coal Bear Nation, which sounds an awful lot like the nickname ascribed to Stephen Colbert's fan base.

"One of our partners came up with the idea, and thought it would be fun and kind of a lark," Malliet said. "It ended up being pretty serious when, all the sudden, we've got a million votes for Coal Bears. It seemed that the votes were coming in at 3,000 per minute or something like that."

While Colbert himself did not encourage fans to vote for Coal Bears, outlets like Deadspin, the forum on SportsLogos.net, and an organization that called itself the Normal Coal Bear Alliance got hold of the story and advocated for the name.

"We let everyone know, obviously this isn't right, and we're going to make sure that name of the team is a legitimate name that people around here will know and respect," Malliet said.

That name, of course, ended up being the Cornbelters. It's a name that has achieved the goals the team set out for, which Malliet confirms every time he sees a person wearing his team's hat during his many travels.

"They always strike up a conversation. If you're wearing a Yankees hat, that doesn't always strike up a conversation," Malliet said. "What I love about it is that, like minor league baseball, it's different and it's fun. That's what we try to be for our fans."

For an independent minor league baseball team, the struggle for branding success is an uphill battle (even in the corn fields of Normal, Illinois, where there are no hills). The ability to take a topic that might not set fans' imaginations ablaze from the outset and turn it into one of the sport's more noteworthy brands is a considerable accomplishment.

Pensacola Blue Wahoos

Pensacola Blue Wahoos
2012–present

Current Team Data

Parent
Cincinnati Reds

Class
Double-A

League
Southern

The wahoo is a fish that is strong, fierce, and delicious. The fish featured in the Pensacola Blue Wahoos' logo is the one that got away. You can tell by the hook in his mouth attached to the broken fishing line that he snapped through pure, brute force.

"The wahoo is actually quite a fighter," said Donna Kirby, the team's director of promotions and community relations since its inception in 2012. "It's a very, very strong fish out there in the Gulf."

While the hook in the fish's mouth is important symbolically, it's often not the first thing fans notice. "A lot of people overlook the hook," Kirby said. "The point of that hook is that he's busted through it. He's not being caught. That wahoo is strong and dominant and he's busting off that hook."

Of course, some actual wahoos out there in the Gulf aren't so lucky. The wahoo is a popular fish among deep sea fishing charters in the Gulf—and yes, it is on the menu at Pensacola Bayfront Stadium. "I kind of feel like it's cannibalistic for me to even mention this," Kirby said, "but when you're filleting wahoo or when you're grilling wahoo, it's delicious. It is so good. It almost has a steak flavor to it."

Given the popularity of the wahoo among sports fishermen and eaters of fish, it's not surprising that the community relates to the team's name. "We get people who send us pictures all the time of, hey I was out fishing this weekend and caught a wahoo," Kirby said. "I always feel weird about it."

The Blue Wahoos of the Double-A Southern League are a Cincinnati affiliate—part of a colorful journey that Reds players take through the minor league system. The name Wahoos was suggested by a number of people in a name-the-team contest held through the *Pensacola News Journal*, but the team had concerns that the name would conflict legally with the University of Virginia, who are officially the Cavaliers but also go by the Wahoos.

BRIAN MAST

"We thought, you know what," Kirby said, "with all the water we've got around here, we've got such pretty skies usually, why don't we tag blue on the front of that and call ourselves the Blue Wahoos?"

While blue is the team's primary color, their accent color, known as rubine red by fans of the Pantone Matching System, has become increasingly prominent. After some initial hesitation about how hot pink would be received by players and fans, the team committed to its unique color scheme with a promotion called Pinko de Mayo in 2012, during which the team wore an alternate jersey in all pink.

"Clobber Fish"

"We put them on the guys and we thought, what are the players going to think of this? They ate it up," Kirby said. "Every time they wore the pink jersey, the team won. So that became quickly, you're never ever taking those jerseys off, right? Every Sunday, they wear those pink jerseys."

Part of rubine red's appeal is that it is unique. "You see so many typical colors across the board," Kirby said. "They're nice, we have nothing against those, but we wanted to have some sort of an accent color that makes it pop, and the pink really did the trick for us on that. It's taken on a life of its own."

The Wahoos' most popular secondary logo is one that the team refers to internally as "Clobber Fish," whose show of strength is perhaps slightly less subtle than the primary logo's snapped fishing line. (Before I spoke to Donna, I thought of this logo as Joe Pesci Fish.) Another popular secondary logo is the P-hook, a fishing hook bent to resemble the letter P. "Guys on the golf course love to have that on their polos," Kirby said.

The Blue Wahoos' mascot, Kazoo, was voted the Southern League's most popular in 2013's "Mascot Mania" contest conducted by Minor League Baseball. (Kazoo could not be reached for comment on how he feels walking around a stadium filled with people eating grilled wahoo.)

P-hook

Initially, there was some resistance to the announcement that a team would be relocating to the well-established city of Pensacola. ("They say it's America's oldest city," Kirby said.) But the team has made being a prominent and socially responsible member of the community a priority, and those initial misgivings have been overcome. The team was the Southern League's nominee for the John Henry Moss community service award in 2013, and their Kazoo Cares Foundation supports local children interested in baseball.

One of the first moments when Kirby felt that the team was being accepted by the community came at a popular public event called Gallery Night when they first unveiled the logo, which was designed by the prolific firm Brandiose. "The crowd went wild. The crowd just immediately embraced it," Kirby said. "I think that was a bonding moment." (It also doesn't hurt in terms of community buy-in that the team's stadium was named 2013's number one minor league ballpark and number 11 overall stadium experience in the USA and Canada by *Stadium Journey*.)

As with all successful identities, the Blue Wahoos make specific connections to their community and surrounding with the choice of a nickname and a strong logo design. In a cluttered and competitive minor league logo landscape, the Blue Wahoos stand out in large part because of a unique color palette. And also, let's be honest, because their logo is just so darned delicious.

Reading Fightin Phils

Reading Fightin Phils
2013–present

Current Team Data

Parent
Philadelphia Philles

Class
Double-A

League
Eastern

The Reading Fightin Phils, Double-A affiliate of the Philadelphia Phillies, have stories to tell. Lots of stories. They play in a historic ballpark that has received tons of accolades. They have the longest-running affiliation with their parent club of any team in the minors. They play in a part of the country called Baseballtown because of roots in the sport that date back to 1858. And they have a regionally famous hot dog vendor who wears a costume that makes it look like he's riding an ostrich.

"That's a tough story to tell," said the team's general manager Scott Hunsicker. "It's an especially tough story to tell if your name's Reading Phillies and your logo is really just an R that's always kind of looked like a P."

After 46 years as the Reading Phillies, the team decided that it was time for a change before the 2013 season. They were walking the fine line between wanting to honor and celebrate their parent club, which plays just 50 miles away, and doing something fun and unique to give them their own identity.

"If you're the Reading Phillies and your logo's basically a Phillies P with a kickstand on it, you're playing hard the Phillies card," Hunsicker said. "While it's cool to be the Reading Phillies, we were always just the little Phillies." (To be fair, the Reading Phillies' logo wasn't always just a P with a kickstand. It featured a train for many years, because of the Reading Railroad, but as Hunsicker points out, "It's not really the most fun, progressive angle to take from an iconic logo standpoint.... Not everyone thinks trains are cool anymore.")

With the beginning of the 2013 season, the team went from one of the most conservative looks in minor league baseball to one of the wackiest. The Reading Fightin Phils, as they are now called, took to the field with a primary logo that featured an ostrich and a cap logo that featured a punching fist. Not only that, but they sometimes wore uniforms with a completely separate name and hot dog-themed identity. Lost amid the wackiness, though, was an attention to detail and an homage to history that baseball fans would love if they had noticed it.

"I think so many people got caught up on the hot dog with the mustard and the different color palette on the uniform and the ostrich with the hair on his leg," Hunsicker said. "If there was one regret through that whole period of time, it was some of the stuff that got missed."

In putting their uniforms together, the team went back in their parent club's history to 1950: "Literally having a game-worn uniform from the Whiz Kids team and putting that under a microscope and replicating the chain stitch and going through pattern after pattern

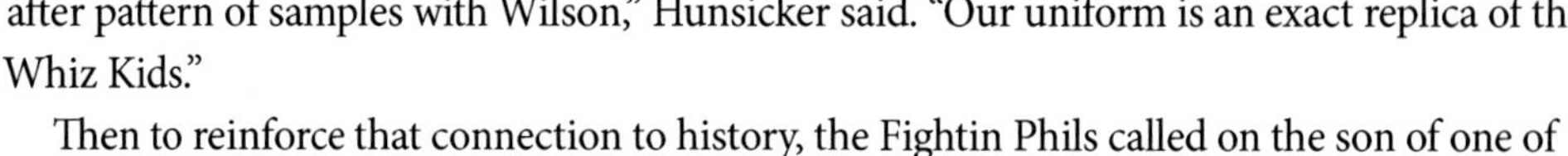

after pattern of samples with Wilson," Hunsicker said. "Our uniform is an exact replica of the Whiz Kids."

Then to reinforce that connection to history, the Fightin Phils called on the son of one of the most beloved figures in Philadelphia sports history. The first night they wore their new uniforms, the ceremonial first pitch was thrown out by Richie Ashburn, Jr., whose father played on that Whiz Kids team and served alongside the legendary Harry Kalas in the broadcast booth for decades. He wore a jersey that was an exact match of his father's, "except it didn't say Phillies, it said Fightin Phils," Hunsicker said.

"I think some of that direct lineage to the Phillies kind of got whitewashed with the ostrich and the Baseball Town and all that stuff," Hunsicker said, "which is a shame because for people that care about that sort of historical perspective, I'm not sure that they really got a chance to hear all that."

What fans did hear about was the team's outrageous new identity—two outrageous new identities, actually—that featured a combatant ostrich and an anthropomorphized hot dog.

The first point of order in developing the new identity was the name. The nickname Fightin Phils, or Fightins for short, is often used by fans as a nickname for the big-league club, so it maintained that connection, but still gave the team some flexibility.

"The most important reason of our long-term success is the Phillies affiliation," Hunsicker said. "Long story short, that's how we arrived at Fightin Phils and how we sort of evolved to use Fightins."

It's worth noting for people who get twitchy about grammar and usage that there is no apostrophe in the abbreviated word "Fightin" in the team's name. One of the reasons for this? "Apostrophes can be tough, even for English majors," Hunsicker said.

Also of note is that Fightin begins with an *F* insted of *Ph*, which would reinforce the alliteration visually. "Eliminating the *Ph* and eliminating the apostrophe was eliminating two more variables," Hunsicker explained. "We ended up with a one-color, simple wordmark with no apostrophe and no *Ph*, which we think is more historically accurate with the way that Fightins fans over the years that did call the Phillies that are kind of used to."

Next up is where things started getting weird. The team's primary logo, designed by Brandiose, features an ostrich, which at first glance has nothing to do with rural Pennsylvania. (Hunsicker did offer, "Agriculture is the number one industry in Berks County, and while ostrich farming is not the number one industry in Berks County, farming is.")

The real connection to ostriches in Reading is the Crazy Hot Dog Vendor, portrayed for more than a decade by Matt Jackson, the team's Executive Director of Graphic Arts and Game Entertainment. The Crazy Hot Dog Vendor dresses like a guy riding an ostrich, slinging hot dogs into the crowd. It's not the sort of connection you typically base a logo on, but the Crazy Hot Dog Vendor is a huge deal in Reading.

"He has achieved that status. It's remarkable," Hunsicker said. "We went through a bazillion different animals and ideas—they weren't all animals—we came to realize that this Crazy Hot Dog Vendor and the fact that he rides an ostrich was worth it."

That said, Hunsicker is aware that not everyone gets the connection. "For people in this region, he really has reached that status," he said. "For people outside of this region, having any ostrich involved with us probably seems completely weird."

Even though the logo is a bit out there, it reflects a time-tested tradition, "It's kind of the 'take an animal, make it kind of cool' model," Hunsicker said. "It's existed forever."

The team's other logos include the letter F with a fist terminating a horizontal stroke and a feathered letter R for Reading. While kids are drawn to the ostrich logos, the other logos appeal to different generations. "We have the feathered R. That's for the old-timers that saw Roger Maris and Rocky Colavito," Hunsicker said. "Then the F-fist hat would be kind of our lead hat. The F-fist is very indicative of today, current."

As if all of this were not enough, the Fightins have a completely different identity, called Baseballtown as an homage to the region's Baseballtown Charities. "Baseballtown has been around for a long time, and it speaks to more than just the Reading Fightins," Hunsicker said. "We've got thousands of kids that have played baseball now directly as a result of Baseballtown Charities."

The Fightin Phils keep live ostriches outside the stadium.

The identity features Bunbino the hot dog and a mustard-themed script, and allows the team to market paraphernalia to fans who may not want to wear Phillies gear.

"We really felt like, well you know what, if the Cubs have a bunch of Wrigley Field stuff and the Red Sox have a bunch of Fenway Park stuff, if you're coming here, we should have a lot of Baseballtown stuff," Hunsicker said. "The easiest way to achieve that is to wear some of it on the field. Because once you wear it on the field it really becomes part of who you are."

"At the same time, though, we didn't feel like we wanted to force the same color palette and everything on Baseballtown," Hunsicker said. "We've always liked that it was a different color palette. It was obviously heavy lifting to figure out a way to possibly accomplish it."

One of the benefits to the team's new identity (or identities) is that they can now participate in the Minor League Baseball Little League uniform program. After years of seeing teams of local children showing up to Reading Phillies games wearing gear from other teams around the country, Reading wanted to see their own brand represented.

"Why do the Toledo Mud Hens and the Durham Bulls and the Lake Elsinore Storm get to have that?" Hunsicker asked. "Not because of the merchandise sales, but just because I think that the people that have come to the games here since 1967 deserve that. Why would a kid in Toledo not be able to learn about us? They didn't even know that we existed."

With so many stories to tell, it's no wonder the Reading Fightin Phils' visual identity is so diverse. They have a rich history, which includes, among much else, the first professional game and the first professional home run of Hall of Famer Mike Schmidt, who would hit 548 dingers for the big-league club. There is more incentive than usual for them to maintain close visual ties with their parent club because of the duration of their relationship with the Phillies as well as their geographic proximity.

But they also exist in a world of increasingly edgy minor league logos, and a boring identity just won't fly. (Technically, ostriches don't fly either, but that's neither here nor there.) It's safe to say that they're the only team in sports that started the process of designing its uniform by analyzing 65-year-old fabric swatches, then based its new identity on a wacky costume worn by one of its hot dog vendors.

They're attempting to walk the rather wide line between tradition and wackiness, and while what most people notice is the fighting ostrich and the grimacing hot dog, it's all built on a foundation of a history that goes back decades.

Richmond Flying Squirrels

Richmond Flying Squirrels
2010–present

Current Team Data

Parent
San Francisco Giants

Class
Double-A

League
Eastern

The Richmond Flying Squirrels, Double-A affiliate of the San Francisco Giants, are among the most popular and distinct minor league baseball team identities out there, but the team name was not well received when it was first announced before the 2010 season. In a city with a storied baseball history that dates back to 1884, a newfangled and unusual logo was not the norm. I spoke with Jon Laaser, the Squirrels' director of broadcasting and media relations, about the team's name and mascot.

"[The reaction] was overtly negative here when we unveiled Flying Squirrels," Laaser said. "But when you get past that shock value and you actually see how things are going to play out, and you see how the team looks in the uniforms and you see how it sounds when you're broadcasting the game and, you know, what it looks like on a T-shirt, it's easier to identify with."

The Flying Squirrels, who were previously the Connecticut Defenders, debuted in 2010, just a year after the Triple-A Richmond Braves moved to Georgia to become the Gwinnett Braves. Baseball fans in the city were glad to have a team, but the Squirrels had some obstacles to overcome.

"We wanted to differentiate between some of the apathy that was associated with the Braves and some of the outdated thinking in terms of promotion," Laaser said.

I had long believed that the name came from a name-the-team contest held by the city's newspaper, *The Richmond Times-Dispatch*. (It says so on Wikipedia!) So I was shocked to learn that the team name in fact has its humble origins in a barber shop poster.

The true story of how the team name originated ("which we haven't made all that public," Laaser said, "but it's probably far enough down the road now that it wouldn't matter") is that Chief Executive Manager Chuck Domino was at a barber shop and saw a poster on the wall with animals indigenous to Virginia. "He saw flying squirrels on there and it jumped out to him," Laaser said. "He immediately said to our vice president Todd Parnell, 'That's what the name is going to be.'"

This prompted a question I've long held about the Squirrels. Are there actually flying squirrels in Richmond? I lived there for a decade and I don't recall ever seeing one. According to the Virginia Department of Game and Inland Fisheries, the southern flying squirrel *(Glaucomys volans volans)* "is present throughout Virginia except in the westernmost tip." According to Laaser, "There are flying squirrels in Virginia, certainly not prevalent, not something you'd see all that much just walking down the street, but not totally out of left field."

The Flying Squirrels are part of an obvious and awesome trend in minor league baseball in recent years towards wacky logos. ("There was wackiness in minor league baseball before we came along," Laaser said.) But there's a limit, according to Laaser, "You can't just throw a name out there and say, 'Yeah, it's wacky, deal with it.' There's an intelligence that goes along with the way you brand it and market it."

With their sleek logo and kid-friendly mascot Nutzy, the Flying Squirrels were trying to create "something that the guy that owns the tattoo shop … something that the surly guy can wear on a hat and feel comfortable in the rough and tumble world that he lives in and something that kids can wear as well."

Clearly, the Squirrels have done their job. They've regularly ranked among the top 25 in minor league baseball merchandise sales in an increasingly competitive marketplace, according to MiLB.com. (This explains why I felt so compelled to buy a Squirrels T-shirt the last time I was in Richmond.)

The Diamond in Richmond, Virginia

I was glad to get a representative of the team on the phone because I wanted an official response to something that I've heard about this logo ever since it was first unveiled: Is it on purpose that the logo is shaped like the state of Virginia?

"We'd love to take credit for that and having the brilliant foresight for that to be the case," Laaser said, "but in the interest of full disclosure, that was somewhat coincidental.… Someone pointed that out to us about a week after we unveiled the logos back in the fall of 2009 and we looked at it and said, 'Well, I'll be damned, they're right.'"

Now well established, ol' *Glaucomys volans volans* has overcome the initial misgivings of fans. The future of the Flying Squirrels themselves may hinge on how things turn out with the team's protracted discussions about plans to (finally, hopefully) build a stadium in downtown Richmond. However, the team's logo and identity are firmly entrenched as one of the most popular in the minors.

Savannah Bananas

Savannah Bananas
2016–present

Current Team Data

Class
Collegiate Summer

League
Coastal Plain

When you go to the website for the Savannah Bananas, a summer collegiate-level team in the Coastal Plain League, the first thing you see, in big, bold, all caps type, is this slogan: WE MAKE BASEBALL FUN. When it comes to telling the story behind the team's nickname, that's pretty much all you need to know.

In many cases, minor league baseball teams tie their nicknames to some quirky, little-known fact about their hometown. (That's the whole point of this book.) So when I started researching this story, I half expected to learn that the town of Savannah, Georgia, had some tie to banana-based agriculture. Perhaps there was a team of banana scientists in a Savannah lab cultivating a climate change-resistant species of the yellow fruit, or the local Piggly Wiggly (which I assume exists) holds the record for most bananas sold in a single week, or a graduate of a Savannah high school is working to fight global hunger through a banana-awareness campaign.

The truth is this: When "Savannah Bananas" was submitted on the first day of a name-the-team contest that brought in more than 1,000 suggestions in the fall of 2015, staff members couldn't get it out of their heads.

"We kept going back to it. Savannah Bananas. Savannah Bananas. Savannah Bananas. Savannah Bananas," said team president Jared Orton. "There's no rhyme or reason to it, except that it just fits." (And also, there *literally is* a rhyme to it.)

The Bananas were about to open up operations in a town that had lost its minor league team, and were fighting for the attention of a fan base that might have been a bit jaded.

"We had a huge lunch event where we announced the name-the-team contest, and literally no one cared," said team owner Jesse Cole. "It was a tremendous struggle for me and my wife as owners, because no one was buying into the team."

So with nothing more than a funny little rhyme for rationale, the team turned to noted designer Dan Simon of Studio Simon to turn this fun name into a legitimate brand.

"The minute that name was told to me, it put a smile on my face," Simon said. "I just couldn't help but smile."

And while smiling is great and all (it's my favorite) the team wanted Simon to think about the project another way.

"Our first question was, can you create an angry, fierce, intimidating banana?" Orton said.

Simon took to the drawing board, and approached the project as seriously as you could expect of a person who has just been asked to create an angry piece of fruit.

"When we talk about these outrageous names that a number of these minor league teams are going with these days," Simon said, "one of the mistakes that is made with the development of those identities is, when you take an outrageous name and you couple it with an equally outrageous piece of artwork, then it's too much. That's why a lot of these identities are poorly received. It's overkill."

As with any project, there was much back and forth about the details. "If you could see some of the emails exchanged," Orton said. "At one point, the banana had teeth. At one point, we're trying to figure out if the banana was left handed or right handed. We're talking about this fruit object."

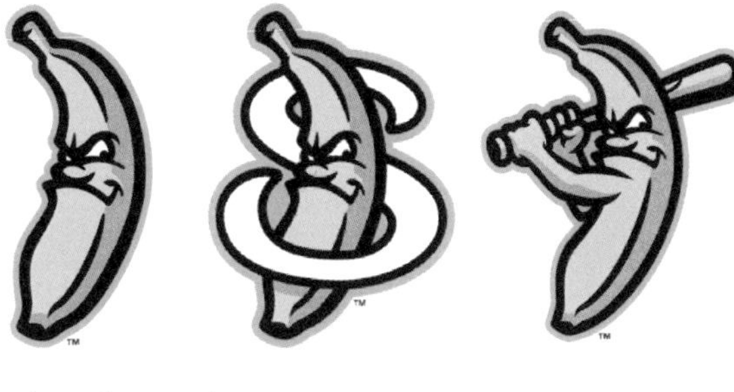

Orton was home for Christmas when Simon delivered the artwork, and he loved it. Orton proudly showed it to his family, who might have wondered what he was putting in his egg nog. "They're like, what are you talking about? What is this logo? This is the dumbest thing we've ever seen in our lives," he said.

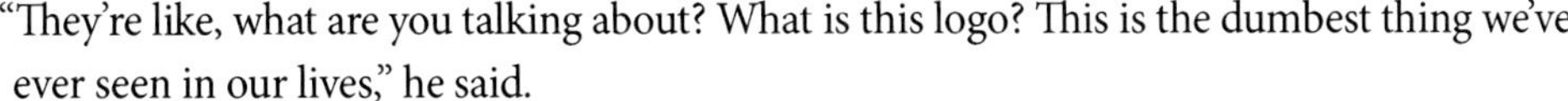

In the end, the brand immediately caught the attention of the national media, not to mention merchandise-buyers from all 50 states. That's the function of a name that people liked and solid design.

"As crazy as it sounds to say these words, that banana looks like he was born to play baseball and he should be playing baseball," Simon said. "That's the key to taking an outrageous direction and getting it to be embraced by fans across the United States and more specifically in the community where the team plays."

All of this might seem a bit much for a collegiate summer-level team, but the branding in that market is following the lead set by professional teams at all levels.

"A number of summer collegiate teams have been using the minor league baseball model as far operations of their business goes," Simon said.

SAVANNAH BANANAS

The team even has its own craft beer, a Banana Cream Ale brewed by Savannah's Service Brewing Company. (If there's one industry that has tried to match the wackiness of minor league baseball step for step, it's craft brewing, so this is a match made in heaven.)

"It is a true banana ale that does taste like bananas," Orton said, "and people love it."

The branding has obviously paid dividends. In a town that had just lost its minor league team, the Savannah Sand Gnats, the Bananas broke the Coastal Plain League attendance record in their first season, selling out 17 of their 24 home games. In 2016, they ranked second in average attendance out of 160 collegiate summer league teams nationwide, trailing only the Madison Mallards. At any level, it seems, a fun name (even one with no real backstory) and a solid brand are going to be successful.

Scranton/Wilkes-Barre RailRiders

Scranton/Wilkes-Barre RailRiders
2013–present

Current Team Data

Parent
New York Yankees

Class
Triple-A

League
International

When I first saw the logo for the Scranton/Wilkes-Barre RailRiders, which features a porcupine riding a rail, one obvious question leapt to my mind: Where the heck did a porcupine riding a rail come from? Turns out I'm not the only one. I spoke with the team's president and general manager Rob Crain, and here's what he had to say:

"I've talked to a lot of folks about our name and our colors, and the main question you get is, 'Where the heck did a porcupine riding a rail come from?'"

The rail aspect of the logo makes perfect sense. It comes from the rich train-related history in northeastern Pennsylvania. Scranton is home to Steamtown National Historic Site, which features railroad museums and functioning historic steam engines. Also, the city was the site of the first functional electric trolley system in 1886, earning Scranton the nickname "The Electric City" (which led to Michael Scott and Dwight Schrute's hilarious rap, "Scranton: The Electric City" on *The Office*). The RailRiders' stadium itself has a trolley barn in left field, and fans can take an actual trolley to games.

"You're kind of going back in history," Crain said. "You're going back to items that have been ingrained in our community, and that's where the RailRiders came from."

So that's where the train part comes from. The second element—a porcupine that probably has a lot of bugs in his teeth—is even easier to explain. "The porcupine is an animal here in northeastern Pennsylvania," Crain said. (It's true that there are porcupines in Pennsylvania. The nocturnal animal naturally has a top speed of two miles per hour—until you put it on a railroad track. Then it's a lot faster.)

What catches most people's eyes, and prompts the obvious question about the logo, is the fact that those two easily explained elements are combined in one logo. Alternate logos feature other mash-ups of porcupines and railroads, including the porcupine train coming right at us, the conductor's hat on a baseball bat, and the porcupine conductor.

The reason that the railroad and the porcupine are combined is also pretty simple: According to MiLB.com, RailRiders and porcupines were the top two vote-getters in the team's name-the-team contest, so rather than choose one, the team went with both. (The team's mascot is a porcupine named Quill.)

The RailRiders, Triple-A affiliate of the New York Yankees, began playing with their new identity in 2013. From 2007 to 2012, the team was known simply as the Scranton/Wilkes-Barre Yankees. The decision to move away from Yankees—a classic name with deep roots—in favor of a porcupine train was met with mixed reactions.

"Changing from a name like the Yankees was one of those that definitely got some attention," Crain said. "The Yankees name here in this market is very polarizing, and you could probably say the same thing around the entire country.… In northeastern Pennsylvania, you've got Yankees fans, you've got Phillies fans, you've got Mets, you've got Red Sox, you've got Pirates, you've got everybody. You've really got to make it, no matter who your big league team is, you are a RailRiders fan because they're the community's franchise."

That said, the team is not trying to distance itself from its Major League affiliate. "When we changed the name, we didn't shy away from our Yankee roots," Crain said. "Our main color is navy. At home we wear pinstripe jerseys just like the Yankees do. We have the interlocking NY on our sleeves on all of our jerseys. The Yankee affiliation, we're very, very proud of. So we didn't want to hide that, but we also wanted to create our own."

The rebranding coincided with a massive renovation of the team's stadium, PNC Field. "One of the things about changing the name, one of the big parts was it was kind of a rebirth for us," Crain said. "The Yankees were, we'll say old stadium, and now the RailRiders are part of the new ballpark.… It was kind of a designation of a new era of minor league baseball here in northeastern Pennsylvania."

Crain emphasized during our conversation that choosing a minor league team name should be a "hyper-local" process. With their new nickname and logo, the RailRiders have seized on not one but two facets of their community, and in doing so have achieved their goal of establishing their own unique identity. The decision to combine two seemingly disparate elements in one logo makes you look twice, and it gives the RailRiders one of the most distinct looks in an increasingly wacky minor league nickname landscape.

Sugar Land Skeeters

Sugar Land Skeeters
2010–present

Current Team Data

Class
Independent

League
Atlantic

There are two things residents of Sugar Land, Texas, associate with their town. The first is the Imperial Sugar Company, headquartered there since moving from Louisiana in 1907. The second is mosquitoes, which are probably going to be a problem when you build a town on swampy marshland.

First, the sweet stuff. While the Imperial Sugar Company's original refinery in Sugar Land is closed, the company keeps its headquarters there. In fact, the Imperial Sugar Company is such an important part of Sugar Land that the city's official seal includes a crown from the company's logo.

So when a new Atlantic League of Professional Baseball team moved to town in 2010, it's no surprise that a name-the-team contest turn up some sweet ideas from fans—but the vote eventually produced a name with a little more bite.

"There were a lot of sugar-related names," said JT Onyett, the team's assistant general manager. "But they did a vote and it came down to the Skeeters."

At first blush, this might be something of a surprise, since mosquitoes—which have tested positive for West Nile Virus in Sugar Land in recent years, and which the city routinely attempts to exterminate using a battalion of trucks roaming the city pumping bug spray into the air—are not exactly beloved in the area.

"Mosquitoes, obviously, are not the best part of living here," Onyett said. "If you've been down here, you know that there are a lot of mosquitoes with the weather and the climate that we have. Mosquitoes are rampant around here."

That said, with a little bit of work and the right marketing, mosquitoes make for a fun identity for an independent baseball team's nickname and logo. (One of the team's major sponsors is a pest control company, which makes light of the fact that it's not trying to exterminate the team itself.)

"Everyone's got a dog or other normal mascot type thing, so having this pest, it kind of takes it to a different element," Onyett said. "I wouldn't say there's a huge benefit to being a bug or a pest, but we definitely have fun with the fact that we are."

But the team didn't just adopt the name Mosquitoes. They went with Skeeters, a common (but not universal) nickname for the pests. Onyett, who moved from southern California to work for the team, was not exactly sure what he was getting into.

"When I started looking at coming out here, I was kind of like, 'A Skeeter?'" said Onyett. "I had never heard of that. My family back in California, when I first took the job, was kind of like, 'What's a Skeeter?' Around here, everyone knows."

The logo attempts to walk that fine line between appealing to both kids and adults, all while trying to make a biting, disease-carrying nuisance a loveable mascot.

"I think our mosquito-looking guy, he looks tenacious enough but still fun," Onyett said. "It's not like there's a clown on the logo or something like that, that an adult would not wear out in public."

While the team went with a mosquito-based logo, they didn't ignore sugar altogether in their identity. The logo set, designed by Brandiose, evokes sugar cane in its lettering. And lest you forget where Texas's biggest sugar company is located, the primary mark features a cartoon mosquito skewering an outline of Texas like a push pin marking a map. And the colors, officially called rawhide yellow, imperial blue, and refinery red, have a kind-of sugary taste them.

Before the mosquitoes moved to town in 2012, the region had not had minor league baseball since the Houston Buffaloes (the first-ever minor league team to be affiliated with a Major League club) left town more than a half-century earlier in 1961. It was important that the Skeeters get it right to get the fans on their side.

"I think a big thing that this team had to do when they came here was get the community buy-in," Onyett said.

They appear to have done something right, because not only do the Skeeters, the first Atlantic League club located anywhere but the Northeast, have solid fan support, they've also caught the attention of some notable names in the sport.

While the Skeeters' roster has seen the likes of Major Leaguers like Jason Lane and Scott Kazmir, the first name that pops to mind for most baseball fans is one with a little more history behind it.

Roger Clemens famously pitched two games with the team in 2012, in part because his son was a catcher with the Skeeters, but also, some speculated, because he might be trying to catch the attention of the nearby Houston Astros.

In 2014, another Skeeters pitcher of note was Tracy McGrady, the NBA star who tried to turn to baseball after his basketball career ended. McGrady pitched half a season with the team before hanging up his cleats.

The Sugar Land Skeeters could have gone with a sugar-based identity and it likely would have been unremarkable. Instead, the Skeeters have taken a bug that most people actively try to kill with their bare hands and attempted to turn it into a fun identity. It's the sort of thing that can backfire if done poorly, but done right, it's one of the more notable identities in independent minor league baseball.

Wichita Wingnuts

Wichita Wingnuts
2008–present

Current Team Data

Class
Independent

League
American Association

Wichita, the largest city in the state of Kansas, is inextricably tied to the aviation industry. During the 1900s, the city produced more airplanes than any other. Six aircraft manufacturers were founded in Wichita in the 1920s and 1930s, and the industry would be responsible for more jobs than any other in the state of Kansas. While aviation in Wichita shifts and changes with the times, it's still a huge part of the culture and economy there.

So it stands to reason that the city's independent minor league baseball team would take on a name related to aviation. The name includes the word "wings," a pretty darned important part of a plane, and "nuts," a pretty darned important part of baseball.

"It can be seen as the fans being nuts for their wings," said Rob Low, the team's Broadcasting and Media Relations Manager.

The whole "Nuts" thing is such a prevalent part of the team's identity that they use just that word on some of their hats and jerseys, and they use it in tongue-in-cheek promotions, as with the "Nut Crusher" pick-up truck that is parked outside the stadium.

Another connection between the Wichita Wingnuts and the aviation industry is that wing nuts are hardware, and hardware is used to make airplanes. Though this is not a relationship you want to analyze too closely, as you'll see below.

"It's supposed to be a play on Wichita's nickname as the air capital of the world," Low said. "It's sort of a tip of the cap to that, with wing nuts being a common piece of hardware for aircraft construction."

I have never built an airplane myself, so being a vigilant journalist, I thought it would be worthwhile to confirm the role of wing nuts in aviation. I reached out to Brian Trosko, an instrumentation engineer with a major aircraft manufacturer.

"I've never seen a wing nut on an airplane," he said. "Whole point of wing nuts is they're easy to fasten/unfasten with just your fingers. That's not what you look for in something that holds an airplane together."

To give the team the benefit of the doubt, though, you could still argue that wing nuts are tangentially related to the industry. The document "Fasteners in the Aerospace Industry" by El Camino College in California—something I never thought I would read—states, "Wing nuts are commonly used on battery connections or hose clamps where proper tightness can be obtained by hand."

So from my perspective at the bottom of this minor league baseball nickname rabbit hole, I say it's legitimate to loosely connect (as it were!) wing nuts with aviation, and that's good enough

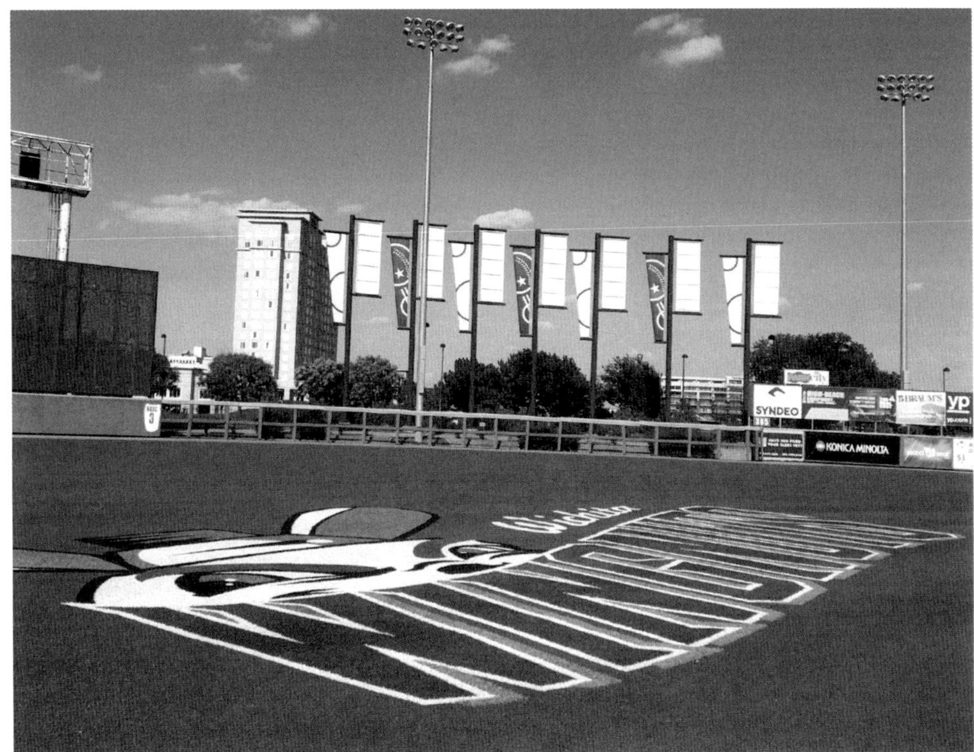

justification for a fun logo and nickname. That said, I hope no one's using wing nuts to actually attached wings to airplanes.

Of course, this connection between the Wingnuts nickname and the aviation industry is news to some—including the players wearing the uniforms. I attended a Wingnuts game and spoke with two players on the team, infielder Zack Cox and outfielder Brent Clevlen.

I asked Zack Cox, 2010 first-round draft pick of the St. Louis Cardinals, in his first season with the team, why they were called the Wingnuts. He paused, then said, "I have no idea." After thinking for a moment, he touched on two basic reasons any team chooses their nickname: creativity and alliteration. "It's pretty unique to be called a Wingnut, and Wichita Wingnuts kind of flows pretty good."

I turned to Brent Clevlen, who has been with the Wingnuts (among other teams) off and on since 2011. "To be honest, I have no idea why we're called the Wingnuts." Then, perhaps highlighting that it takes a special kind of nerd to care this much about the origin stories of minor league baseball nicknames, "I've never had anyone ask me about the name before."

The Wingnuts had a tough act to follow when they debuted in 2008. They assumed the Wichita baseball mantle from another team with a red W logo, the Double-A Wichita Wranglers. The Wranglers played in the city from 1987 to 2007 as affiliates of the Padres and Royals, featuring the likes of Johnny Damon, Alex Gordon, and Andy Benes, before leaving to become the Northwest Arkansas Naturals.

The Wingnuts' logo was created by Associated Advertising in Wichita, and it found immediate success when it was unveiled. In a bracket-style tournament conducted by CNBC in 2008, the Wingnuts were selected by tournament organizer and then-CNBC Sports Business Reporter Darren Rovell (yes, that Darren Rovell) as one of the 64 best minor league baseball logos. They advanced through fan voting all the way to the championship match-up before finally losing to the Southern Illinois Miners.

"We were originally a 12-seed, if you will, and we got all the way to the final round," Low said. "And this was before we had even taken the field for a game."

The Wingnuts' identity is pretty much exactly what you'd want from an independent minor league team. It has some bad-pun double entendres, it's loosely related to an integral aspect of the local community, and it features a grimacing baseball logo with red stitching eyebrows. Now I just hope that the team will share this article around the clubhouse so the next time some really cool person at a trendy party wants to know why they're called the Wingnuts, they'll have an answer at the ready.

Dearly Departed

DEFUNCT TEAMS AND BRANDS

Nothing lasts forever, and so it is with many minor league baseball teams. The chapter that follows features teams who are no more, lost to rebranding, relocation, or contraction. While the teams are no more or the logos are no longer in use, there are just some brands will live forever. Some of these articles are in the present tense because they were written before the teams succumbed to whatever brought them down.

Sam Lynn Ballpark in Bakersfield, California, was built "backwards" so that the sun set over the center field wall, blinding batters.

Bakersfield Blaze

Bakersfield Blaze
1995–2016

Final Team Data

Parent
Seattle Mariners

Class
High-A

League
California

What Happened
The Blaze were disbanded by the California League after the 2016 season.

The 31-year-old electronic board that tells the time and temperature in center field at Historic Sam Lynn Ballpark might actually work, but the team does not turn it on. It's not an energy-saving technique; it's more about keeping fans in the stands sane.

"We don't use it," said Bakersfield Blaze assistant general manager Philip Guiry, "because we don't really need to tell people that it's 110 degrees outside and it's 8:00 at night."

But if the team is trying to keep from reminding fans about the insufferable heat in central California's San Joaquin Valley, it's a little incongruous that their mascots are named Torch and Heater, and the actual team name conjures Bakersfield's crazy hot temperatures.

"There's not much behind our name," Guiry said. "It's hot in Bakersfield. Blazing hot, some would say. Bakersfield Blaze. The end."

It also doesn't help that Historic Sam Lynn Ballpark was built in 1941 "facing backwards," as Guiry puts it. That is, during an evening game, the batter looks west, right into the (blazing) setting sun. This means that games in the dead of summer have to start as late as 8:00 to avoid blinding batters.

Perhaps because fans of the Blaze want to avoid the reality that their team is named for extreme temperatures, there are other origin stories. One such story, according to Guiry, is that during a game against Visalia in the early 1980s, the field's sprinklers went off. The team's mascot tried to stem the tide by stepping on a sprinkler head, and ended up flooding the third-base side of the infield.

"And so Visalia's pitching coach, I think, was like, 'If you just pour a little gasoline on that, it will just burn off all the water, dry it right up,'" Guiry said. "They did that and they just burned the field. So for half the season, we just played with a scorched third-base side. People have told me that's why they changed the name to the Blaze."

The only problem? "It's not true," Guiry said, "but it's a fun story." (Don't misunderstand: The fire happened. It's just not why they're called the Blaze.)

That said, there may yet be a little more to the team's identity than just the blazing heat. The use of black as a team color relates to the area's substantial oil industry ("Bakersfield is the Texas of California," Guiry said) and the orange has to do with nearby agriculture, specifically those addictive, tiny citruses called Cuties that my children eat like popcorn.

The Blaze's primary logo is a simple, traditional baseball script set in a typeface called MVB Mascot. Their original logo from 1995 was sketched on a napkin by a season-ticket holder when the team adopted the new name, then refined by a professional designer,

One way to cool off in Bakersfield is to participate in the ALS ice bucket challenge on the field during a game, which I did with the help of Philip Guiry (he's the one on the left) and mascot Heater in 2014.

The original logo

according to Guiry. Other logos along the way have included what I thought was a Toronto Maple Leaf homage and what Guiry calls the "graffiti logo," which was not exactly met with much critical acclaim. "We try to distance ourselves from it because it's kind of ugly," Guiry said. (Regarding my theory on the Maple Leafs logo: The Blaze, currently the Single-A affiliate of the Cincinnati Reds, have changed affiliations more than a dozen times since the 1940s, but they have never been affiliated with the hockey team from Toronto.)

In 1978, the team (then unaffiliated) sported what Guiry calls "the best logo in baseball history." The Bakersfield Outlaws (one of nine names the team has had since 1941) wore pill box hats and had the name of a commercial sponsor on the front of their uniforms. And yes, the logo is classic. As Guiry puts it: "SPURS AND CLEATS! I love that damn logo."

The Blaze hosted a reunion of Outlaws players and gave away retro T-shirts at a game in 2015. But for Guiry, one throwback night during the season might not be enough. He'd like to see the team consider adopting the name Outlaws again, if only just to get fans' minds off the blazing heat. "I'm trying to get us to go back to that," he said.

The Blaze's current identity, which would be its last, is fairly bland (it's a dry heat), but the team's rich and varied history gives them a lot to tap into for throwback promotions. They have been the Badgers, Boosters, Bears, and, of course, Outlaws, among many other names over the years.

While the Blaze have gone away from literally representing fire on their logo, their name and mascots still embrace the region's high temperatures. Fans know that it's hot out, but they never know what they're going to see at a game—it could be a hot young prospect, a pitcher hurling fireballs, blazing speed on the basepaths, or third base spontaneously combusting. Of course, they won't be seeing any of that until the sun goes down.

Brevard County Manatees

Brevard County Manatees
1994–2016

Final Team Data

Parent:
Milwaukee Brewers

Class
High A

League
Florida State

What Happened
The Manatees moved to Kissimmee, Florida, to become the Florida Fire Frogs.

If the rumors are true, the reason that there was a minor league baseball team called the Manatees is that fans wanted a Major League team called the Manatees, but the powers that be wouldn't allow it. Here's Kyle Smith, general manager of the Single-A Brevard County Manatees of the Florida State League:

> The rumor has it that there was a name-the-team fan voting for the Florida Marlins. The fans picked Manatees, but Wayne Huizenga didn't like the name of that, or somebody didn't like the name of that, and decided to go with Marlins. And as a reconciliation, they decided that, okay, we'll name our minor league affiliate in Brevard, our spring training home, we'll name them Manatees.

And while a Major League Baseball team named after a marine mammal that looks like a floating bratwurst with flippers might have been the greatest thing ever, Smith sort of gets it.

"I understand," he said. "If I were them I would do the same thing. It's not sleek, it's not fast, it's not sexy. Where Marlins is sleek and fast and kind of sexy, a sea cow is not."

While manatees are not sexy, they are endearing (not to mention endangered), and they hold a special place in the heart of the local community on Florida's Atlantic coast. "Save the Manatees foundation is 50 miles away," Smith said. "It's obviously a big deal down here."

Introduced in 1994 as the Single-A affiliate of the Florida Marlins, the Manatees joined the baseball world wearing teal (because it was the '90s and that was the law). They switched to red, white, and blue (or bleu, blanc, et rouge) when they became an Expos affiliate in 2002, and they maintained that color scheme even after they became a Brewers affiliate in 2005. The Manatees logo and mascot are notable for being decidedly not fierce, much like another teal Marlins affiliate introduced at the same time.

"We might be one of the first teams—[Portland] Sea Dogs are another perfect example—of the first wave of those kind of cutesy, non-imposing, cartoony logos," Smith said.

"You can't make a manatee fierce," Smith continued. "What kind of alternate logo could we do? Do we just have a hat that's a snout and whiskers? That's not imposing. The only thing we can do is give him like an axe or knife. Well, we're not going to do that."

The team played off their mascot's lovable image with a tongue-in-cheek "Fear the Sea Cow" slogan that was intended to be used just for one season, but fans took to it and it has been used ever since. "Anything with that on it became our number one seller," Smith said, "so we've kind of stuck with that as our mantra."

The team's primary logo features the team's mascot, Manny the Manatee, holding a baseball bat and wearing a cap. The team's cap logo features an interlocking BC and Manny tossing a baseball in the air.

The Manatees made a specific design decision regarding the logo on Manny's cap to avoid creating an *Inception*-style infinite loop of cartoon manatees.

"On Manny's hat is just the BC," Smith said, "it's not the actual logo because obviously that would be kind of strange. It's kind of like that one baseball card, like there was 10, 15 years ago, where the guy, it's a baseball card of him holding that baseball card."

The team uses the primary logo on all materials outside of the local community because the letter pairing of BC can mean a lot more than just Brevard County. "If I wear that in the Orlando area or I go back to Minnesota," Smith said, "people think it's British Columbia or Boston College or something like that." (It made me think of the Brooklyn Cyclones, but my head is pretty much always in a minor league baseball cloud.)

The most recent addition to the Manatees' identity is a wordmark that's an homage to their parent club.

"We introduced a new script logo that we use on our road and alternate jerseys," Smith said. "It's the way the Brewers spell out Brewers in cursive: Starts with a B and has seven letters. Well, so does Brevard. We took that script and created Brevard."

Some of the Manatees' sales can be attributed to the affinity many people have for this affable, vulnerable animal.

"I think we sell a lot of merchandise online to folks that have no idea who we are or what we do," Smith said. "Obviously they know it's baseball because there's a baseball in the logo, but a lot of people just buy it from somewhere because they like manatees."

Another selling point is that the only place you see this nickname in sports is in Brevard County, Florida.

"It's a unique name that nobody else in sports has," Smith said. "So that's one thing we have going for us, as opposed to the Tigers or something like that." (Take that, Detroit. Or Clemson. Or Auburn. Or Princeton. Or Japan's Hanshin Tigers. Or Korea's Kia Tigers. Or Norway's Frisk Tigers. Etc.)

Because of these feelings that I have about manatees (the animal), I feel a little bit guilty when I think about the fact that the first time I saw the baseball team's logo, I thought it looked like the label of a can of manatee meat. Again, let me reiterate that I support the noble manatee and long for the day conservation efforts succeed thoroughly enough that it's removed from the endangered species list. And I very much like the team's logo—but something about it made me think of cat food.

In the end, we're only left to wonder what would have happened to logos and team names in the Majors if the Marlins had been the Manatees instead. Would the Rockies and Diamondbacks, introduced the same year and five years later respectively, have been cartoon dinosaurs and cacti instead of sleek mountains and snakes? Or would the Miami Manatees have been laughed out of the big leagues and everything would have just returned to normal?

We do know that the wave of kid-friendly cartoon logos in the minors has continued with a vengeance in the two decades since the inception of the Brevard County Manatees. In that sense, the Manatees have been baseball fashion makers—fat, sausage-shaped, marine mammal fashion makers—who helped move the trend along.

Casper Ghosts

Casper Ghosts
2008–2011

Final Team Data

Parent
Milwaukee Brewers

Class
Rookie

League
Pioneer

What Happened

The team relocated to Grand Junction, Colorado, to become the Rockies.

Imagine you're a logo designer and you've been tasked with creating a brand for a minor league baseball team. You're free to let the creativity flow, but you have a few constraints to consider:

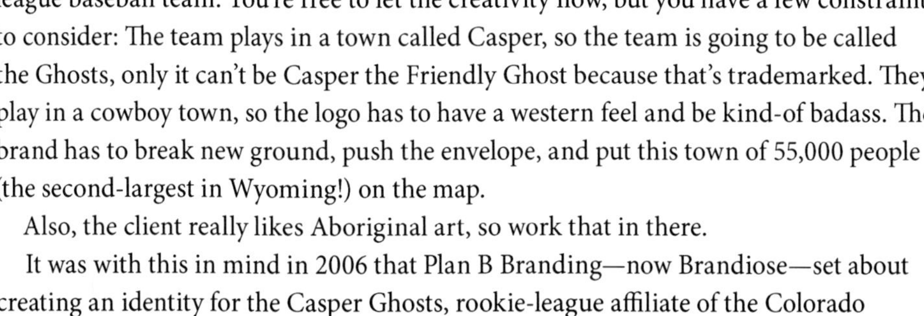

The team plays in a town called Casper, so the team is going to be called the Ghosts, only it can't be Casper the Friendly Ghost because that's trademarked. They play in a cowboy town, so the logo has to have a western feel and be kind-of badass. The brand has to break new ground, push the envelope, and put this town of 55,000 people (the second-largest in Wyoming!) on the map.

Also, the client really likes Aboriginal art, so work that in there.

It was with this in mind in 2006 that Plan B Branding—now Brandiose—set about creating an identity for the Casper Ghosts, rookie-league affiliate of the Colorado Rockies. They had been the Casper Rockies since moving to Wyoming in 2001, but the team's CEO Kevin Haughian had a bigger, bolder vision.

As Brandiose's Jason Klein tells it, Haughian approached the design firm with this message: "I really just want something that's out there, that's never been done before, that really breaks the mold, gets people talking."

The project would take two years, the longest Brandiose has spent on a single identity, according to Klein. It would result in a logo that is well-known for being the first on-field glow-in-the-dark cap in professional baseball, but less well-known for being inspired by indigenous artwork from the other side of the world.

"He was really into Aboriginal art," Klein said of Haughian. "He said, I want to see if we can create a ghost character out of Aboriginal art. At first, our thought was all these dots are going to make things really difficult because Aboriginal art is mostly made of dots. How are we going to embroider all this?"

Klein and his Brandiose partner Casey White turned to a 19th-century printing process developed by artist and printer Benjamin H. Day Jr.—a process popularized in paintings by pop artist Roy Lichtenstein in the 1960s.

"We started looking at Ben Day dots, how dots connect," Klein said. "Could we create a logo where the thread continues from dot to dot that wasn't just separate dots on a cap?"

It took a lot of back and forth between the team and the design firm getting sizes and shapes to work correctly, but dots became an integral part of the logo. With Aboriginal art and the Ben Day printing process being such important influence in the design process in this already-unique identity, you can't help but wonder how many fans knew where those dots in the logo came from.

"Probably zero," Klein said. "I don't think it was even in the press release. That's one of those unique examples where every designer has some sort of reference that maybe the world never is privy to, yet inspires something unique."

Of course, with the Ghosts playing in a small Wyoming cowboy town, there was no lack of inspiration for concepts. The Brandiose guys found a way to put themselves in a ghostly, western mood—"We listened to 'Ghost Riders in the Sky,' that song, over and over and over," Klein said. With Johnny Cash ringing in their heads, they set to work.

Early concepts included a ghost bat (which looks to me like a possessed version of a Lowell Spinners logo that would come later) and an eerie cowboy, among others.

A visit to Casper's Wonder Bar inspired concepts that combined ghosts and cows.

Concept sketches via Brandiose

"Casey and I were really, really into this skull … and less into the Ben Day dots because it was so abstract," Klein said. "Looking back, whether fans would have loved one or the other, or if the skull would have given the team as much publicity, we'll never know."

One part of the identity where the western feel shined through was with the script, which accomplished two tasks at once. "I really feel it was cowboy and ghostly at the same time," Klein said. "It just had a ghost town feeling to it."

In the ephemeral world of minor league baseball, nothing is constant, and four seasons after their debut, the Ghosts vanished. After the 2011 season, the team left Casper for Colorado's western slope and became the Grand Junction Rockies. This is a shame not only because it's boring when minor league teams adopt their parent clubs' identity, but Grand Junction Ghosts would have been a perfectly good team name. Minor league teams have based their identities on less than simple alliteration, and sticking with an established identity in a new town is certainly valid.

That said, Klein has no regrets.

"I'm glad that we were able to create something that made history," he said. "It was a very cool little design experiment that we were able to do, where someone pushed us in trying something new from an artistic perspective. I think that was really cool to be a part of that."

The Ghosts' claim to fame is that they were the first team to wear a glow-in-the-dark logo on their cap, but the story behind the Ghosts' brand goes a lot deeper than that one factoid. The number and variety of influences on this identity are surprising, to say the least.

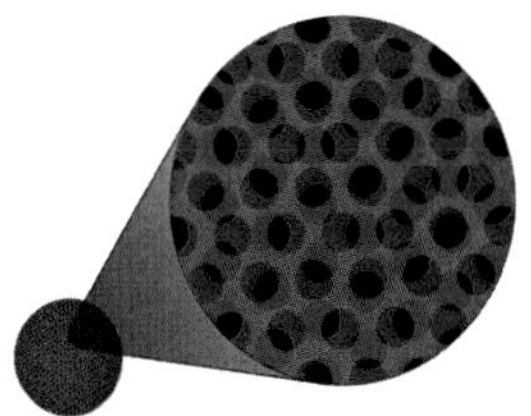

Ben Day dots

Laredo Lemurs

Laredo Lemurs
2012–2017

Final Team Data:

Class
Independent

League
American Association

What Happened
The Lemurs ceased operations before the 2017 season.

This is an objective, scientifically proven fact: Lemurs are awesome. Also, people love lemurs. It's science.

Here's another scientific fact for you: Laredo, Texas, is not close to the island nation of Madagascar, which is located in the Indian Ocean and is the only place in the world where lemurs live in the wild.

So when a new team in baseball's independent American Association opened its doors in Laredo, Texas, in 2012, the fact that it was called the Lemurs might have seemed like a stretch. Team leaders, including owner Mark Schuster and manager Pete Incaviglia, had three criteria for deciding on the new nickname: It had to be kid-friendly, it had to be unique in all of sports, and it had to have a tie to the history of Laredo.

That third item might have been a sticking point in calling the team Lemurs were it not for some digging (as it were) by the team. I spoke with Lemur manager, longtime Major Leaguer Pete Incaviglia, who credits Schuster with discovering the rationale for the name. "Mark did a real good job of going through the history of the lemur," Incaviglia said. "Way back when, in the dinosaur era, I guess there were a bunch of lemurs that lived in Laredo."

In researching the area, Schuster had discovered the work of Dr. James Westgate of Lamar University.

"We have one lake in Laredo, and it's Lake Casa Blanca," Schuster said. "And this archeological dig was at Lake Casa Blanca, and he found all of these lemur-like creatures—bones, stuff like that, that had been fossilized—in the area."

"While they weren't specifically the lemurs that we know today—they have evolved over time—these were lemur-like creatures," Schuster said. (Note: Curt Schilling could not be reached for comment on this point.)

As for appealing to children, Incaviglia put it succinctly: "All kids love a lemur."

In fact, the choice of Lemurs as a mascot means that the team has pop culture doing a lot of their marketing for them. "We all know the movie *Madagascar* and King Julien, 'We've got to move it, move it!'" Schuster said. "I thought, we have a 20-year lease at the stadium, these kids grew up watching *Madagascar*—and there's going to be *Madagascar 19, 20, 21*—they're going to keep making them from here until forever." (My own kids also loved PBS's *Zoboomafoo*, which features a talking lemur.)

While people do love lemurs, the team name itself was not well received when it was first announced—which seems to be par for the course with unique minor league team names.

Schuster knew the backlash was coming, and even warned city officials to that effect.

"I absolutely took a beating from everybody in the market," Schuster said. "I met with the city a few days before making the announcement and I said, 'Listen, I just want to let you know that we're going to name the team the Lemurs, and I want you to know that the reaction is going to be completely negative, so just be prepared.'"

Knowing that the negative reaction was coming allowed Schuster to use it to his advantage. "It's an opportunity for me also to get some media attention," he said. "I was on every TV station, every radio show defending myself as to why we named this team the Lemurs."

LAREDO LEMURS

Manager Pete Incaviglia

The choice of lemurs as a baseball mascot is a bit unusual, and probably requires some defending. "The animal itself is fat and lazy," Schuster said. "Lemurs, when they're sitting around, they sit on their ass and their belly hangs out."

I reached out to Chris Smith, education specialist at the Duke Lemur Center, one of the premier lemur research facilities in the world, which has a fun lemur logo of its own. Smith pointed out that the ring-tailed lemur, the species featured in the team's logo, is well suited to baseball because it's adaptable, eats almost anything, and lives in large social groups, just like baseball players. The ring-tailed lemur has poor eyesight, though, so another variety of lemur might have worked better. According to Smith, red-ruffed lemurs have an alarm call heard over a half mile away, good for heckling. Aye-ayes have the biggest brain, suitable for coaching. And Coquerel's sifaka have an eight-foot vertical jump. "You might want those guys snatching those homers from over the wall," Smith said.

Smith is glad to see lemurs featured in a baseball logo, but he did have one concern. "The great American game mixed with the most endangered mammal group means that lemurs get a kind of cultural penetration that is difficult to achieve otherwise," he said. However, "their graphic designer makes lemurs look so mean!"

Schuster addressed this point in conversations with Jason Klein of Brandiose, the firm that designed the logo.

"Jason and I went back and forth on this about what the animal should convey," Schuster said. "We thought if we made him happy, jolly, whatever, that it doesn't convey that we're competitive and that we're a team to be reckoned with. And so we went with the opposite of what a lemur really is."

Alternate versions of the logo feature the lemur carrying a Texas-ish flag, an LL for Laredo Lemurs, and, as described by Brandiose's Casey White, a "sleeve patch featuring a tiny Lemur digging his claws into the player's sleeve."

Schuster wanted to have a live lemur in the ballpark, which fans would see as they attended games, and which could travel to local schools to educate children about the endangered mammal. There was one insurmountable obstacle to that plan, though: "The problem is in Laredo, Texas, we're about two and a half hours from, you know, American civilization, which is San Antonio," Schuster said. "You really need to have a veterinarian close by that can work on primates, and that was sort of the obstacle that we were unable to overcome."

The next best thing to a live lemur in the ballpark is the team's mascot, Pancho, who was designed by the original Phillie Phanatic, Dave Raymond, and who Schuster says is more popular than the team's players.

In the end, these logos and mascots have one purpose, which the Lemurs accomplish with gusto. "You know, minor league baseball is fun. Minor league baseball is about family entertainment," Incaviglia said. "And to have a neat mascot to go with your logo makes people want to come out and enjoy baseball."

The Lemurs have a solid enough fan base to call "Lemur Nation," the team sells gear to fans of both Lemurs (the team) and lemurs (the animal) all over the world, and you can be sure that the next *Madagascar* sequel is right around the corner.

New Britain Rock Cats

If you're like me, you'll be humming "Stray Cat Strut" the rest of the day after reading the story of the New Britain Rock Cats. After all, if ever there was one, Rock Cat mascot Rocky is a feline Casanova, a ladies' cat. If they made a movie about Rocky, he'd be played by a young John Travolta, or possibly Henry Winkler.

Rocky made his debut in the mid 1990s, but he's a throwback to the 1950s, a time when cats were cool, and cool cats wore leather jackets.

When the New Britain Red Sox switched parent clubs in 1995 to the Minnesota Twins, the team rebranded as the Hardware City Rock Cats. Their first logo was created by noted cartoonist Guy Gilchrist, who draws the Nancy comic strip (among much else) and also created the Portland Sea Dogs logo. For Gilchrist, a lifelong baseball fan and longtime Connecticut resident, the Rock Cats project was a labor of love.

"We never really thought of the character as a logo," he said. "We thought of the character as being the spirit of the town." And that spirit, one of grit and industry and iron, is reflected in that first Rock Cats logo. Gilchrist said:

> I made up a character and named him Rocky, sort of after Rocky Balboa, where he was just the tough guy.... It had a good feel to it, you could do rock n roll with it, he had the leather jacket, and that was all sort of 1950s, sort of retro cool.

The logo features a rough-and-tumble cat out on the town. *(He slinks down the alley looking for a fight, howling to the moonlight on a hot summer's night.)* The letters HC for Hardware City are formed by an urban building and a moon, and Rocky's tail is shaped like the number 9, a subtle nod to Gilchrist's favorite player, Ted Williams. (Though Gilchrist points out that the Twins' famous number 9, Tony Oliva, was no slouch either.)

The 1950s look and feel of the Rock Cats' early logo was an homage to the heyday of the team's longtime and legendary owner, Joe Buzas, whose career as a baseball team owner spanned dozens of teams and nearly six decades before he passed away in 2003.

"Joe Buzas is absolutely one of my favorite baseball people," Gilchrist said. "Without his tenacity, and without his world-famous—I'll say thriftiness—without all of that, baseball would not have survived in New Britain.... He took every shortcut he possibly could because in those days you absolutely had to." *(He's flat broke but he don't care. Struts right by with his tail in the air.)*

New Britain Rock Cats
1997–2015

Final Team Data

Parent
Colorado Rockies

Class
Double-A

League
Eastern

What Happened
The Rock Cats moved to Hartford, Connecticut, to become the Hartford Yard Goats in 2016.

Guy Gilchrist's Hardware City Rock Cats logo

The city of New Britain's nickname, Hardware City, is a reference to the town's history as a home to manufacturing, specifically Stanley Black and Decker's headquarters. But there was a problem with incorporating the city's nickname into the official name of the ballclub.

"People couldn't find Hardware City on the map," Gilchrist said. "So we took that stuff out and changed it to the New Britain Rock Cats."

After one year as the Hardware City Rock Cats, the team switched in 1996 to the name it has had ever since, the New Britain Rock Cats. Gilchrist created a new and much simpler logo that incorporated Rocky's face, complete with sunglasses and giant Elvis hair, over the letters NB. Then in 2007, the team abandoned the rock 'n' roll Rocky altogether and went with the version they have today.

"It looks like they've taken the shades off of Rocky and stuff like that," Gilchrist said. "But, that's okay."

With the final version of the team's primary logo so far removed from its roots, some of the history and the original intentions of the design—the actual meaning of the term Rock Cats—were lost. Tim Restall, the Rock Cats' general manager, experienced that firsthand.

"When I first came on, I asked people, what's a Rock Cat?" he said. "Not a lot of people could tell me what the history of the Rock Cats was. Some people said it was with regards to rock 'n' roll, some people said it was with regards to the quarries in the area."

To reconnect Rocky with his rock 'n' roll roots, the team unveiled a new alternate logo designed by the prolific firm Brandiose in 2014. The new logo featured Rocky in full rock 'n' roll regalia, singing into a baseball bat microphone—and that big hair returned.

"Internally, we call him Rocky Elvis, because of the jumpsuit and things like that," Restall said.

The new alternate logo featured a color unique to baseball, and one that fits with Rocky's throwback rock 'n' roll image. "We were told by Brandiose that it was one of the first on-field hats to have metallic red," Restall said, "which we thought was pretty cool, especially when you're going with a rock 'n' roll, having metallic with gold on a jump suit." *(Wishes he could be as carefree and wild, but he's got cat class and he's got cat style.)*

When the team announced the new alternate logo, there was some consternation. Restall said that fan feedback on Rocky Elvis was positive, but he pointed out that the Rocky that fans came to know and love would be there for the duration.

"Everyone is afraid of change," Restall said. "We said, it's not replacing the logo, it's a new alternate logo."

Over the years, the Rock Cats have had logos with three different letter pairings. The HC for Hardware City in the original team name was brought back briefly in 2011 in an alternate logo that reflects the team's parent club, the Minnesota Twins. The team re-learned a lesson from those early days with that logo, according to Restall: "I think it was confusing. People didn't know what HC was." Another little-used alternate logo, with NB for New Britain, introduced in 1996, was meant to resemble another version of the Twins logo. And finally, the claw-themed RC for Rock Cats, updated most recently in 2007, is still used prominently.

From the team's early days, when Guy Gilchrist would custom design Rocky logos for charity events and oversee production of dolls and other paraphernalia to ensure they met his standards, the team worked hard to make sure Rocky was a prominent part of the New Britain community.

“The character was doing things like reading or encouraging kids to stay in school, all that kind of stuff,” Gilchrist said.

That sort of involvement continued. According to Restall:

> He's our spokesperson. He's our flagship. We put him out everywhere.... I think Rocky on one Saturday went to 42 little league openings. He is constantly out in the community, whether he's at the hospital, he's at little league games, store openings, anything like that. He's the brand of the Rock Cats, so we constantly get him out into the community.

Rocky was part of the team's larger effort to create an entertaining ballgame experience for the casual fan. “The baseball fan knows where we are. They know where the Double-A baseball team plays, who's coming in, and what the prospects are and all that,” Restall said. “But when we market, we market the fun, the nachos, the kids area, the in-between inning promotions. That's the stuff that we focus on.”

Gilchrist, who speaks about baseball with the passion of a true fan, sees minor league baseball and this sort of entertainment as the sport's salvation. With many fans priced out of attending Major League games, and World Series games starting as late as 9:00 on the east coast, the minors and their family-friendly entertainment are a haven for baseball fans.

“[The minors] are going to be the survival of baseball,” Gilchrist said. “It's wonderful. They play day games. Kids get to be right up close, and get autographs from their heroes and stuff. I truly believe it will save baseball.”

What can you say about a cat who's part of something like that? *Singing the blues while the lady cats cry, wild Rock Cat, you're a real gone guy.*

Brandiose's Rocky

New Orleans Zephyrs

New Orleans Zephyrs
1993–2016

Final Team Data

Parent
Miami Marlins

Class
Triple-A

League
Pacific Coast

What Happened

The Zephyrs rebranded as the New Orleans Baby Cakes before the 2017 season.

On its own, the word *zephyr* does not exactly instill fear. It refers to a gentle wind, rolling in from the west and rustling the daffodils (or whatever) as it heads east.

That said, the city of Denver sits just to the east of the Rockies, and the wind that often comes charging out of the mountains and whipping through the city can be a force. So to think there was a connection between the Triple-A Denver Zephyrs, who first took the field in 1985, and a word that means west wind was not much of a stretch. Thankfully, the team was not actually named for a mild breeze.

The Denver Zephyrs, who had been the Kansas City Blues (1901–1954) and the Denver Bears (1955–1984), were actually named for a stainless steel passenger train that ran between Chicago and Denver from the mid 1930s into the 1970s. The overnight train took about 16 hours to cover more than 1,000 miles on its route.

When Major League Baseball expanded in 1993 and the Colorado Rockies entered the National League, the Zephyrs needed to find a new home. They moved to New Orleans, where they would keep the name Zephyrs, even though the city had no connection to the famous train (or west winds, for that matter). As luck would have it, there was another connection.

"There happens to have been a very famous roller coaster at the old Pontchartrain Beach Amusement Park that was called the Zephyr," said Zephyrs Director of Media Relations Dave Sachs. "It was this huge white wooden roller coaster, and it was this famous landmark in the city for decades."

It was an amazing coincidence that allowed the New Orleans Zephyrs to capitalize on an established brand—and save the team a lot of time and money in rebranding.

"You basically wonder if the guys at the time were like, 'Eh, we can get away with this,'" Sachs said. "They were allowed kind of to be lazy in keeping the name and the logo and not really changing anything except for from Denver to New Orleans."

The Pontchartrain Beach Amusement Park closed in 1983, but the Zephyrs pay homage to the roller coaster with a mural outside a stadium concession stand called The Last Ride.

For 12 seasons after relocating, the New Orleans Zephyrs, now an affiliate of the Miami Marlins, kept the logo from the Denver Zephyrs, which was basically a baseball whose stitches formed a Z. In 2005, the team launched its first major update to their identity in three decades with a new logo based on their mascot.

"They rebranded and went to kind of a cartoony thing, trying to market to kids," Sachs said.

The new logo featured Boudreaux the nutria, which turns out not to be a dietary supplement, but rather a distinctive rodent also known as a coypu or river rat. It was a word I had never heard before, so I asked for an explanation.

"He's a nutria, like a water rat," Sachs said. "You can find them in the drainage ditches around town. They're a little like possums, kind of. They're nutria."

In 2010, the Zephyrs adopted their final look, which was based on the *fleur de lis*, the flower-based French symbol closely associated with the city of New Orleans—including several of its sports teams.

Everyone is familiar with the New Orleans Saints *fleur de lis*, but also at the time, the then-New Orleans Hornets featured a logo that they called the fleur de bee. Not to be outdone, the Zephyrs had an alternate logo that they call the fleur de Z.

The timing for the Zephyrs to adopt the *fleur de lis* could not have been better in terms of civic pride.

"We rebranded right around the time the Saints won the Super Bowl," Sachs said. "Everyone associates the *fleur de lis* with New Orleans, and we hopped on board with that, took advantage of it."

The Zephyrs, of course, put their own twist on the iconic symbol in their primary logo. "The middle part of the *fleur de lis* is a baseball bat," Sachs said. "I don't know if people actually notice it. They see the *fleur de lis* logo and think, 'Oh, it's just like the Saints.' We actually do have the baseball bat as part of the logo.

The Zephyrs' typeface, featured on the wordmark on their home uniforms and a Z cap logo, also recalls some of New Orleans' local heritage.

"It's that kind of French Quarter font that you might see when you're walking around in the older parts of town—kind of classical" Sachs said. "You'll see that on restaurants and stuff down in the French Quarter."

The purpose of the 2010 rebrand, according to Sachs, was to create a classier look. Rather than featuring a cartoon water rat in the logo, they would let Boudreaux the mascot appeal to kids on the field, but their new identity, based on a symbol from European antiquity and type that echoed signage from restaurants in the city's French Quarter, would be more refined.

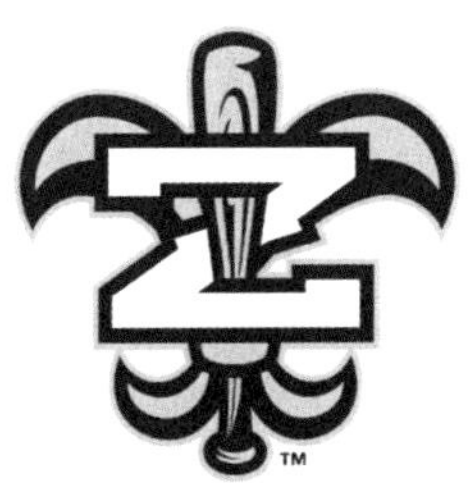

"That was kind of the focus of changing the logo," Sachs said. "We wanted to go away from the cartoony logo and go with more of a classic, clean look. We banished Boudreaux from all the logos."

The New Orleans Zephyrs have one of the more obscure back stories in the minors. The significance behind the name of the team shifted from a famous train to a famous roller coaster when the team moved from Denver to New Orleans, then a series of logos over the years have featured a clip art baseball (essentially), a rodent that lives in drainage, and a *fleur de lis*—none of which have anything to do a train, a roller coaster, or even a west wind.

That said, their classic look in an ever-wackier minor league logo landscape was something of a breath of fresh air—or maybe just a gentle breeze.

Oklahoma City RedHawks

Oklahoma City RedHawks
2009–2014

Final Team Data

Parent
Los Angeles Dodgers

Class
Triple-A

League
Pacific Coast

What Happened
The team was renamed the Oklahoma City Dodgers before the 2015 season.

The Triple-A Oklahoma City RedHawks play in Chickasaw Bricktown Ballpark, the centerpiece of Oklahoma City's hopping, rejuvenated, brick-covered Bricktown entertainment district. It's a beautiful ballpark—voted one of the 10 best in the minors by *USA Today* readers—and everything about it pays homage to the city's baseball history.

Statues of Mickey Mantle, Johnny Bench, and Warren Spahn grace the park's entrances, along with the busts of seven other players, all of whom were either born in the state or spent significant portions of their lives there. Even the ballpark's location on the map—between Mickey Mantle Drive and Joe Carter Avenue—pays tribute to those with ties to the state of Oklahoma.

So it stands to reason that a team in a city with such deep baseball roots would choose to represent itself with a brand that feels classic, even if that brand has not been around that long.

"Based on the stadium and the surrounding area, to have more of a traditional name and traditional look is good," said Alex Freedman, the RedHawks' play-by-play broadcaster and director of media relations.

The franchise adopted the name Oklahoma RedHawks in 1998 when they moved into their new stadium. The nickname references the state's natural heritage. "The definition really has to do with the state of Oklahoma," Freedman said. "The formal name is the red-tailed hawk, also known as a red hawk, which is an indigenous, almost raptor-like bird here in Oklahoma that's kind of similar to an eagle."

Amazingly, the name was not chosen by fan voting, but was simply chosen by team owners because it was meaningful. "There was not a contest or anything like that," Freedman said. "They wanted something to do with Oklahoma that was indigenous and would show off a fighting spirit."

The RedHawks rebranded in 2009, adding the word "City" to become the Oklahoma City RedHawks. Their new logo embraced the city's airport code turned nickname, much like a certain NBA team that debuted the year before in 2008.

"They wanted to change the logo more to show off and stress Oklahoma City rather than a RedHawk logo," Freedman said. "The letters OKC have become a very big deal as a way to identify the city."

While the RedHawks' primary logo and cap insignia are text-based, an alternate logo that features a hawk with a bat in its mouth is still popular, and appears on the team's batting practice hat. I asked Freedman, who is from St. Louis, if anyone ever remarked on a resemblance between the team's mascots, Cooper and Rudy, and the Cardinals' Fred Bird. He said that no one had, but that the alternate RedHawks logo gets noticed.

"There have been a couple times when I've been [in St. Louis] during the holidays and I've worn that and just random people would ask, 'Is that a new Cardinals hat that I don't know about?'"

Astros prospect Jonathan Singleton's locker in 2014. The author did not have the foresight to take a close-up photo of 2017 World Series MVP George Springer's locker, just to the left.

The franchise was born in 1962 as the Oklahoma City 89ers, a reference to the Oklahoma Land Run of 1889. The name was popular, but the change to RedHawks coincided with a move to Chickasaw Bricktown Ballpark, so the timing worked.

"I think people were probably pretty accepting of it because they were getting this brand-new stadium, and a really nice stadium at that," Freedman said.

But whenever there's change, especially with a team that dates back to the 1960s, there will be some resistance. "There's still nostalgia," Freedman said. "When I go out in the community, they're like, 'Yeah the ballpark is great, but I remember all these times at All Sports Stadium…' Even though it was a dump, people have very fond memories of it."

And nostalgia for the old ballpark naturally comes with nostalgia for the old brand. "A lot of them would want to keep the 89ers name," Freedman said. "Even today, on Twitter, there are people who want us to go back to being known as the 89ers."

The team addresses this nostalgia with retro giveaways that feature the old name and logos.

While some fans are looking to the past, the team went through some exciting changes during the 2013–14 offseason, and they are looking to the future. Shortly after the season ended, the Dodgers dropped the Albuquerque Isotopes as their Triple-A affiliate and signed on with the RedHawks, who had previously been an Astros affiliate. This precipitated a domino effect that resulted in six Triple-A teams switching parent clubs.

As a Dodgers affiliate, Oklahoma City is open to the possibility of changes to their brand, and it's something they've been getting asked about a lot.

"We'd be foolish not to explore it," Freedman said. "What that will mean is yet to be determined, but we'll just have to wait and see. I know we're going to incorporate it somehow."

With a strong, classic-feeling logo and one of the best ballparks in minor league baseball, it's a good time to be a RedHawks fan. They have a storied history, a good thing going right now, and a future filled with possibility. And they play in a city with a really cool airport code.

Savannah Sand Gnats

Savannah Sand Gnats
1996–2015

Final Team Data

Parent
New York Mets

Class
Single-A

League
South Atlantic

What Happened
The Sand Gnats relocated to South Carolina to become the Columbia Fireflies before the 2016 season.

A lot of sports teams choose to represent themselves with fierce, intimidating creatures: Tigers, Diamondbacks, Sharks, Chihuahuas, etc. But none of these sounds quite so awful as the swarming, biting insects that infest coastal Georgia twice a year. Sand gnats, colloquially referred to as biting midges, punkies, sand flies, sand fleas, and no-see-ums, are most appropriately called "Flying Teeth" by the website *Butterfly Kingdom*.

An article called "The Biting Truth of 'No-See-Ums'" says this about the charming little guy: "They are very small flies (about 1/25–1/10 inch long) whose small but bladelike mouthparts make a painful wound out of proportion to its tiny size. Welts and lesions from the bite may last for days." Yeah, they said "small but bladelike mouthparts"! And if you're wondering where you might find sand gnats, you just have to check a map to see if you are "South of the Gnat Line," which is a real, live, actual thing that you can find online.

"It doesn't just bite you," said Jeff Berger, communications and graphics manager for the Single-A Savannah Sand Gnats. "It kind of rips your skin open a little bit."

People who live south of the gnat line use chemical products, repellents, and home remedies to try to stave off the tiny beasts, usually in vain. The best solutions seem to be to stay inside or simply pack your bags and move away (which is precisely what the Sand Gnats are going to do—more on that below). It begs the question, why would a team adopt a name that serves as a daily reminder of a community's biggest scourge?

When the Savannah Cardinals changed parent clubs from St. Louis to Los Angeles before the 1996 season, a rebrand was in order. The team looked for an identity that was unique and specific to the city. "Everybody that comes down here and hangs out here for a while, you kind of get to learn what a sand gnat is just because you want to know what just bit you," Berger said. "It's definitely unique and it definitely symbolizes what is Savannah."

Then, after a pause, Berger added this: "Everybody down here seems to like it, from what we gather."

The logo has remained unchanged since 1996, so clearly fans do like it, in spite of the fact that it's a reminder of the fact that every spring and fall, the air is filled with invisible razor blades that leave welts and gashes in residents' skin for days.

"They just like how fierce it is," Berger said. "It's a muscular bug holding a bat with a big fang on it, and sunglasses, so it looks pretty cool. People are kind of attached to it."

The logo features Gnic (pronounced "Nick") the Gnat, an anthropomorphized bug with those signature dagger teeth, a warped baseball bat (maybe a Wiffle bat left out in the sun?), and sunglasses. And coming from that era of unchecked steroid use in the mid-1990s, there's one unmistakable trait Gnic exhibits. "We always liked just how buff the guy is," Berger said. "I mean, it's just a bug, but he's ripped out of his mind."

Gnic wears a hat with a white emblem on it, which Berger says is the subject of frequent questions. "It says 'SSG,' for Savannah Sand Gnats," he said.

The purpose of the SSG logo on Gnic's hat is to prevent an Inception-style infinite loop of gnat logos, which would occur if Gnic were wearing the team's regular cap logo, which is Gnic. "It's just an easier thing to put on a hat—instead of putting him again, and then it's a never-ending cycle of a gnat wearing a gnat hat," Berger said.

Gnic was the team's on-field mascot during the Sand Gnats' early years, but he was ultimately demoted, because baseball is a business and sometimes you just have to make difficult decisions.

MIKE SAMPOGNA

"We had to retire him because he wasn't doing so hot," Berger said. "The team wasn't performing, so we brought in the new performer."

Enter Gnate the Gnat, the team's mascot since 2005 and lead dancer of "The Gnaturals." ("We really play into the G and the N here," Berger said.) Not only have the Sand Gnats performed better under his watch, winning the league championship in 2012, but Gnate won the South Atlantic League's Mascot of the Year award in 2012, 2013, and 2014.

Sadly for fans of painful welts and invisible biting insects, the Sand Gnats played their final season in Savannah in 2015, and the nickname was retired when the team moved to Columbia, South Carolina, for the 2016 season. "We haven't announced any new team name yet," Berger said back in 2015, "but it's not going to be Sand Gnats. You don't get any sand gnats in the midlands out there in Columbia."

The Sand Gnats became the Columbia Fireflies when they moved to South Carolina, drawing to a close a two-decade era of one of the weirder logos in minor league baseball. When the era of wacky minor league baseball logos was in its infancy back in the mid-1990s, the Sand Gnats took to the field sporting a cartoon version of a hateful, horrible, biting insect. It was a risky move that would still be paying dividends if negotiations between the team and the city of Savannah on a new stadium had not fallen through. On August 29, 2015, the Sand Gnats hosted Gnate Appreciation Night, and the celebration continued throughout the team's playoff run. When the lights went out in Savannah after that last game, though, we said goodbye to a fun, weird logo—but those horrendous bugs will be there forever.

ACKNOWLEDGMENTS

This book exists because **Chris Creamer** discovered an obscure blog that I had been writing about the origins of minor league baseball logos and asked me to write for his very popular site, SportsLogos.net, which I had been a fan of for years. His support and insight have helped grow the scope and size of this collection of articles immensely.

I am grateful to all of the baseball executives and front-office personnel who took time out of their days to talk to me, sometimes conjuring stories that went back decades. I am also grateful to the logo designers who have been so generous with their time to talk to me about their work. In particular, **Jason Klein** of Brandiose, **Dan Simon** of Studio Simon, and **Todd Radom** of Todd Radom Design have always been readily available whenever I've reached out.

Thank you to the many individuals who have graciously provided photos for this book, including **Stephen Bobb, Scott Castiglia, AJ Chlebnik, Rick Curti, Chris Evans, Seth Gallagher, Jared Ham, Elista Istre, Heidi Kay, Brian Mast, Mike Sampogna, Peggy Simme, Josh Spangler,** and **Steve & Tammie Stiles**.

Finally, I am grateful to the individuals in my life who have enabled my minor league baseball addiction. **Jeremy Soule, Chris Trebon, Stephen Bobb, Scott Castiglia, Al Langlois, Jon Langlois, Scott Mealey, Stew Smith, Rob Wright,** and **Mike Zimmer** have masterminded some amazing baseball-centric road trips in recent years (pictured), which has fostered the love that has driven this project.

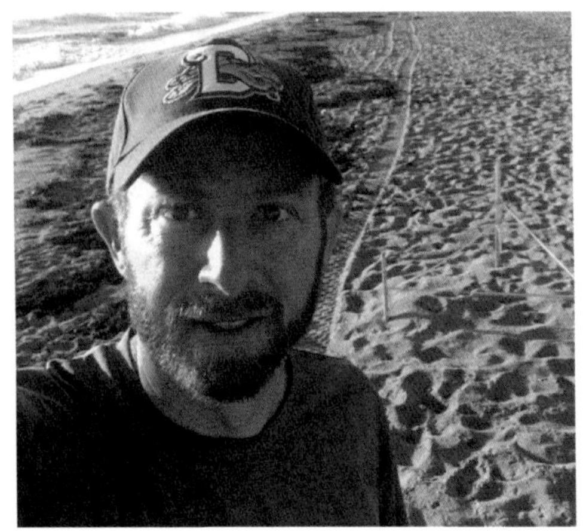

ABOUT THE AUTHOR

Paul Caputo is a grown man who serves ice cream in plastic helmet sundae cups to dinner guests. He has an MFA in visual communications from Virginia Commonwealth University and a bachelor of arts in French and journalism from the University of Richmond (the only college or university in North America whose mascot is Spiders). He is a Philadelphia sports fan, but he's not so bad. Reach him at pauljcaputo@gmail.com.

Made in the USA
Monee, IL
20 January 2020

20593442R00145